INTRODUCTION TO UNIVERSITY TEACHING

Sara Miller McCune founded SAGE Publishing in 1965 to support the dissemination of usable knowledge and educate a global community. SAGE publishes more than 1000 journals and over 800 new books each year, spanning a wide range of subject areas. Our growing selection of library products includes archives, data, case studies and video. SAGE remains majority owned by our founder and after her lifetime will become owned by a charitable trust that secures the company's continued independence.

Los Angeles | London | New Delhi | Singapore | Washington DC | Melbourne

INTRODUCTION TO
UNIVERSITY TEACHING

RICHARD BALE • MARY SEABROOK

⑤SAGE

Los Angeles | London | New Delhi
Singapore | Washington DC | Melbourn·

$SAGE

Los Angeles | London | New Delhi
Singapore | Washington DC | Melbourne

SAGE Publications Ltd
1 Oliver's Yard
55 City Road
London EC1Y 1SP

SAGE Publications Inc.
2455 Teller Road
Thousand Oaks, California 91320

SAGE Publications India Pvt Ltd
B 1/I 1 Mohan Cooperative Industrial Area
Mathura Road
New Delhi 110 044

SAGE Publications Asia-Pacific Pte Ltd
3 Church Street
#10-04 Samsung Hub
Singapore 049483

Editor: James Clark
Assistant editor: Diana Alves
Production editor: Martin Fox
Copyeditor: Elaine Leek
Proofreader: Neil Dowden
Marketing manager: Lorna Patkai
Cover design: Naomi Robinson
Typeset by: C&M Digitals (P) Ltd, Chennai, India
Printed in the UK

Library of Congress Control Number: 2021932762

British Library Cataloguing in Publication data

A catalogue record for this book is available from the British Library

ISBN 978-1-5297-0724-3
ISBN 978-1-5297-0725-0 (pbk)

˙⁺ SAGE we take sustainability seriously. Most of our products are printed in the UK using responsibly sourced ˙s and boards. When we print overseas we ensure sustainable papers are used as measured by the PREPS ˌystem. We undertake an annual audit to monitor our sustainability.

CONTENTS

ABOUT THE AUTHORS

Richard Bale is a Senior Teaching Fellow in Educational Development in the Centre for Higher Education Research and Scholarship (CHERS) in the Educational Development Unit at Imperial College London. He is a linguist by background, and prior to working in educational development he held roles such as Head of Modern Languages, Lecturer in Applied Linguistics and Teaching Fellow in German, Translation and Interpreting. Richard holds a PhD in corpus-based interpreter education, a Master's (MEd) in University Learning and Teaching, a PGCE in Modern Languages, a BSc (Hons) in Linguistic and International Studies, and he is a Senior Fellow of the Higher Education Academy (SFHEA). His first book, *Teaching with Confidence in Higher Education: Applying Strategies from the Performing Arts*, was published in 2020 by Routledge.

Mary Seabrook leads the Graduate Teaching Assistant Development Programme at King's College London, is a Senior Teaching Fellow and a Senior Fellow of the Higher Education Academy (SFHEA). She has experience in a wide range of educational settings, including schools, adult and further education, the Open University and voluntary sector. Before taking up her current post, she worked as a self-employed Education Consultant, undertaking a range of teaching, research and development projects. She was previously Senior Lecturer in Medical Education at Guy's, King's and St Thomas' School of Medicine and her PhD explored the changing culture and values of medical education. Drawing on many years of observing doctors in educational roles, her book *How to Teach in Clinical Settings* was published in 2014 by Wiley-Blackwell.

ABOUT THE AUTHORS

ACKNOWLEDGEMENTS

We would like to thank our editors at Sage, Diana Alves and James Clark, for commissioning the book and for their support and guidance throughout the writing process. We are also very grateful to the following people for reviewing chapter drafts: Kristina Arakelyan, Lauren Cracknell, Alistair Morey, Jayne Pearson, Chenée Psaros, Sandra Takei and Mira Vogel. Thanks also to Sandra Takei for providing Activity 9.3, to Mark Anderson for providing the storyboard template featured in Chapter 8, to Kerry Dobbins and other anonymous reviewers for their helpful feedback on our book proposal, and to all the colleagues who contributed the case studies that feature throughout the chapters. We would also like to thank Advance HE, Guild HE and Universities UK for granting permission to print the UK Professional Standards Framework, which enabled us to map the chapters to the dimensions of the UKPSF. Finally, we are very grateful to the many colleagues, students and course participants who have helped to shape our ideas and practices over the years.

INTRODUCTION

Welcome to *Introduction to University Teaching*. Our aim in this book is to provide an accessible, reader-friendly guide to some of the key issues, topics and practices of relevance to anyone working in a teaching and learning support role at UK universities. You may have just started teaching, or maybe you are preparing for your first teaching sessions in the near future. Or, perhaps you have been teaching for some time, and now you would like to reflect on and formalise your practice as a means of professional development.

Who is this book for?

This book is aimed at colleagues who are relatively new to teaching in higher education. We focus on issues of particular relevance to staff who support learning and teaching at universities, but whose primary roles are not explicitly teaching-focused. This means the book is aimed at colleagues working in a broad range of disciplines and functions, and with a variety of remits. These include, among others:

- Doctoral Researchers
- Graduate Teaching Assistants (GTAs)
- Teaching Assistants
- Postgraduate students who teach
- Postdoctoral Researchers
- Research Assistants
- Learning Technologists
- Learning Designers
- Librarians
- Disability Advisors
- Specific Learning Difficulties Tutors
- Careers Advisors
- Education Administrators
- Education Managers.

Regardless of your job title, if you are involved in aspects of learning and teaching, either directly or indirectly, the chapters in this book will be helpful to you.

Structure of the book

We have structured the book into 12 chapters, each discussing a particular aspect of teaching and learning practice. However, the various topics are linked, so we have provided cross-references between chapters at relevant points. Each chapter contains activities and points for reflection, where we encourage you to relate the chapter content to your own practice and experience. You could do this on your own or in collaboration with other colleagues who are also teaching. Each chapter begins with three learning outcomes. These help you to understand what our intentions are, providing a guide for what you are likely to learn by reading the chapter and completing the activities. We conclude each chapter with a brief 'over to you' section, where we invite you to reconsider the chapter learning outcomes and think about how you will incorporate what you have learned into your ongoing teaching practice. A further feature of this book is a tool for your professional development. As a teacher in higher education, you have the opportunity to have your teaching experience recognised in the form of a teaching fellowship awarded by an organisation called Advance HE, formerly the Higher Education Academy (HEA). We introduce this organisation in more detail below. We have also mapped each chapter to the framework that is used to evidence your practice and gain fellowship – the UK Professional Standards Framework (UKPSF) (see Table 0.1). We explore the benefits of gaining fellowship when we discuss your career development in Chapter 12. Finally, we have included case studies from teachers in various roles, all of whom have kindly given permission for extracts of their fellowship applications to be included at relevant points throughout this book. These case studies help to illustrate the points made in the chapters, and they also provide examples of reflective writing from successful fellowship applications.

What are Advance HE and the UKPSF?

The UK Professional Standards Framework (UKPSF) is a set of professional standards for all colleagues involved in teaching and learning support in higher education. The framework is overseen by an organisation called Advance HE, which was formed in 2018. Advance HE is a sector-wide organisation for equality and diversity, learning and teaching, and leadership and governance in higher education. Prior to 2018, responsibility for the learning and teaching part of Advance HE – as well as the UKPSF – sat with the Higher Education Academy (HEA). The HEA advocated for evidence-based teaching and awarded fellowships to recognise university teachers' practice and expertise. To this day, recipients of fellowships are entitled to use postnominal letters, depending on the category of fellowship awarded. These are:

- Associate Fellow (AFHEA)
- Fellow (FHEA)
- Senior Fellow (SFHEA)
- Principal Fellow (PFHEA).

The category of fellowship awarded depends on the kind of role the applicant has in relation to teaching and learning. This means it is not about hierarchy or status. For example, an eminent professor who has little or no teaching responsibilities may not be eligible to apply for any category of fellowship. Colleagues reading this book are likely to have roles that align with Associate Fellowship or Fellowship, so we will focus on these two categories in this book.

Regardless of the category of fellowship, applicants must show how their practice aligns with the UKPSF. This is usually done by writing a series of reflective accounts (see the case studies throughout the chapters of this book), although some universities and programmes also accept other formats, such as oral presentations. The UKPSF consists of three dimensions:

- five Areas of Activity (A) – these outline the kinds of activities undertaken by colleagues who are teaching and supporting learning in higher education
- six aspects of Core Knowledge (K) – these represent what colleagues who are teaching and supporting learning in higher education need to know in order to carry out the activities competently
- four Professional Values (V) – these are the values that colleagues who are teaching and supporting learning in higher education should hold and demonstrate in their practice.

In Figure 0.1, you can see the three dimensions of the UKPSF and how they relate to each other. The Areas of Activity are depicted at the top, and the Core Knowledge and Professional Values underpin these activities. As mentioned above, the category of fellowship suitable for you depends on the scope of your role in teaching and learning support. This is recognised in the extent to which your practice needs to be mapped to the UKPSF:

- For Associate Fellowship, also called Descriptor 1, you are required to provide evidence of your practice in two of the five Areas of Activity. In addition, you need to evidence at least Core Knowledge K1 and K2, and any (but not necessarily all) of the Professional Values.
- For Fellowship, also called Descriptor 2, you are required to provide evidence of your practice in all five Areas of Activity, all six aspects of Core Knowledge and all four Professional Values.

To show how the chapters of this book map to this framework, we have provided an overview in Table 0.1 of indicative mappings to the UKPSF. This will help you to identify which aspects of practice you might be able to evidence by incorporating reflections on each chapter and topic into your practice. You can find more detailed information about the UKPSF and requirements for each category of fellowship in the Further Resources at the end of this Introduction.

Areas of Activity

A1 Design and plan learning activities and/or programmes of study

A2 Teach and/or support learning

A3 Assess and give feedback to learners

A4 Develop effective learning environments and approaches to student support and guidance

A5 Engage in continuing professional development in subjects/disciplines and their pedagogy, incorporating research, scholarship and the evaluation of professional practices

Core Knowledge

K1 The subject material

K2 Appropriate methods for teaching, learning and assessing in the subject area and at the level of the academic programme

K3 How students learn, both generally and within their subject/disciplinary area(s)

K4 The use and value of appropriate learning technologies

K5 Methods for evaluating the effectiveness of teaching

K6 The implications of quality assurance and quality enhancement for academic and professional practice with a particular focus on teaching

Professional Values

V1 Respect individual learners and diverse learning communities

V2 Promote participation in higher education and equality of opportunity for learners

V3 Use evidence-informed approaches and the outcomes from research, scholarship and continuing professional development

V4 Acknowledge the wider context in which higher education operates recognising the implications for professional practice

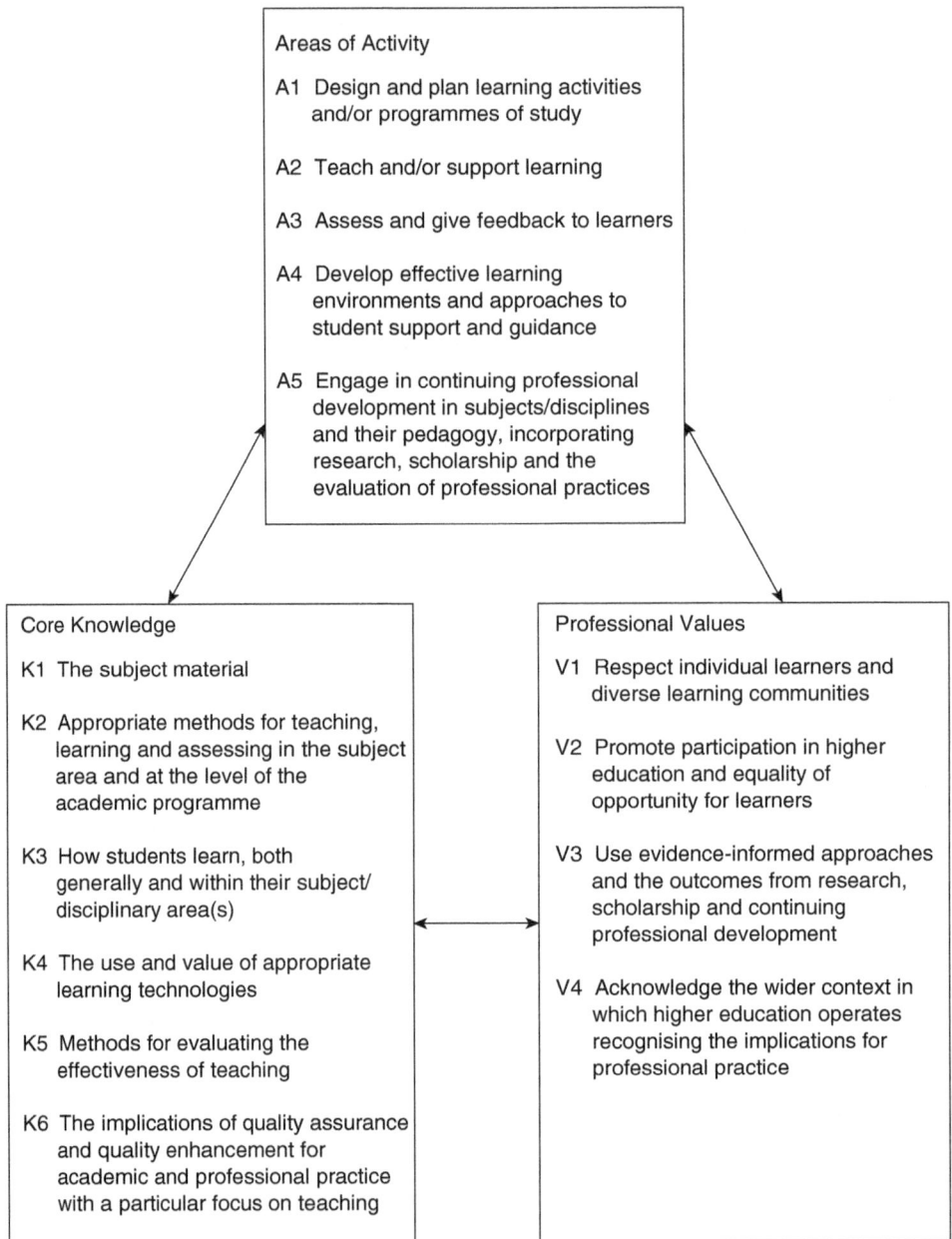

Figure 0.1 The dimensions of the UK Professional Standards Framework (UKPSF)

Introduction to the chapters

In the first chapter, we begin by providing some brief contextual information about UK higher education, and then invite you to think about your role in teaching and supporting learning, and how you describe your identity within your institution.

Table 0.1 Indicative mappings to the UKPSF by chapter

Chapter	Indicative UKPSF mapping
1	A5, K6, V4
2	A2, A5, K2, K3, V3
3	A1, K2, V1
4	A1, A2, A3, A4, K2, K3, V1, V2
5	A1, A2, A3, A4, K2, K3, K4, V1, V2, V3, V4
6	A1, A4, K2, K3, V1, V2
7	A2, A3, A4, K2, K3, V1, V2
8	A1, A2, A3, A4, K2, K4, V1, V2, V4
9	A1, A2, A3, A4, A5, K1, K2, K3, K4, V1, V2, V3, V4
10	A1, A3, K2, V3
11	A2, A3, A4, A5, V4
12	A1, A2, A3, A4, A5, K1, K2, K3, K4, V1, V2, V3, V4

Then, in Chapter 2, we ask what we mean when we use the terms 'teaching' and 'learning'. Whilst our focus is on practice, we provide an overview of some of the prevailing learning theories which you might find helpful when conceptualising how you teach and how your students learn. In Chapter 3, we explore the planning stage of teaching. We focus on key components to consider when designing learning and teaching sessions, whether you are planning an individual session or (perhaps in future) an entire course.

The next chapters focus on teaching and learning in specific contexts. Chapter 4 discusses teaching in small groups, such as tutorials, whereas Chapter 5 explores large group teaching in lectures. Chapter 6 looks at teaching and learning in other settings, such as laboratories and in fieldwork, and Chapter 7 discusses teaching in one-to-one contexts, such as project supervision.

In Chapters 8 and 9, we explore topics that are integral to our teaching practice, namely the use of digital technologies to enhance learning and teaching, and the importance of inclusive practice. Then, in Chapter 10, we discuss the vital aspect of teaching practice that is assessment and feedback. Chapter 11 identifies some of the challenges that you might encounter in your teaching, and suggests some potential approaches and ways to address these challenges. Finally, Chapter 12 encourages you to look beyond this initial exploration of learning and teaching, and to think about how you can evaluate your teaching and develop your career as a university teacher. Professional development is integrated throughout this book in the form of reflection as well as encouraging you to evidence your practice against the UKPSF by applying for Associate Fellowship or Fellowship.

Further resources

Advance HE – the website of the organisation that awards fellowships (AFHEA and FHEA): www.advance-he.ac.uk/

UKPSF download: www.advance-he.ac.uk/knowledge-hub/uk-professional-standards-framework-ukpsf

1
STARTING TO TEACH IN HIGHER EDUCATION

Learning outcomes

After reading this chapter you should be able to:

- Explain key features of a university teacher's role
- Recognise connections between various identities, e.g. teacher, researcher, mentor
- Identify your own training context and reflect on additional academic development needs.

Introduction

In this chapter, we will explore some of the thoughts you might have as you begin teaching in higher education. We start by providing some brief context about the current state of play in UK higher education. We then invite you to explore fundamental questions about your identity, and how you see yourself within the university system. These questions – and your reflections – lead us on to a discussion of some of the key features of your role in teaching and learning as well as aspects of work which you should not be expected to do. We will also introduce the concept of scholarship of teaching and learning (SoTL), and encourage you to add 'scholar' or 'teacher–researcher' to your list of roles. Finally, we identify the range of training and support that is available for teachers in higher education, and encourage you to find out what is offered at your own institution.

A brief note on the UK higher education context

The higher education sector has undergone, and continues to undergo, rapid change in recent years, and this makes it an exciting time to start teaching in universities. To understand the context in which we teach nowadays, it is perhaps useful to go back to significant events of the 1990s and the noughties. In the mid-1990s, the UK government commissioned a report on the future of higher education. The report, led by Sir Ronald Dearing, made 93 recommendations and paved the way for many of the changes in funding and growth of the sector that we see today. A key recommendation of the report (Dearing, 1997) was that teaching staff receive training in teaching during their probationary period. Thirteen years later, the Browne Review (Browne, 2010) highlighted further the need for teaching staff in universities to have the opportunity to obtain teaching qualifications. The report also stated that universities would be required to publish information about teaching qualifications of academic staff.

> It will be a condition of receipt of income from the Student Finance Plan for the costs of learning that institutions require all new academics with teaching responsibilities to undertake a teaching training qualification accredited by the HE Academy, and that the option to gain such a qualification is made available to all staff – including researchers and postgraduate students – with teaching responsibilities. Anonymised information about the proportion of teaching-active staff with such a qualification should be made available at subject level by each institution. (Browne, 2010: 48)

This was an important milestone because, as is clear from the quote above, Browne recommended that teaching training be made available to *all staff* whose roles include elements of teaching and supporting learning. Since the Browne Review, many universities now stipulate that teaching staff must gain professional recognition of their teaching by achieving Fellowship of the Higher Education Academy (Ayres, 2018). All this means that teaching staff are increasingly expected to have teaching qualifications and/or attend training, and this includes training programmes for part-time teaching staff, such as Graduate Teaching Assistants (GTAs) (Winter et al., 2015) and other colleagues who support students' learning.

The dependence on part-time teaching staff has increased in recent years (cf. Muzaka, 2009; Standen, 2018), and this has further highlighted the need for high-quality, comprehensive training for such colleagues, who are often working (and/or studying) in a variety of roles, such as postgraduate researchers, postdocs, librarians, learning designers, learning technologists and so on. This means there is a great opportunity for teachers, regardless of job titles and substantive roles, to gain training and qualifications in teaching and to enjoy higher status as educators.

Funding of higher education and the Teaching Excellence Framework (TEF)

The professionalisation of teaching in higher education is partly a result of changes in how we fund universities. Depending on when you studied, and in which country of the UK (if you attended higher education in the UK), you may have received a grant to pay for living costs during your studies, or, after the Dearing Report, you may have paid tuition fees up to £1,000 a year. Fast forward to the current day, you might be charged in excess of £9,000 per year in England and Wales, over £4,000 in Northern Ireland and over £1,000 in Scotland, depending on your age.

As students now usually pay fees, the quality of teaching is receiving greater and greater scrutiny, and perhaps rightly so. An important development in quality assurance has been the Teaching Excellence and Student Outcomes Framework (TEF), which is an exercise in assessing teaching excellence in universities, currently only in England. The name of this framework – 'teaching excellence' – highlights a difficulty when comparing and benchmarking teaching quality across institutions; namely it is difficult to conceptualise what we mean by 'excellence', and therefore attempts to assess teaching excellence across different institutions and a wide range of disciplines bring great challenges. Nevertheless, the emergence of the TEF might be viewed optimistically as it signals a change in the status of teaching in higher education alongside research, which has undergone a similar assessment exercise, the Research Excellence Framework (REF) – formerly the Research Assessment Exercise (RAE) – since the 1980s.

The policies of the last 30 years or so show a shift from public to private funding, with competition and marketisation at the heart of the funding model. Since 2015, the cap on undergraduate student numbers was lifted by the UK government, meaning universities in the UK could recruit as many undergraduate students as they could attract. The aim was partly to improve access to higher education; however, in a competitive market, where most of the funding is derived from students' tuition fees, it is in the interests of universities to attract as many students as possible. This has implications for staffing and teaching resources, with a broad range of higher education staff now involved in teaching and supporting learning. The marketisation of higher education has also shifted the relationship between students and their universities. In a survey conducted by Universities UK in 2017, just under half of undergraduates (47%) said they considered themselves to be customers of their universities.

This consumer mentality adds to the increasing scrutiny of teaching quality and, whilst we might not agree that education should be a commodity, this creates new opportunities for teachers, and the sector as a whole, to reflect on how we teach and how we train and support colleagues who teach and support learning in higher education.

Student surveys

There are various mechanisms by which students' opinions on their university experiences are sought. One such survey is the National Student Survey (NSS), which takes place annually. The NSS, which is commissioned by the independent regulator for higher education in England, the Office for Students (OfS), asks final-year undergraduates about their experiences of studying their particular course at their chosen institution. The survey consists of 27 questions on eight aspects of the student experience, with responses rated on a Likert scale from 'definitely agree' to 'definitely disagree'. The eight aspects included in the survey are:

- Teaching on the course
- Learning opportunities
- Assessment and feedback
- Academic support
- Organisation and management
- Learning resources
- Learning community
- Student voice.

The survey culminates in a score for 'overall satisfaction', and students have the option of adding qualitative comments in response to the questions. The NSS is one instrument used by universities to monitor teaching practice at a departmental and an institutional level, and this feedback can be used to improve practices for current and future students. Having said this, several criticisms have been levelled at the NSS, not least due to the focus on 'satisfaction' scores rather than actual levels of quality. Institutions also run campaigns detailing why students should be satisfied, highlighting that good results in the survey have a positive impact on the institution's standing in league tables, and hence on the value of degrees awarded by that university.

If you are teaching postgraduate students, it is also useful to be aware of how postgraduate taught and postgraduate research students are surveyed. Postgraduate taught (e.g. Master's) students are surveyed via the Postgraduate Taught Experience Survey (PTES), which takes place annually and is organised by Advance HE – the organisation that oversees the award of Higher Education Academy Fellowships, which you may be applying for. Advance HE also organises the annual Postgraduate Research Experience Survey (PRES), which aims to find out about the experiences of students studying for research degrees (e.g. MPhil, PhD).

Activity 1.1

Your institutional context

Take some time to familiarise yourself with the context of your own institution:

- Does your institution subscribe to Advance HE? If so, what support is available for teachers who would like to gain recognition as a Fellow (FHEA) or an Associate Fellow (AFHEA)? Is gaining fellowship compulsory in your institution?
- What was the outcome of the most recent TEF at your institution and in your department?
- What were the results of the most recent NSS for your institution? Look at this for the institution as a whole as well as the results for your department.
- Do the same for the most recent PTES and PRES.

A senior colleague in your department might be able to direct you to answers to these questions. Alternatively, if your institution has an educational development unit (sometimes called different names, such as centre for learning and teaching), staff in that department will be able to answer these questions or direct you to the relevant information.

Who are you? What is your role in the university?

Having explored a bit of the wider context, let's come back to you and your own position. Universities are diverse and complex institutions consisting of a range of people performing a variety of important roles. For some colleagues, their main role may contribute to one or both of the key areas of focus in the work of the university, namely teaching and research. Others may have a different role, which relates to teaching and/or research less directly. As you are reading this book, we can probably assume that your role involves aspects of learning and teaching either as the main part of your remit or as a smaller but significant part of your work.

Reflection

What is your role at your university? How are you involved in teaching and supporting learning? You could answer this question by thinking about the job title on your contract, but it is also useful to think about this in more detail: What tasks do you do day-to-day? If a friend or a family member asks what you do, what do you tell them; how do you describe your work? How do you see your professional identity? How does teaching relate to your other roles?

Discussion

Some roles at universities have very clear remits in teaching and/or research, such as lecturer, professor, teaching fellow, research assistant or postdoctoral researcher, for example. However, as is probably evident from your own reflections, universities employ a whole host of colleagues whose work makes a significant contribution to teaching and research. These might include librarians, learning technologists, learning designers, doctoral researchers and graduate teaching assistants, education managers, programme managers, administrative assistants ... The list of roles and job titles is potentially endless. The important point is that colleagues in these roles have an impact on students and their learning. Whether you describe yourself first and foremost as a teacher, a librarian, a doctoral researcher, an academic, and so on, gives you an insight into how you see yourself in the university; what is your (academic) identity? Academic identities are complex, dynamic and changeable, and developing a teacher identity can be challenging (Dugas et al., 2020; Van Lankveld et al., 2017). It is important to identify your core values in relation to your work so that you can construct an authentic identity as a teacher (Fitzmaurice, 2013). Whatever your role, it is important to consider how you personally, specifically, support teaching and learning. If you are a learning technologist, for example, perhaps you do not often teach directly, but your work has an impact on how others teach and how students learn. Or, perhaps you are a doctoral researcher and you work as a graduate teaching assistant in your department. How much of your time is spent on teaching-related activities? How do you see yourself: first as a researcher, second as a teacher? Ask yourself questions like this and keep your responses in mind as you work through the topics in the other chapters in this book. It would also be interesting to see whether your sense of identity (as a teacher or otherwise) changes as you gain more experience in teaching and learning.

What does the university teaching role entail?

As we have seen above, the range of teaching and learning support roles in higher education is diverse. In addition to lecturers and professors, who are perhaps the obvious teachers (and researchers) in universities, there is a plethora of teaching and learning support roles. Colleagues whose remit is heavily focused on teaching, such as module leads, are often expected to take responsibility for all aspects of the teaching encounter, from designing the learning activities and assessments, to ensuring the learning environment is conducive to learning. In terms of the UKPSF and Fellowship, this means all five Areas of Activity and all aspects of Core Knowledge and the Professional Values need to be evidenced in the teacher's practice. In your own teaching practice, you are likely to be taking responsibility for specific aspects of learning and teaching, or you may be co-teaching. Your precise remit, depending on whether you are a GTA, a librarian, a learning technologist, etc., will need to be clarified by colleagues in your department, but here are some responsibilities you can expect to have in your teaching practice:

- Understand how your teaching sessions fit within the wider module or programme of study. What are the module learning outcomes and how do your sessions help students to meet these outcomes?
- Plan your teaching sessions in advance. What will you do during the sessions? What will your students do? How will you encourage your students to engage actively during the sessions? What will students need to do to prepare for each session?
- Help students to learn during your sessions. How will you facilitate students' learning? How will you make students feel safe and included?
- Draw students' attention to information in the module handbook, such as assessment information and deadlines. How will you help students to prepare for their assessments?
- Provide regular opportunities for students to receive formative feedback. What methods will you use to assess your students formatively? How will you provide feedback? Will there be opportunities for students to provide feedback to each other?
- Mark students' assessments and provide feedback and grades in a timely manner, in accordance with departmental policies. How will you ensure you assess fairly? Are there any types of assessment that you should not mark? You can check this with your departmental module lead.
- Signpost students to relevant pastoral support and other services in the university.

Equally as important as knowing what your role entails is understanding what your role should *not* entail. In your role, you are unlikely to be expected to take responsibility for the following:

- Design the module or syllabus. If teaching is a subsidiary part of your role, the syllabus and modules are likely to be designed by other colleagues, such as module leads.
- Design assessments. If you are not designing modules or syllabi, you are not likely to be involved in writing learning outcomes, which means you will not be expected to design assessments. In order for a course to be constructively aligned (see Chapter 3), you would need to be involved at all stages, from writing learning outcomes, to planning learning and teaching activities, to designing assessments.

- Know all the answers to students' questions. This applies to any teacher, but it is important to recognise that you are not expected to know the answers to an infinite number of questions. Of course, you need to be prepared for your sessions and know the key content, but as a facilitator of learning, it is not your role to have all the answers; it is more about guiding students and helping to facilitate their learning.
- Excessive response to students outside of class time. Depending on your context, you may have set 'office hours' when you can meet students, or you may agree to respond to student queries by email. However, you should agree with your colleagues – and with your students – what can be expected of you regarding response to teaching-related emails outside of your scheduled teaching time.

Teaching and research: scholarship of teaching and learning (SoTL)

At the start of this chapter, we invited you to reflect on your role in the university, where there is often a distinction between teaching, research and professional service roles. However, as the target audience of this book, you are likely to be in a role that crosses this divide. Maybe you are a librarian who also facilitates workshops on information literacy; perhaps you are a learning technologist who advises academics on technology-enhanced learning; maybe you are a postgraduate researcher who teaches undergraduates in your role as a graduate teaching assistant. Regardless of your role, and regardless of whether you have an explicit research component in your work, there are opportunities to take a scholarly approach to your teaching. This brings us to the scholarship of teaching and learning (SoTL).

The concept of scholarship of teaching, in contrast to the more general scholarship of discovery (research), was first cited by Boyer (1990), who wrote about the need to move away from the tendency to pit teaching versus research. For Boyer, teaching itself ought to be subject to scholarship and enquiry. Since then, various conceptions of SoTL have been proposed, but some of the key characteristics are summarised by Trigwell et al. (2000), who suggested that SoTL is characterised by a teacher who:

- takes a scholarly approach to teaching by reading work published by others – this includes scholarship of teaching and learning in general and in the teacher's specific discipline
- is a reflective practitioner who asks questions about their own teaching practice and about their students' learning – this leads to action in the form of investigating practice and trying to find solutions to identified problems
- shares their own work with others – this might be in the form of a publication in a journal, a talk at a conference, a blog post, etc.
- takes a student-centred approach in their practice – this means that the focus in any scholarly enquiry is on student learning, not just on teaching practice.

The key aim of SoTL, and the dissemination of findings from teachers' projects, is not just to increase teaching expertise as a form of continuing professional development;

the focus instead is on improving students' learning, which makes SoTL as a concept inherently student-centred. SoTL is also an inclusive scholarly endeavour, as anyone involved in teaching and learning can engage in such scholarship; it is not something reserved for academic or research staff. While there are many ways of disseminating projects which could be categorised as SoTL, there are now several journals explicitly focused on SoTL, such as the *Journal of Scholarship of Teaching and Learning* (since 2001), the *International Journal for the Scholarship of Teaching and Learning* (since 2007), *Teaching and Learning Inquiry* (since 2013) and *Open Scholarship of Teaching and Learning* (since 2021). You can find links to these journals in the Further Resources at the end of this chapter.

If we return at this point to your reflections on your role at the university, the concept of SoTL might give you a different perspective on the work that you do in learning and teaching. In university teaching, we are all part of a scholarly community, regardless of whether our primary remit is in disciplinary research. So, in addition to your other roles that you reflected on earlier, you might now consider adding 'scholar' or 'researcher' to your remit, if you did not already do so. You are already engaging in reflective practice through reading this book, and you may have already started reading some of the literature on learning and teaching. As you continue to teach, you may start to identify aspects of your practice that you would like to engage with in a scholarly way, and subsequently disseminate this in a form of publication.

Activity 1.2

Identifying areas of practice for scholarly investigation

From what you have read so far about the scholarship of teaching and learning, can you identify any areas of your teaching practice that you could investigate?

There is now a growing National Teaching Repository, led by Edge Hill University and funded by Advance HE, which consists of teaching resources, ideas and strategies submitted by colleagues teaching at a variety of institutions. There is also a dedicated section on SoTL. Have a look at some of the submissions for inspiration: https://figshare.edgehill.ac.uk/The_National_Teaching_Repository. If you do not currently have any ideas for your own potential SoTL projects, return to this point at a later date. We also revisit the concept of SoTL and scholarly enquiry in Chapter 12.

Training contexts for university teachers

So far, we have looked at your role(s) in teaching and learning as well as the wider context of higher education in the United Kingdom. As we come to the end of this chapter, and before exploring the other topics in the subsequent chapters, it is important to reflect on your current skills and experiences as a teacher in higher education, and to identify any training and professional development you might engage with as you progress. As we said earlier in this chapter, there is now a general expectation in universities that teachers receive training and/or qualifications in learning and teaching. One aspect of this, which we have already started to think about in this book so far, is recognition of your teaching practice through Advance HE fellowships, such as Associate Fellowship (AFHEA) and Fellowship (FHEA). However, in addition to this, there is a range of qualifications and professional development opportunities offered by different universities to help teachers to reflect on and develop their practice on a continuous basis.

Activity 1.3

Professional development provision at your institution(s)

Take some time to find out what professional development provision is provided at your institution in relation to learning and teaching practice. This might be in the form of workshops, qualifications, mentoring and so on. Make a list of the opportunities and think about which options are most applicable to you at your current stage in your teaching experience. A colleague in your department or colleagues in educational development may be able to offer advice on the opportunities that are most relevant to you personally.

From your investigation of the training context for teachers at your institution, you may come across a variety of opportunities. These might include:

- a one-off induction about teaching in your particular context
- one-off workshops on various topics in educational practice, e.g. facilitating small group learning, making teaching more inclusive, teaching in laboratory settings, designing authentic assessment
- mentoring and peer review of teaching
- professional recognition through Advance HE, e.g. AFHEA, FHEA
- academic professional apprenticeships in teaching and/or research (see Further Resources at the end of this chapter)
- postgraduate qualifications in education, such as Postgraduate Certificate, Postgraduate Diploma and Master's degrees in education.

Depending on the institution, some or all of these professional development provisions might be available to teachers, and academic professional apprenticeships and postgraduate qualifications up to Master's level may even be offered free of charge to those who are currently teaching at the institution. As we come to the end of this opening chapter, we encourage you to reflect on your own training needs with regards to teaching practice, and to find out what professional development is available at your institution.

Over to you

We hope this chapter has provided an opportunity for you to reflect on your role in teaching and learning at your university, and to consider the different facets of your professional identity. As you start your teaching, you should feel empowered to find out exactly what is expected of you, but also identify aspects of teaching-related work that should not form part of your role. You should also take some time to explore the professional development opportunities offered by your institution, and plan which training options are most relevant to you at this point in your teaching practice. As you read on through the other chapters in this book, we hope to stimulate ideas about other aspects of teaching, which might prompt you to engage with further development opportunities as they become relevant to you in your practice.

Further resources

The following three websites link to the main student surveys mentioned in this chapter:
The National Student Survey (NSS): www.thestudentsurvey.com/index.php
The Postgraduate Taught Experience Survey (PTES): www.advance-he.ac.uk/reports-publications-and-resources/postgraduate-taught-experience-survey-ptes
The Postgraduate Research Experience Survey (PRES): www.advance-he.ac.uk/reports-publications-and-resources/postgraduate-research-experience-survey-pres

The following webpages link to the four SoTL journals mentioned in this chapter:
Journal of the Scholarship of Teaching and Learning: https://scholarworks.iu.edu/journals/index.php/josotl/index
International Journal for the Scholarship of Teaching and Learning: https://digitalcommons.georgiasouthern.edu/ij-sotl/
Teaching and Learning Inquiry: https://journalhosting.ucalgary.ca/index.php/TLI/index
Open Scholarship of Teaching and Learning: https://osotl.org

The website of the Institute for Apprenticeships and Technical Education provides information about the academic professional (level 7) apprenticeship:
www.instituteforapprenticeships.org/apprenticeship-standards/academic-professional

References

Ayres, R. L. (2018) Impact assessment in higher education: a strategic view from the UK. *Information and Learning Science*, 119 (1/2): 94–100.

Boyer, E. L. (1990) *Scholarship Reconsidered: Priorities of the Professoriate*. Princeton, NJ: Carnegie Foundation for the Advancement of Teaching. https://files.eric.ed.gov/fulltext/ED326149.pdf (accessed 22 January 2021).

Browne, J. (2010) The Browne Review: Securing a sustainable future for higher education. www.gov.uk/government/uploads/system/uploads/attachment_data/file/422565/bis-10-1208-securing-sustainable-higher-education-browne-report.pdf (accessed 22 January 2021).

Dearing, R. (1997) The Dearing Report: Higher education in the learning society. www. educationengland.org.uk/documents/dearing1997/dearing1997.html (accessed 22 January 2021).

Dugas, D., Stich, A. E., Harris, L. N. and Summers, K. H. (2020) 'I'm being pulled in too many different directions': academic identity tensions at regional public universities in challenging economic times. *Studies in Higher Education*, 45 (2): 312–26.

Fitzmaurice, M. (2013) Constructing professional identity as a new academic: a moral endeavour. *Studies in Higher Education*, 38 (4): 613–22.

Muzaka, V. (2009) The niche of Graduate Teaching Assistants (GTAs): perceptions and reflections. *Teaching in Higher Education*, 14: 1–12.

Standen, A. (2018) Where teaching meets research: engaging postgraduate teaching assistants with research-based education. In V. C. H. Tong, A. Standen and M. Sotiriou (eds), *Shaping Higher Education with Students: Ways to Connect Research and Teaching*. London: UCL Press. pp. 41–52.

Trigwell, K., Martin, E., Benjamin, J. and Prosser, M. (2000) Scholarship of teaching: a model. *Higher Education Research and Development*, 19 (2): 155–68.

Universities UK (2017) Education, consumer rights and maintaining trust: what students want from their university. www.universitiesuk.ac.uk/policy-and-analysis/reports/Documents/2017/education-consumer-rights-maintaining-trust-web.pdf (accessed 22 January 2021).

Van Lankveld, T., Schoonenboom, J., Volman, M., Croiset, G. and Beishuizen, J. (2017) Developing a teacher identity in the university context: a systematic review of the literature. *Higher Education Research and Development*, 36 (2): 325–42.

Winter, J., Turner. R., Gedye, S., Nash, P. and Grant, V. (2015) Graduate Teaching Assistants: responding to the challenges of internationalisation. *International Journal for Academic Development*, 20: 33–45.

2

CONSIDERING HOW WE LEARN AND HOW WE TEACH

Learning outcomes

After reading this chapter you should be able to:

- Explain key learning theories and how these are relevant to your practice
- Describe different approaches to learning and consider how teaching promotes learning
- Evaluate how knowledge of theory can support the development of your teaching practice.

Introduction

In this chapter, we introduce some of the most prevalent theoretical perspectives on learning and teaching and consider how students approach learning. By exploring a range of theories, we encourage you to reflect on how you teach, how your students learn and why you teach in the ways that you do. Knowledge of theory can help us to articulate how we carry out our practice, and also give us confidence that our methods are grounded in evidence. It is also important to consider what we mean when we say we are 'going to teach' or 'my students are learning'. We start by reflecting on these two concepts: learning and teaching.

What does it mean to learn and to teach?

It is a matter of common experience that we all learn in different ways, at different paces, and that we enjoy different approaches. We have also all experienced different approaches to teaching, some of which we might remember for positive reasons and others we might avoid emulating in our own practice. The important point is that there is no one 'good' way of learning or a 'best' way to teach. What 'works' for one learner or teacher may not have the same intended effect for someone else. This complexity and variety is what makes learning and teaching exciting.

—— **Reflection** ——————————————————————————

Think about something you have learned in the past. This could be something in an academic subject, a skill used in everyday life, learning to play a musical instrument, etc. What does it mean 'to learn'? How would you conceptualise this process of learning? What made the process successful (or unsuccessful)?

Discussion

Depending on your existing values and beliefs about learning, you may have conceptualised learning in various ways, such as mastering a skill by practising regularly; listening to a teacher give a lecture; reading materials and producing your own notes; observing a more competent person perform the skill at hand; learning with and from your peers; explaining the topic/demonstrating the skill to someone else. The extent to which the learning was successful reveals something about your own values about learning. Perhaps the example you thought of reveals that you are good at learning on your own, or that you prefer to learn from experience and observation, or that you prefer to learn with and from others.

Reflection

Now think about something you have taught. Again, this could be in a formal setting in an academic subject, or you could think about teaching a friend or a family member something informally. What does it mean 'to teach'? How would you conceptualise this process of teaching? What made the process successful (or unsuccessful)?

Discussion

Your conceptualisation of teaching might depend on the example you chose for reflection, but also on your previous experiences of being taught. Perhaps your own experiences of being taught have involved a teacher/expert providing you with information and knowledge on a subject, or a practical demonstration of a skill, or perhaps you have been taught with greater distance between the teacher and you as the learner. Or, perhaps your beliefs about teaching mean there is no need for a teacher – as a physically present, more knowledgeable person – at all. The success of the teaching encounter may have been based on the relationship between learner and teacher; the motivation of the learner; the teacher's ability to engage students and explain concepts; the teacher's ability to facilitate discussions and group work. Your thoughts here reveal how you might define learning and teaching, and help to stimulate some reflection on how these two activities are different and how they interact with each other. It is useful to reflect on this in any case, but it is also something that you will need to do if you apply for fellowship. Case Study 2.1 is an extract from an Associate Fellowship personal statement, which outlines the applicant's role in learning and teaching.

Case Study 2.1

Extract from an AFHEA Personal Statement: Bridget McNulty, Graduate Management Trainee, Human Resources Division

I am currently employed as a Graduate Management Trainee. This three-year scheme aims to provide a strong foundation for future leaders in higher education through exposure to different facets of the university sector, of which learning and teaching activities play a fundamental part. I graduated from the University of Oxford with a BA (Hons) in English and Modern Languages in 2018. I have had experience of teaching and supporting learning with a range of diverse learners both in the UK and through international employment.

Since starting my current role, I have led a review of the institution's Success Guides – online resources tailored to student priorities – and created original content to meet the

(Continued)

needs of learners for the Education Office. Currently, in the Provost and President's Offices, I am exploring methods of engaging students in the development and implementation of both the Academic Strategy and the Sustainability Strategy, considering how strategic themes can be embedded in the curriculum.

I am committed to facilitating the learning of others and to my own professional development, recently achieving PRINCE 2 Practitioner (2019). I am proactive about fostering innovative approaches to student support; since the lockdown during the pandemic, I have collaborated with the Centre for Academic English to launch a virtual Conversation Club to tackle social isolation among our international students and enable them to develop their informal language skills. Formal recognition of my experience in teaching and supporting learning would enhance my understanding of teaching contexts and my authenticity as a learning support practitioner, which would be an asset for my personal and professional development.

Until we take some time to reflect on learning and teaching, it can be tempting to think of these two terms as being part of one activity. However, learning and teaching are different activities. Related but different. A teacher might teach a student to carry out a particular technique in a laboratory, for example. But the student is then unable to carry out the technique on their own. In this case, the teacher has done their job; they have *taught*. But the student has not *learned*. Teaching is one potential way of stimulating learning, but teaching does not necessarily lead to learning. Reflecting on how you view the roles of teachers and learners is a good way of starting to understand your own values and beliefs about learning and teaching. We have begun this process by thinking about our own experiences – both as learners and as teachers – but it is also useful to consider what learning theories tell us about how we learn and how we teach. Some of your own reflections so far are probably underpinned by different theoretical approaches, and theory can help us to make sense of our experiences. We will look at some of the most prominent learning theories and consider how these relate to our own learning and teaching experiences.

Teacher-centred versus student-centred theories of learning

When thinking about theories of learning, a useful question to ask is: where does learning take place? Your answer to this question will reveal which school of thought aligns with your understanding of what it means to learn and to teach. Some of the responses to this question might include:

- Learning takes place inside the heads of learners.
- Learning takes place in classrooms and lecture halls, with teachers leading the action.
- Learning takes place anywhere, both in formal and in informal spaces.

- Learning takes place in the social space between learners and teachers.
- Learning takes place online across networks.

A traditional view of teaching is that knowledge is transmitted from the teacher's head to the learner's head. This is a one-way process and a clear example of a teacher-centred conceptualisation of teaching, as opposed to learning. Without delving into the student's head, it is impossible to know whether any learning has taken place. This transmission model of teaching is what traditionally takes place in a didactic lecture, where a teacher or professor speaks, from the position of an expert, and students' heads (or notepads and laptops) are filled with information. Beyond this, there are three broad paradigms which have been proposed over the years: behaviourism, cognitivism and constructivism. These are summarised briefly here.

Behaviourism – cognitivism – constructivism

Behaviourism focuses on observable behaviours, or changes in behaviours, displayed by the learner. In a behaviourist approach, the learner is presented with a cue or some kind of input, which stimulates a response. The teacher might reinforce or discourage the learner's response by using reinforcements or punishments after the learner has displayed a behaviour in response to the stimulus. Examples of this might include some form of verbal reinforcement, such as 'excellent work!', or awarding students a small percentage of a module mark for participation in class. An influential proponent of behaviourism was American psychologist B. F. Skinner, who studied the causes of behavioural responses and the subsequent consequences of a learner's actions. Skinner called this process *operant conditioning*, whereby a behavioural response is either reinforced or punished in order to encourage or discourage repetition of the behaviour in the future. Reinforcements and punishments can both be either positive or negative: in each case, positive refers to the addition of a stimulus and negative refers to the removal of a stimulus, but both lead to a desired change in behaviour. For example, a teacher might praise a student for a piece of good work to encourage this behaviour (positive reinforcement) or a teacher might remove a homework assignment if students concentrate and demonstrate a good understanding of the topic during class (negative reinforcement). In both cases, the aim is to reinforce, to encourage, the desired behaviour. Similarly, punishments can be positive – adding an unpleasant stimulus to discourage repetition of the behaviour – or negative – removing a pleasant stimulus with the same aim of discouraging the displayed behaviour.

Cognitivism is a reaction to the behaviourist view of learning, contesting the notion that we merely respond to stimuli and change our behaviours in response to reinforcements and punishments. Theories in this paradigm stem from cognitive psychology, a key proponent of which was the Swiss child psychologist Jean Piaget. In the cognitive approach, learning takes place in the learner's head, and emphasis is placed on mental processing, thinking, memory and problem solving. Behaviours are observed, but any changed behaviour is seen as a result of cognitive processing in the learner's brain. A key difference between behaviourism and cognitivism is the role of the learner. From a behaviourist perspective, the learner is a passive recipient of environmental stimuli, whereas cognitivists view learners as active participants, with a focus on active processing of information.

Constructivism and cognitivism share many common characteristics, and some theorists consider constructivist approaches to be part of cognitivism. The premise of constructivism is that learners have their own, pre-existing experiences and knowledge; hence, the learning experience is unique to each individual learner, depending on the learner's own interpretation and process of meaning making. A key point of distinction between constructivist and behaviourist and cognitivist views of learning is the philosophical assumption that underpins these paradigms: behavioural and cognitive theories approach learning from a point of objectivity – that there is a real world and a set of truths, and teaching is about providing learners with this objective knowledge. Constructivist theories, on the other hand, place emphasis on subjective experiences of the learner, approaching learning as a process of interpretation and construction of knowledge based on previous experience. From a constructivist perspective, the teacher provides opportunities for the learner to engage in active discovery without assuming the role of knowledge provider.

Table 2.1 summarises the key points in these three paradigms, highlighting the role of the teacher, the role of the learner and how learning is conceptualised in each case.

Table 2.1 Summary of behaviourism, cognitivism and constructivism

	Behaviourism	Cognitivism	Constructivism
Teacher's role	Provides stimulus material and encourages desired responses through reinforcement and punishment	Proposes strategies for learners to incorporate new knowledge within existing knowledge, focusing on organisation of knowledge in the learner's memory	Facilitates the learner's discovery of new concepts by asking questions and providing space to construct meaning on the basis of prior experiences and existing knowledge
Learner's role	The learner is a passive recipient of stimuli administered by the teacher. The learner's behaviour is changed by the teacher's reinforcements and punishments	The learner is an active participant in the learning process, engaging in reorganising, memorising and storing of information, and adding to/changing existing mental models	The learner is an active participant in the learning process, engaging in interpretation and meaning making based on previous experiences
Concept of learning	Transfer of learned responses, from reinforcements and punishments, to new situations	Recall and retrieval of information from cognitive structures and application to different contexts	Interpretation of knowledge based on previous experience and subjective discovery of new knowledge

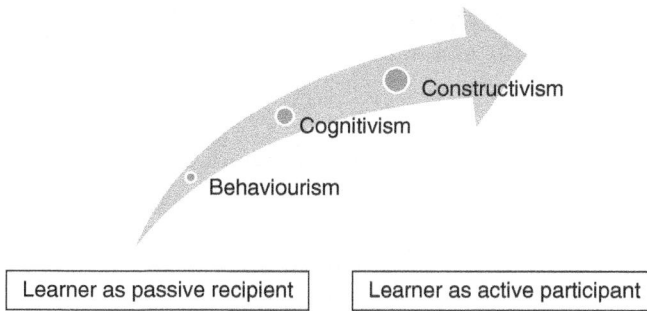

Figure 2.1 Behaviourism to constructivism: passive recipients to active participants

From this initial overview of learning theories, one point to emphasise is the different role played by the learner and the teacher in each conceptualisation of learning. As shown in Figure 2.1, there is a gradual (or perhaps sudden) shift from learners as passive recipients to more active participants as we move along the continuum from behaviourist to constructivist views of learning. In this way, these theories of learning move from teacher-centred, focusing on what the teacher does, to more student-centred views of learning as we move towards constructivist approaches.

From learning as an individual activity to learning as a social activity

The three paradigms discussed above provide us with some useful ways of conceptualising what it means to learn and to teach. A common thread in all three approaches is that learning is considered to be an individual activity. Now we turn our attention to theories that view learning as a social, interconnected activity.

Active learning

In discussions about learning and teaching and higher education, it is very likely that you have heard the term 'active learning', referring to approaches that place emphasis on students engaging in activities rather than listening passively to a teacher. This is not a theory, but rather an overarching term for a variety of activities and teaching methods aimed at engaging students in their learning. Active learning is not a new idea; as far back as the 1980s, Chickering and Gamson (1987: 4) wrote: 'Learning is not a spectator sport. Students do not learn much just sitting in classes listening to teachers.' Since this time, a growing body of evidence has shown that we learn more when we are actively engaged in the learning process (e.g. Freeman et al., 2014). Since 2000, there has even been a peer-reviewed journal dedicated to educational research in this area: *Active Learning in Higher Education*. It is also important to note that active learning techniques have been in use for many years in the compulsory education sector. If you think back to your time at school – in primary and/or secondary school, how often did you sit and listen to a lecture for a prolonged period of time? It is likely that you learned in active ways, partly because children are unlikely to sit and concentrate, and behave, for long periods of time! Active learning encompasses a broad range of activities, from pausing a lecture to allow students to think and process ideas, to group work, to the use of drama-based methods. We explore some of these methods in Chapter 4 in particular. Returning to our previous discussion about different theoretical paradigms, we can say that students engaged in active learning are constructing their own knowledge – in constructivist terms – using existing experiences to make sense of new information. In a classroom where active learning is taking place, students often construct knowledge collaboratively, with their peers in groups, and hence we also need to consider the social interactions involved when learning is taking place.

Social constructivism

Social constructivism, like constructivism, views learning as a subjective, meaning-making activity based on the learner's existing knowledge and previous experiences. The difference between these two theories is the emphasis on social interaction in social constructivism. This view of learning was developed by Soviet psychologist Lev Vygotsky, who argued that learning cannot be separated from its social context. If we go back to the questions above about where learning takes place, one potential answer from social constructivism would be that learning takes place in the social spaces and social interactions between learners and between learners and teachers. This makes for an inherently active conceptualisation of learning: (social) interaction with others by its nature rules out a passive learning experience. Vygotsky also diverged from constructivist views of learning by emphasising the role of language and culture in learning. From a social constructivist perspective, we do not simply construct knowledge based on our own individual experiences; instead, we socially construct knowledge collaboratively, based on our linguistic, cultural and social context. Here is one example given by Vygotsky (1978): If you think of a round, black shape with two hands, you do not simply see the shape and the colour of the object. You contextualise this and you – we – are able to describe and make sense of this object, which we call a clock. The linguistic and cultural means of calling this object a clock are derived from collaboration and co-construction. But what does all this mean for your own students' learning?

The answer to this question lies in another important aspect of social constructivism: Vygotsky's zone of proximal development (ZPD), which he defined as 'the distance between the actual developmental level … and the level of potential development … under adult guidance, or in collaboration with more capable peers' (Vygotsky, 1978: 86). This concept is usually illustrated using three concentric circles (see Figure 2.2), where the central circle represents what the learner can do unaided, the middle circle represents what the learner can do with guidance and collaboration – the zone of proximal development – and the outer circle represents what the learner is unable to do, even with assistance. An adapted version of the ZPD was created by German educator Tom Senninger (2000), who describes the central circle as the comfort zone, where little learning takes place. Then he describes the ZPD as the learning zone, and the outer circle as the panic zone, where learning does not, and cannot, take place.

The concept of the zone of proximal development encapsulates the social aspects of learning, and can be useful in helping us to pitch learning activities at the appropriate level – not too low in the learner's comfort zone and not too high in the panic zone, where the learner is likely to become stressed and demotivated. Within the zone of proximal development, the teacher can plan support activities to gradually enable the learner to perform the task unaided. The American psychologist Jerome Bruner coined the term 'scaffolding' to describe how a teacher can reduce the complexity and element of choice in a learning task in order to allow the learner to focus on the skill at hand (Bruner, 1978; Wood et al., 1976). Examples of scaffolding could include breaking a complex concept into smaller, more manageable chunks and teaching discrete parts before asking students to engage with the whole topic (see Case Study 2.2). Or, the teacher might demonstrate or model something to the students before asking them to perform the task themselves.

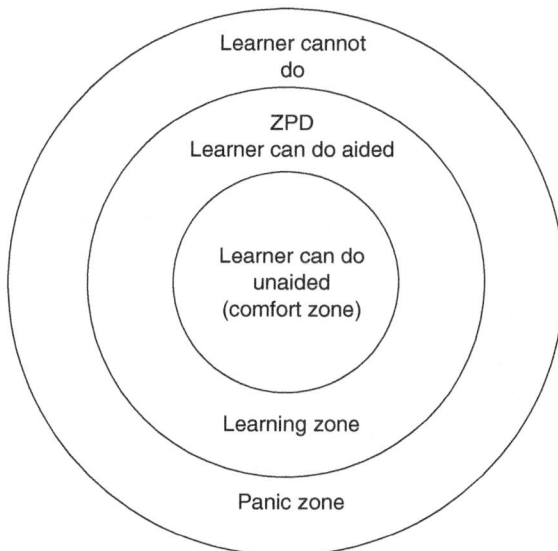

Figure 2.2 Zone of proximal development. (Adapted from Vygotsky, 1978 and Senninger, 2000)

Case Study 2.2

Scaffolding using seminar breakdown sheets: Anna Grimaldi, GTA in International Development

My most long-standing approach to planning seminars has been to use a 'breakdown sheet'. The sheet presents an overview of all the components (readings, concepts, themes, objectives) of that week's materials, providing students with context; it provides activities for the seminars; and it can be stored and used for revision later on for exams or essay-writing. One example is a sheet used for a politics class which compares two authors' social movement theories. The sheet includes prompts to each authors' key arguments for students to fill out in groups as revision, a table to apply the theories to existing social movements (with a pre-written example), an individual exercise to write a concise sentence comparing the theories, and a list of debate questions that provoke students to evaluate and critique authors through a think–pair–share exercise. According to one student: 'In other seminars, the focus seems to be on either the readings, or critical thinking, but in Anna's seminars we blend the two and that is something I have always appreciated.' I continue to develop the sheet following student feedback, such as by including a box for 'key words and phrases' as extra support for those who didn't arrive at university prepared for a given subject. I also made the sheets available online, open to editing from all students so that they can continue to work on them collaboratively outside class. Finally, I share my sheets with other GTAs, so that students across the year group have access to the same materials. In future, I would use this model when designing my own modules to fully integrate materials.

Learning through observation, social interaction and from each other

As we have seen from the theories introduced so far, there is a gradual shift from viewing learning as a passive, individualistic process to an active, social and interconnected activity. There are several other perspectives on learning which have social interaction at their heart, and we will take a brief look at some of these here.

Social learning theory, posited by Albert Bandura (1977), is often seen as the bridge between traditional behaviourist theories and cognitive theories. Bandura suggested that we learn from each other by observing, modelling and imitating. Part of this is Bandura's concept of self-efficacy, which is a learner's belief that they are able to perform a particular task. Bandura explains that there are four factors which influence a learner's self-efficacy:

- mastery experiences – confidence gained through overcoming challenges and exerting effort to learn the skill at hand
- vicarious experiences – opportunities to see people we consider to be similar to ourselves successfully completing the task
- social persuasion – receiving positive reinforcement and feedback that we are able to complete the task
- emotional and physical state – experiencing positive or negative emotional arousal from performing the task, and hence feeling motivated or demotivated.

Related to social learning theory is Lave and Wenger's (1991) *situated learning theory*, which views learning as something that happens in context as part of everyday life. These everyday-life contexts lead to learning in what Wenger (1998) calls *communities of practice*. We are all usually members of multiple communities of practice. For example, you may be part of a disciplinary or work-based community of practice of artists, engineers, medics, learning technologists or librarians. You may also be a researcher and participate in a variety of activities, such as carrying out (collaborative) research, presenting at conferences, reviewing peers' work, and so on. As you are reading this book, you are also probably becoming part of a teaching community of practice, in which you learn from colleagues and share and exchange ideas about teaching practice. Similarly, your students will be part of various communities of practice, such as a cohort of learners on a particular degree programme, a member of a student society, a (apprentice) colleague during a placement or an internship, and so on. This concept of learning emphasises the importance of context, focusing on the learner's emerging and developing competence in the given setting. A key part of learning in communities of practice is the development of the learner's identity as they participate in the work of the community.

A more recent theoretical perspective, which views learning as social and interconnected, is *connectivism*. This approach emerged as an attempt to help us understand how students learn in the digital age. Connectivism was first proposed by Siemens (2004), foregrounding the use of the internet and digital technologies in learning, and emphasising how knowledge is shared between people and across networks. This perspective differs from earlier theories, such as constructivism, as learning is not considered to be constructed within individuals or even within groups of learners, but instead the knowledge derived from social interaction can be shared and stored within and across networks. Connectivism shifts our focus away from learning taking place inside the heads of learners. With digital technologies and mass sharing of information online, this approach considers that learning takes place across networks of people, facilitated by digital technologies. The emergence of connectivism led to the first massive open online course (MOOC) offered by the University of Manitoba in 2008, which attracted over 2000 non fee-paying students from the general public. Since then, learners have been able to connect from all areas of the world in MOOCs offered by companies such as Future Learn and Coursera.

Activity 2.1

Relating theory to practice

Consider the theoretical perspectives on learning and teaching that you have just read about. Do any of the ideas in particular resonate with you? Do you disagree with any of the perspectives introduced? The following questions might help you to reflect on how these theories relate to your practice:

- What do students tend to find difficult or challenging in your discipline?
- Which theoretical perspectives help to explain these challenges?
- How can any of the theories discussed help you to help your learners?
- What difficulties or challenges do you find in your teaching?
- Can any of the theoretical perspectives help you to understand and overcome these challenges?

We have now looked at some key theoretical perspectives on learning and teaching and considered how these might help us to understand challenges experienced by learners and teachers. Now we turn our attention to the learners themselves and ask: how do our students approach their learning?

Students' approaches to learning

When considering how students approach learning, three terms usually feature prominently: surface, strategic and deep. This is based on the seminal work conducted by Marton and Saljö (1976a, 1976b) in Sweden. Marton and Saljö were interested in students' approaches to learning. They asked students to read a text and then to answer questions about the text. Marton and Saljö identified two broad approaches to the task of reading and engaging with the text, illustrated by the quotes from students in group A and group B below (Marton and Saljö, 1984: 43–5):

Group A:

'... the only thing I was thinking about was that I'd got to hurry. What happened was that I read a couple of sentences and then I didn't remember what I'd read because I was thinking all the time, 'I've got to hurry to get this done' ... I kept on thinking that I'd got to remember what I'd just read ...'

'Well I only concentrate on trying to remember as much as possible ...'

'You get distracted. You think "I've got to remember this now". And then you think so hard about having to remember it: that's why you don't remember it.'

Group B:

'… I stopped and thought about what they were actually saying … if there was something I thought wasn't right, and so on. You also stop and then (wonder) if that really follows that, sort of, is it really logical, what they've written. That sort of thing is what you stop for.'

'… and what you're thinking about then, it's, sort of, what was the point of the article?'

'Well, it was sort of the whole aim of [the article] – if that is what is meant. The whole aim of the article was what I was thinking of, sort of.'

Reflection

What do you notice about the students' approaches to learning? What are the key features of the approaches in the quotations in group A and group B?

Discussion

From the quotations in group A, it is clear that the students were focused on memorising the text rather than understanding and engaging with the content. The focus on memorising and recall seemed to lead to anxiety and feeling under pressure, even though there was no time limit on the reading task. The students were concentrating on surface-level facts and words contained in the text rather than trying to understand the overall message. Imagine listening to a speaker and trying to repeat the words, almost verbatim, just after the speaker utters the words sentence by sentence. You would probably be able to repeat many of the words, but you would be unlikely to grasp the bigger picture; to understand the overall message. On the other hand, the quotations in group B illustrate a different approach to the task. The words, and the text itself, are not the focus of the students' attention. Instead, the students aimed to understand the author's intentions, and considered how the ideas in the text related to their existing knowledge and beliefs. This led to a questioning and critical reading of the text rather than accepting the author's ideas at face value.

If you think of your own students, or if you think back to when you were studying, you may identify (in yourself or in others) times when you just learned what was required, memorised the necessary content, and then completed the assessment. This is what Marton and Saljö referred to as surface learning (1984), illustrated by the quotations in group A above. On the other hand, you may have students who at times are more motivated to gain a broad, contextual understanding of the topic, and who seem to enjoy learning, discussing and making meaning. This is what Marton and Saljö referred to as deep learning (1984), shown by the students in group B above. Later, Entwistle and Ramsden ([1983]2015) added strategic learning, which refers to a focus on goals (perhaps a particular grade in an assessment) and a tendency to learn in both surface and deep ways depending on various factors, such as the perceived value of the topic of study and how much time the student has to prepare for an upcoming assignment. These different approaches to learning are not fixed traits or ways of permanently labelling students. Learners might approach learning tasks in different ways at different times depending on their perception of the task at hand and depending on their motivation.

Activity 2.2

Deep, surface and strategic learning

Consider the concepts of deep, surface and strategic learning. For each approach to learning, reflect on the following:

- What are students' intentions? What is their focus?
- What do students do? How do they learn?
- What is the impact on students' learning?
- How can you encourage your students to adopt a deep approach to learning? Is it always desirable to discourage surface and strategic approaches to learning?

Each approach to learning is likely to be very apparent by observing what students do: whether students ask questions; what kind of questions they ask; what learning materials they engage with; how they engage with learning materials. Table 2.2 summarises a few of these observations. An important point to highlight is that a deep approach to learning is likely to result in longer-term learning, as the subject material is placed in context and the learner is engaged in constructing meaning. In some ways, our education systems encourage students to adopt surface and strategic approaches to learning. We talk often about the grades required for entry into particular universities; we emphasise assessments and we often hear the criticism that we 'teach to the exam', simply training students to learn information for the purposes of a test, which often leads to short-term learning. However, as teachers, we are in a good position to encourage students to move beyond surface and strategic approaches. First, it is important that our conversations with students do not place assessment at the heart of the learning experience. We can focus instead on *why* the topics are being studied; what is the importance and how does the subject matter relate to other modules in the programme and to the world beyond the university classroom. By providing opportunities for students to question knowledge, to be critical and analytical, we can encourage students to construct their own meaning and to feel a sense of ownership of their learning. Having said all this, perhaps it is a sign of learner autonomy to be able to recognise when to be strategic, i.e. when to dedicate more time to deep learning and when to learn in a surface way. For example, in the internet age, simple facts can be looked up at the click of a button so it is perhaps strategic not to hold all this information in your head all of the time. We might say, then, that a truly deep learner is one who knows when and how to adapt the approach to learning to the task at hand.

Table 2.2 Overview of surface, strategic and deep learning

	Surface	Strategic	Deep
What is the student's intention?	To recall information; to replicate what has been taught	To pass an exam; to 'do well' in an assignment	To make connections between concepts; to understand
What does the student do?	• Focus on content • Skim read materials • Make and copy notes • Memorise facts • Accept knowledge at face value	• Focus on selecting content • Skim read materials to find points of focus • Focus on assessment – 'will this be on the exam?'	• Focus on broader context • Read beyond the course materials • Ask questions • Think critically • Make connections between concepts/topics/subjects
What is the impact on learning?	Retention of content, often in the short term	Understanding of selected, strategically learned content	Interconnected, contextualised understanding, often in the long term

A note on learning styles

In your own experience as a student, you may have completed a questionnaire to identify your preferred learning style. Perhaps, for you, learning occurs more successfully when information is presented visually, or aurally, or perhaps you need to move, feel, touch and experience things in order to learn. Since the 1970s, several learning styles theories have been proposed, aiming to categorise learners according to how they learn best, and, in turn, how teachers can teach in different ways to ensure each individual student learns. At face value, it would be difficult to disagree with this aim. Who would not want to ensure that all students learn and that their teaching is inclusive? However, unfortunately, the evidence supporting learning styles theories is scant at best. Learning styles theories propose that an individual's learning style remains constant in different subjects, settings and contexts. Learning styles also predict that learners perform better when they are taught according to their preferred learning style. However, across many studies in a variety of disciplines and countries, there is no evidence that either of these statements is true (cf. Willingham et al., 2015). Instead, it is perhaps more fruitful to focus on differences in prior knowledge and abilities of learners, so that we can help them to engage actively in meaning making and in constructing their own knowledge. As we mentioned earlier, the aim of learning styles – to teach in ways that help individual students to learn more successfully – is a noble one. However, the evidence simply does not support the categorisation of learners in this way. Of course, this does not mean we should forget about how we can make our teaching more inclusive. We will explore the important issue of inclusivity, and how we can make our teaching more inclusive, in Chapter 9.

How does all this theory help your practice?

As you have seen in this chapter, there is no one, unified theory of learning and teaching. There is also disagreement on the validity of some theoretical perspectives. You might ask, then, what is the point of theory? How does this help my practice? Theories provide us with principles on which we can base our practice. Theories also help us to make sense of complex phenomena and give us the means and vocabulary to discuss and articulate our experiences. And what could be more complex than a set of multifaceted, social, human activities like learning and teaching?

Activity 2.3

Considering how theory underpins aspects of your practice

Think about what you do as a teacher, such as how you design activities, how you teach certain topics, how you give feedback, how you encourage students to do things and how you discourage students from doing other things. Consider how any of these elements of your practice are underpinned by any of the theoretical perspectives you have read about.

When you start to reflect on what you do as a teacher, it soon becomes clear that many elements of your practice are already underpinned by a variety of theoretical perspectives, and this can give us confidence that our work is grounded in some form of evidence. You may have found that it was sometimes difficult to assign one particular theory to an aspect of your practice. This shows that the theoretical ideas presented in this chapter are not mutually exclusive; there is often some overlap. In addition to your own reflections, Table 2.3 shows some other examples of teaching practice along with suggestions for how these practices are underpinned by theory.

Table 2.3 Examples of teaching practice and corresponding theoretical underpinning

Example of teaching practice	Theoretical underpinning
Opportunities for targeted practice and repetition	Behaviourism
Clear structure and content pre-determined by the teacher	Behaviourism
A clear focus on student learning outcomes; provision of feedback linked to learning outcomes	Behaviourism
Use of (strict) routine in class so that students know what to expect in your classes	Behaviourism
Use of rewards, incentives, 'punishments', e.g. 5% of module mark for participation in class; 10% penalty for late submission of an assignment	Behaviourism
Activities designed to stimulate recall of prior knowledge, e.g. prompt questions, session summaries	Cognitivism
Breaking topics down into more manageable chunks – to prevent cognitive overload	Cognitivism
Highlighting links between new knowledge and existing knowledge – assimilation of new knowledge	Cognitivism/Constructivism
Opportunities for students to 'get out of their heads', e.g. using mind maps, concept maps	Cognitivism/Constructivism
Use of real-world examples, analogies and metaphors	Cognitivism/Constructivism
Use of stimulus material to promote discussion and exploration	Constructivism
Opportunities to reflect on the learning that has taken place	Constructivism
Opportunities to learn from role models (e.g. work placements, invited speakers/lecturers)	Social learning theory
Opportunities to learn from peers (e.g. peer-assisted learning schemes)	Social learning theory
Use of positive feedback to increase students' self-efficacy	Social learning theory
Creation of a positive learning environment to motivate learners	Social learning theory
Identify what learners already know and pitch learning in the zone of proximal development	Social constructivism
Use of group work with shared goals and endeavours	Social constructivism/ Community of practice
Use of whole-class discussions and debates – emphasising different (cultural) viewpoints and use of language	Social constructivism
Opportunities to apply learning to situated contexts, such as work placements, field trips, visits to companies, external organisations, etc.	Social constructivism/Situated learning/Community of practice
Opportunities to work in teams (e.g. problem-based learning, team-based learning)	Social constructivism
Opportunities to collaborate with others remotely (e.g. using online discussions, social media, MOOCs)	Connectivism/Social constructivism
Use of online (perhaps authentic) activities and assignments, such as blogs, vlogs, video creation, etc.	Connectivism
Collaboration between different groups of learners remotely (e.g. one cohort studying in the UK and another in Germany)	Connectivism/Social constructivism

In a very concrete way, knowledge of theory can help us to rationalise and justify our decision making. You could design the curriculum, teach the same topic and assess your students in many different ways. What led you to select your chosen method or teaching technique? Did it work? How do you know? How else could you do it? Knowledge of theory encourages us to be *reflective* teachers; to have a rationale and to move beyond thinking about *what* we teach and to consider *how* and *why* we practise in the ways that we do. This element of reflection and approaching teaching in a considered way is essential for ongoing development and, as mentioned in the Introduction, it is also important if you decide to apply for fellowship, evidencing your practice against the UKPSF.

— Case Study 2.3 —

Theoretical underpinning for active learning activity: Quentin Coutellier, GTA and doctoral researcher in a business school

Lecture theatres favour, at best, bidirectional exchanges, i.e. communication between students and the lecturer (Bonwell and Eison, 1991). They need to be rearranged to foster cooperation between students in a social constructivist approach: rows could be broken down slightly to form smaller discussion groups. Some lecture theatres at my institution are currently being refurbished to facilitate more dynamic, interactive teaching. This novel configuration opens up for various entertaining activities in which the lecturer becomes a mediator, e.g. having students simulate board meetings, so students peer review their work (Marburger, 2005). This also leaves more space for the lecturer to walk around and interact with students while he keeps [they keep] presenting slides, and other material on screen, using a remote laser pointer. For example, I aim to divide students into teams in the lecture theatre, so they tackle the business case from different perspectives, i.e. marketing team, management team, R&D team, board of directors. By doing so, they will have to defend their business recommendations using one common dataset, therefore each team remains able to fact check decisions. While the lecturer can introduce programming mechanisms, and still acts as 'data expert', students are encouraged to identify the best graphs, the best models from a toolbox which is left for them to explore. Using this common dataset, the lecturer can also simulate in real time additional variables, in accordance with other business courses, e.g. refining function parameters based on the material covered in business economics courses that students are already familiar with at this stage of the semester. My supervisor approves this idea and agrees that this will facilitate compromises between demonstrative delivery modes, and interactive exploration of programming resources, through which students help and challenge each other (Olitsky and Cosgrove, 2014).

Over to you

As we have said above, theory can enable us to make sense of our practice and help us to make decisions that mean teaching leads to learning. Some of the ideas discussed here may resonate with you and you may have realised that aspects of your practice are underpinned by particular theoretical approaches. On the other hand, there may be concepts that you do not find helpful. At this point, it might be useful to return to the reflection questions at the beginning of this chapter:

- How do you conceptualise learning?
- How do you conceptualise teaching?

Has your thinking changed since you initially reflected on these questions? In addition, you could think about the following:

- Which area of theory do you consider to be most important for teaching in your context? Why?
- Are there any theoretical perspectives that you disagree with?

You might find it useful to write down your responses to these questions and return to them at various points during your teaching to see if your views change.

Further resources

This book provides an accessible overview of key theories and thinkers in education.
Aubrey, K. and Riley, A. (2016) *Understanding and Using Educational Theory*. London: Sage.

This book is an edited volume bringing together key contemporary learning theorists, with chapters written by the theorists themselves.
Illeris, K. (ed.) (2018) *Contemporary Theories of Learning: Learning Theorists … in Their Own Words*, 2nd edn. Abingdon: Routledge.

References

Bandura, A. (1977) *Social Learning Theory*. New York: General Learning Press.
Bonwell, C. C. and Eison, J. A. (1991) Active learning: creating excitement in the classroom. *ASHE-ERIC Higher Education Report*. Washington, DC: School of Education and Human Development, George Washington University.
Bruner, J. S. (1978) The role of dialogue in language acquisition. In A. Sinclair, R. J. Jarvelle and W. J. M. Levelt (eds), *The Child's Concept of Language*. New York: Springer.
Chickering, A. and Gamson, Z. (1987) Seven principles for good practice in undergraduate education. *AAHE Bulletin*, 39 (7): 3–7.
Entwistle, N. and Ramsden, P. ([1983] 2015) *Understanding Student Learning* (Routledge Revivals). Abingdon: Routledge.

Freeman, S., Eddy, S. L., McDonough, M., Smith, M. K., Okoroafor, N., Jordt, H. and Wenderoth, M. P. (2014) Active learning increases student performance in science, engineering and mathematics. *Proceedings of the National Academy of Sciences*, 111 (23): 8410–15.

Lave, J. and Wenger, E. (1991) *Situated Learning: Legitimate Peripheral Participation*. Cambridge: Cambridge University Press.

Marburger, D. R. (2005) Comparing student performance using cooperative learning. *International Review of Economic Education*, 4 (1): 46–57.

Marton, F. and Säljö, R. (1976a) On qualitative differences in learning I – outcome and process. *British Journal of Educational Psychology*, 46 (1): 4–11.

Marton, F. and Säljö, R. (1976b) On qualitative differences in learning I – outcome as a function of the learner's conception of the task. *British Journal of Educational Psychology*, 46 (2): 115–27.

Marton, F. and Saljö, R. (1984) Explaining differences in outcome. In F. Marton, D. Hounsell and N. Entwistle (eds), *The Experience of Learning: Implications for Teaching and Studying in Higher Education*. Edinburgh: Scottish Academic Press.

Olitsky, N. H. and Cosgrove, S. B. (2014) The effect of blended courses on student learning: eidence from introductory economics courses. *International Review of Economic Education*, 15: 17–31.

Senninger, T. (2000) *Abenteuer leiten – in Abenteuern lernen*. Münster: Ökotopia.

Siemens, G. (2004) Connectivism: a theory for the digital age. CiteSeerX – Connectivism: A learning theory for the digital age (psu.edu) (accessed 22 January 2021).

Vygotsky, L. S. (1978) *Mind in Society: The Development of Higher Psychological Processes*. Cambridge, MA: Harvard University Press.

Wenger, E. (1998) *Communities of Practice: Learning, Meaning and Identity*. Cambridge: Cambridge University Press.

Willingham, D. T., Hughes, E. M. and Dobolyi, D. G. (2015) The scientific status of learning styles theories. *Teaching of Psychology*, 42 (3): 266–71.

Wood, D. J., Bruner, J. S. and Ross, G. (1976) The role of tutoring in problem solving. *Journal of Child Psychiatry and Psychology*, 17 (2): 89–100.

3

UNDERSTANDING COURSE DESIGN AND PLANNING TEACHING

Learning outcomes

After reading this chapter you should be able to:

- Identify the key components of any course
- Define what you want students to learn (formulate intended learning outcomes)
- Plan a teaching session to help students achieve these outcomes.

Introduction

In this chapter we will discuss aspects of teaching design. During the early stages of your teaching career, you are unlikely to be expected to design courses. However, an understanding of the different elements of a course will help you to appreciate the context within which you teach and ensure that your teaching is coherent with the other elements. In the first part of the chapter we describe the key elements of any course and in the second we demonstrate how you can use these to plan individual teaching sessions. In time, you may be involved in redeveloping or designing new courses yourself.

Understanding course design

There are various models of course design; one of the most commonly used is that of Biggs and Tang (2011), shown in Figure 3.1.

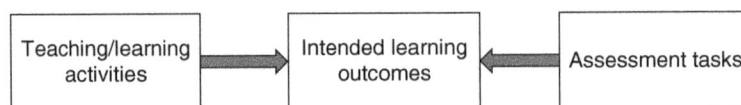

Figure 3.1 Three elements of course design

The *intended learning outcomes* describe what you want students to be able to do by the end of the course, for example to be able to conduct an experiment or analyse a text. (The term is often shortened to *learning outcomes*, although strictly speaking the latter are what students have actually learnt by the end of the course.) The learning outcomes are at the centre of the diagram because they determine the other two aspects. Some of you may be more familiar with the terms 'aims' and 'objectives'. Aims represent broad goals for a course, and objectives (or learning objectives) are similar to learning outcomes in specifying precisely what students are expected to achieve. Aims are usually teacher-centred whereas objectives and learning outcomes are student-centred.

The *teaching/learning activities* are the methods by which you help students to achieve the learning outcomes you have set, for example using small group work, practical sessions or e-learning.

The *assessment tasks* are how you check whether students have achieved the intended learning outcomes. Assessments can take place at various stages, from the formal exams and assignments that count towards students' final grades (known as *summative assessment*) to more informal methods such as quizzes, class discussions or homework, which help you to ascertain progress along the way (known as *formative assessment*).

If you have a look at the curriculum for a course on which you teach, you should see these three elements clearly represented.

We will now look at two examples of a short course on Presentation Skills to illustrate various aspects of course design. Imagine you wanted to take a course to improve your presentation skills: look at the two outlines in Table 3.1 and consider which one you would choose and why.

Table 3.1 Two outlines for a Presentation Skills course

	Course A	Course B
Learning outcomes	*By the end of the course you will be able to:* • Identify the needs of your audience and plan suitable content • Plan and structure a presentation in a clear and logical way • Design PowerPoint slides to create impact and engagement	*By the end of the course you will be able to:* • Design a presentation to entertain or educate your audience • Speak clearly with varying tone, pace and intonation • Present with confidence and handle unexpected or difficult questions
Learning and teaching activities	Online tutorials on planning techniques, with a chatroom in which students submit and comment on each other's presentation plans and can ask questions of the tutor	Live lectures on giving effective presentations from experienced speakers Voice projection workshop given by actors to practise vocal techniques
Assessment tasks	Students submit a written presentation and PowerPoint slides for a specified audience	Students give a 10-minute presentation to fellow students and the tutor, followed by a question and answer session

Reflection

Think about which of the three aspects of course design were most important in your choice. Was your decision based on the intended learning outcomes, or the teaching and learning activities or the assessment tasks? Now imagine that you were taking this course as part of a Master's programme and the results counted for 15% of your overall grade. Would you choose the same course?

Discussion

The two courses differ in various aspects:

1   In terms of the learning outcomes, Course A focuses mostly on planning the content of the presentation, whereas Course B is more about delivery. If you chose according to the learning outcomes, did you choose a course that would build on your strengths or address your weaknesses?

2   In terms of teaching and learning activities, Course A includes online study which you could do in your own space and time at your own pace, whereas Course B involves attend-

ing lectures and a workshop. Was this a deciding factor for you? Both courses include practical elements but one involves working with actors whereas the other involves writing and reviewing the content of a presentation. Some people would find one (or both) of these quite scary and may choose based on what they want to avoid.

3   Finally, the assessment tasks vary. If you have been teaching for a little while, you may have noticed that students tend to be very interested in, and aware of, how they are being assessed from the start of the course. They may ask questions such as 'Will this be in the exam?' or 'Will we be assessed on this?' Some students choose their modules almost entirely based on the assessment method. Did you? And did this change when you knew that the assessment counted towards your grade?

This activity illustrates that you can have two courses on the same subject but with different content and designs. Understanding the bigger picture of any course(s) to which you contribute will help you to focus your teaching appropriately and be able to answer students' questions.

An important aspect of Biggs and Tang's model is what they call *constructive alignment*. The term 'constructive' in this context refers to the constructivist model of learning which is explained in Chapter 2. 'Alignment' is about the coherence of the course in terms of how well the three elements fit together.

An example of a well-aligned activity that most people are familiar with is learning to drive. The learning outcome is to be able to drive safely on public roads, for which you have to pass a theory test and then a practical driving test. The teaching and learning activities are normally studying the Highway Code at home, including practice on mock questions, and having driving lessons or practice with a suitable instructor. The assessment tasks comprise a computerised test of the Highway Code and a practical test of driving. Here, the three elements of course design are well aligned: studying factual knowledge independently provides suitable preparation for the theory test whilst the driving lessons provide practice and feedback on the specific techniques and manoeuvres required in the practical driving test. The assessments are appropriate to what is being tested and ensure that you have the relevant skills and knowledge. This may seem quite obvious, but there are many courses which are not well aligned.

Consider a course to teach critical evaluation of academic papers. This is a generic skill required in most disciplines. The course starts with a lecture explaining in detail how to go about critically evaluating a paper and posts an example of a good critique online for students to study at home. Later, the students are assessed by asking them to list the key criteria for evaluating a paper.

Reflection

How well do you think the various elements are aligned? How would you teach this skill?

Discussion

These elements are poorly aligned because the teaching methods do not provide opportunities for students to practise the skill in question, and the assessment does not test the skill directly. A better aligned model could have the lecturer provide a written guide on critiquing a paper, followed by students working in small groups to apply the guidance to a recent paper. Students could be assessed by submitting an individual, written critique of a different paper. In this model, students practise the skill in a group where they can learn from each other as well as getting feedback from the tutor, and are then tested directly on the skill individually.

Poorly aligned courses provide inconsistent messages to students and may reduce motivation if students cannot see the links between what they are asked to do and how they will be assessed. So it is worth evaluating your own courses so that you are aware of potential issues.

Reflection

Review any course(s) you are teaching on and identify the intended learning outcomes, teaching and learning activities and assessment tasks. How well are they aligned? And if not well aligned, how do you think this might impact on you and the students?

Discussion

Well-aligned courses make life easier for you, as students can see the purpose of what they are doing. Sometimes people worry that they are 'teaching to the test' but if the test is well designed, then that is fine – in fact, it is only fair that you are helping students towards that goal. If there is a mismatch, then you may need to explain the relevance of what you are teaching to the students (for example if you are teaching presentation skills but the assessment is an essay). You could also try to make your teaching activities particularly engaging to increase motivation. Or you may consider, with the agreement of the course leader, amending some of the activities to give students more opportunities to practise for the assessments.

Designing a teaching session

The same principles of design outlined above apply to designing a single teaching session, and in this section we will discuss how you can plan a tutorial, seminar, lecture or even a one-to-one session with a single student. Not all teachers new to university teaching will be required to do this. For example, Graduate Teaching Assistants may be given a session plan by their course leader/module convenor and expected to work to this. However, if you continue teaching, it is likely that at some point you will be expected to plan your own sessions.

You will get the most from this section if you pick a real session you will be teaching (or if not applicable, choose a topic and a group of learners that you could be teaching in future) and use it as an example to which you apply the steps below. For the purposes of this book, the planning process has been divided into five steps:

- Research your learners
- Define the intended learning outcomes
- Plan the teaching and learning activities
- Plan the assessment tasks
- Evaluate your plan.

Each part is described below and an outline plan that you may like to use is given in Figure 3.2.

Topic:	Date:
Learner Profile: stage of course, previous/future topics in course, size of group, expected knowledge base, student expectations, common misconceptions/difficulties.	
Intended Learning Outcomes (Learning Objectives). What do you expect students to be able to do by the end of the session?	
Teaching/Learning Activities: How will you engage students in learning about the topic? What will you do and what will the students do?	
Assessment Tasks: How will you check what students have learnt?	

Figure 3.2 Outline teaching plan

Research your learners

Firstly, find out as much as possible about your learners. How many are there? What stage of the course are they at? What previous teaching have they had? What do they know already? What will they want from your session? You can note your findings in the first section of your teaching plan (Figure 3.2).

This is important groundwork because it will help you to plan appropriately, and to pitch your teaching at the right level for the students. Of course, within any group there will be a variety of levels of knowledge, but you need to get a sense of where students are, what they know, understand and can do already.

A colleague once described how he was invited to give a lecture at an international conference. He gave his presentation and then invited questions. When he heard the first question he was shocked because he realised that the person asking hadn't understood the first thing he'd said – and therefore would have understood little of the rest of the talk. Afterwards he realised that he had made assumptions about the level of the group rather than finding out.

So how can you research your learners? Options include:

- contacting the students directly, for example
  - circulating a short survey asking what they hope to gain from the session and any concerns or questions
  - circulating a quiz to assess current knowledge and understanding
- checking information held by the university (e.g. students' previous qualifications)
- asking colleagues who have taught the same students or the same course previously.

Case Study 3.1 gives an example of this kind of initial research.

Case Study 3.1

Initial assessment: Chenée Psaros, Academic Skills Advisor

It is often a challenge for me to get to know many of the students I teach as I deliver one-shot workshops. It can be difficult to assess where students are in their journey, especially as the workshops are often mixed with undergraduates at various levels and postgraduates. At the beginning of the session, I always ask students to tell me what they hope to achieve from the session and which faculty they are from. In all the workshops I deliver, I ask students to participate in an initial assessment activity that will inform me about their current knowledge of the topic I am teaching (Brabazon, 2007). In the *Academic integrity* workshop this is an anonymous poll due to the sensitive nature of the questions; and in the *Critical thinking* workshop, this is a discussion because a collaborative environment accommodates a variety of responses. The information I collect from these activities informs me where to

(Continued)

pitch my class. It allows me to select the content I think would be most useful for a particular group. At the end of the session, I return to the initial assessment as a tool where students can self-assess what they have gained from the session. I have often observed students' positive evaluation of how much more they knew at the end of the session.

Define the intended learning outcomes

Once you have information about your learners, you can start to plan what you want them to gain from the session. You may be given the intended learning outcomes, either in writing or verbally, or you may have some choice over this. If the latter, consider what you would want your students to achieve by the end of the session. This might be broad goals or aims such as:

- understanding a particular concept or concepts
- gaining or applying specific knowledge
- being able to perform certain skills – either practical or academic, or
- developing certain attitudes, values or professional behaviour.

When thinking about these (Activity 3.1) you might like to consider focusing on the following:

Threshold concepts (Meyer and Land, 2003) are central concepts within a discipline that are essential to progression and mastery. 'Threshold' denotes the idea of a gateway that opens up new understandings, perspectives or ways of thinking about something. Examples might include sustainability (geography), the biopsychosocial model (health disciplines), figurative speech (language), cultural relativism (social sciences) and inertia (physics). These concepts may be challenging for students if they are at odds with existing knowledge, attitudes or understanding, but once understood they are usually irreversible and won't be forgotten.

Bottlenecks (Middendorf and Pace, 2003) are the places where students typically get stuck. This may be for cognitive or emotional reasons, for example because they lack essential background knowledge or feel their religious or political beliefs are being challenged. Focusing your teaching on these areas of difficulty may be a better use of your time than trying to cover the whole topic.

Activity 3.1

Setting aims

Make a list of broad aims for your teaching session and prioritise them.

Keep these handy for later activities.

It's also worth checking at this stage how the course and your particular topic is assessed and ensuring that your aims are coherent with the assessments.

Now we are going to turn these broad aims into intended learning outcomes. To do this, imagine that you have taught the class and now want to check their learning. How could they show you that they had achieved the aims? Describe precisely how they could convince you of their learning. Table 3.2 gives some examples.

Table 3.2 Aims translated into intended learning outcomes or assessment tasks

Aims	Intended learning outcomes
Translate a literary text into Spanish/Chinese, etc.	Produce a clear and accurate translation of a set text into Spanish/Chinese, etc.
Understand the concept of osmosis	Explain how osmosis works
Understand the theories of two philosophers	Compare and contrast Aristotle's and Kant's philosophies of education
Know the key events in recent Indian history	Draw a timeline of the 20th century showing 10 key events in Indian history and justify your choice
Appreciate the importance of obtaining a patient's consent for treatment	Describe the implications of not obtaining informed consent – for both the patient and healthcare professional
Design a city of the future	Draw a scale map of a future city showing all amenities and residential areas
Assess a mathematical proof	Critique a proposed proof and identify flaws or errors in the logic

Reflection

What do you notice about the structure of the intended learning outcomes?

Discussion

If you look closely, you will see that all the learning outcomes start with a verb that describes what students are expected *to do* (rather than to know, understand or be aware of/appreciate). This is important because you can only judge what a student knows or understands by how they use that knowledge. It also means that learning outcomes are student-centred rather than teacher-centred; in other words they describe what the student has learnt rather than what you have taught (and there can be a big difference).

Another feature of learning outcomes is that they give more detail about the level of learning required. For example, if teaching about plagiarism, you could ask students to:

1   define plagiarism
2   explain the rationale for rules against plagiarism
3   analyse sample texts to identify cases of plagiarism.

These represent progressively more demand in terms of understanding and applying the concept. Back in the 1950s, an educational psychologist, Benjamin Bloom, compiled a range of learning outcomes and organised them into taxonomies that are still widely used today (Bloom et al., 1956). There were taxonomies for the cognitive domain (knowledge), the psychomotor domain (skills) and the affective domain (attitudes and values). The most commonly used is that for the cognitive domain. It was revised in 2001 and this version is shown in Figure 3.3.

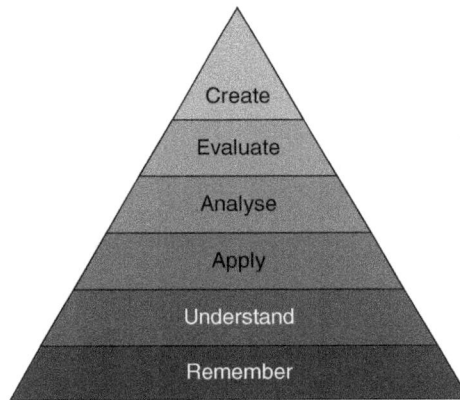

Figure 3.3 Bloom's taxonomy, as revised by Anderson, Lorin and Krathwohl (2001)

The taxonomy is useful because, even at university level, much teaching is directed at the lower levels – focusing on knowledge (remembering) and understanding. Whilst these areas are obviously important, knowledge is easily accessible nowadays and teachers' time is usually better spent helping students to understand and apply knowledge in more complex ways. The taxonomy can help you to plan teaching (and assessment) that helps students to develop the higher-level thinking skills required at university level. So when writing learning outcomes, rather than asking students to describe or list something – which requires simple factual recall – you could ask them to explain or analyse it, which requires a greater level of understanding and application of knowledge. It is not necessary to start at the bottom of the hierarchy and work up. You may start by asking students, for example, to analyse a case study, which requires them to draw on the lower levels, and if necessary find the relevant information themselves.

Table 3.3 shows the categories of the taxonomy, describes the nature of the cognitive ability required by the student and gives a list of verbs that can be useful when writing learning outcomes, assessments or devising questions to use in class.

Table 3.3 Verbs related to Bloom's taxonomy

Taxonomy category	Cognitive activity required	Related verbs
Create	Creativity Invention	Write, propose, develop, formulate, synthesise, create, adapt, combine, construct, develop, design, imagine, invent, plan, propose.
Evaluate	Judgement	Judge, choose, defend, conclude, recommend, support, criticise, appraise, value, grade, prioritise.
Analyse	Induction Deduction	Justify, analyse, categorise, correlate, assess, relate, distil, conclude.
Apply	Application	Build, solve, test, consider, apply, use, select, construct, plan, relate, transfer.
Understand	Explanation Comparison Illustration	Classify, compare, contrast, demonstrate, differentiate, predict, re-order, estimate, distinguish between, illustrate, give examples of, rearrange, rephrase, explain, interpret, summarise.
Remember	Memorisation Repetition Description Knowledge recall	Define, describe, identify, list, name, recall, show, label, find, match, recall, quote, recognise, recite.

Good learning outcomes are sometimes said to be 'SMART' in that they are:

- **S**pecific (describe precisely what students will be able to do)
- **M**easurable (i.e. can be assessed)
- **A**chievable (realistic within the given time frame)
- **R**elevant (cover topics that students need to learn) and
- **T**ime-framed (state the expected time within which the learning should be achieved).

Now look back to the broad aims you identified earlier and translate them into learning outcomes in Activity 3.2.

Activity 3.2

Writing learning outcomes

From your broad aims, specify the learning outcomes you hope the students will achieve and enter these into your teaching plan (Figure 3.2). You can use the format:

(Continued)

By the end of this session, I want students to be able to:

-
-
-

When you have written them, evaluate whether your learning outcomes meet the 'SMART' criteria.

Reflection

How did you find the process of writing learning outcomes? What do you think are the advantages and disadvantages of using them?

Discussion

Teachers often find that writing learning outcomes helps them think more clearly about what they are trying to achieve, and to prioritise which aspects of the topic are most important. Also, by focusing on what students will be able to do (rather than on what they will teach), it helps them to become more student-centred. Well-constructed learning outcomes also make planning teaching/learning activities and assessment tasks much easier because there is a clear direction to follow. For students, learning outcomes can help them to understand the level of learning required and act as a checklist against which they can evaluate their progress. On the negative side, learning outcomes can appear restrictive or reductionist, forcing teachers to reduce sometimes complex learning goals into over-simplistic statements. Learning outcomes can appear dry, particularly if you are using those written by others. Also, the concept of learning outcomes suggests that you can predict what students will learn when in fact their learning may be different from or more varied than you expect.

Planning teaching and learning activities

Once you have clear learning outcomes, it can be fairly straightforward to plan your teaching and learning activities – note the emphasis on what both you and the students do. This is useful to ensure that students are actively engaged in learning rather than expected to passively acquire information from the teacher. However, in practice, there is often not a clear distinction so we mostly refer to teaching/learning activities.

So, returning to some previously quoted learning outcomes, you can see in Table 3.4 some suggestions of teaching and learning activities that could help students to achieve them.

Table 3.4 Planning teaching/learning activities

Learning outcome	Potential teaching activities	Potential learning activities
Explain how osmosis works.	Show a computer animation Explain osmosis and take questions	Students work in pairs to explain the concept to each other Students answer a quiz on osmosis
Compare and contrast Kant's and Aristotle's philosophies of education	Provide online material for students to study prior to class Set a group work task and review students' answers at the end	Students bring notes from their online studying and then work in small groups to compare the two philosophies
Design a city of the future	Ask students to brainstorm factors to take into account when designing a city of the future Show photographs of some futuristic cities and discuss their design philosophies	Students work individually to design a city within certain parameters Students then present their work for critique by their peers

When planning teaching and learning activities, think back to the concept of constructive alignment, and ensure that the activities are well aligned with the learning outcomes.

Planning assessment tasks

When planning a single teaching session, the assessment tasks are not formal ones like exams or essays but are ways to check that students have learnt what you intended. They can be simple things like asking students to summarise key points or do a short quiz. Sometimes you will have seen the students demonstrate their learning during the session (e.g. in a workshop setting), so you may not need an additional assessment task at the end.

Table 3.5 gives examples of teaching/learning activities and appropriate assessment methods for different types of learning. Use this to help you complete your teaching plan (Activity 3.3).

Activity 3.3

Planning teaching/learning activities and checking learning

Based on your learning outcomes from Activity 3.2, identify appropriate teaching and learning activities that would help the students to achieve them. There will be various options – try to choose activities that have the students practise or apply the skills, knowledge or professional behaviour that they need to learn.

Then complete your plan by ensuring that you have a way of checking student learning. This may already be inherent in your plan or you may wish to add a further activity at the end.

Table 3.5 Matching teaching/learning activities and assessment tasks to learning outcomes

	If your learning outcomes require students to develop **knowledge and understanding**, consider:	If your learning outcomes require students to develop **practical or academic skills**, consider:	If your learning outcomes require students to develop **values, attitudes or professional behaviour**, consider:
	↓	↓	↓
Teaching and learning activities	Online materials including interactive elements such as quizzes	Demonstration (live)	Discussion
		Video tutorial	Debate
	Private study followed by tutorials	Practical workshop	Role play
		Individual practice with feedback	Hearing personal accounts (e.g. from clients, patients, colleagues)
	Individual or group research projects	Simulation (e.g. with mannequins, computer simulation)	Reflection
	Interactive lectures		Case studies
	Guest speakers	Role play	Expert panel
	Discovery method (students are guided to find out for themselves)	Real life experience (e.g. through placements)	Writing and critiquing position statements
		Problem-solving exercises	
Assessment tasks	Quizzes	Observations of performance	References,
	Short answer or multiple choice questions	Log book	Observations (e.g. from workplace, colleagues)
		Video-recording of practice	
	Problem-solving questions		Reflective writing
		Tasks requiring application of skills or problem solving	Role play
	Essays		Simulation
	Oral presentations		
	Question and answer		

Evaluate your plan

When you have completed your plan, check that you have allowed sufficient time for the various activities and remember that you may need to be flexible during the session. Having a plan should help you to focus and organise learning appropriately, but it is also important to be responsive to the group, so that if, for example, students take longer than expected on an activity that you consider important, you may decide to let it overrun and cut something from later on. As a new teacher, it is often useful to have a back-up plan, so think about something extra that you can add in if the session goes quicker than you expect and something you can leave out (or give as homework) if you overrun.

After the session, it is useful to review your plan again and make notes on how it went, particularly if you will be teaching this session again in future. Consider the extent to which the learning outcomes were achieved as this will impact on future sessions (if you are teaching the same group again). You may conclude that you need to revisit the same topics or you may feel that students are ready to move on. Further ways to evaluate your teaching are discussed in more depth in Chapter 12.

Case Study 3.2 comes from an Associate Fellowship of the Higher Education Academy application by a GTA who describes how he went about designing a statistics course for his Graduate School. Notice how he uses previous evaluations to modify the learning outcomes and how he tries to make the course accessible and relevant to the learners.

— Case Study 3.2 —

Designing a course: Brett Thomas, GTA and doctoral researcher in Electrical and Electronic Engineering

I've developed a three-hour course named 'Basic Statistics', which I delivered recently for the Graduate School. This course and two other new statistics courses were previously delivered as one very large course lasting about nine hours over two days. Learner feedback suggested that this course was too long and too didactic and that the purpose of what they were learning wasn't made clear. For example, they were able to calculate the mean or mode of a data set – the issue was knowing when or why they would want to do this.

I was given the opportunity to design every aspect of the course, from the content and associated PowerPoint to supplementary material. My goal was to shorten the course, make it more engaging and effective and update the material if necessary.

I first analysed the content to assess its relevance and to structure it into a more logical progression. I re-ordered the course into clear modules: for example, I grouped nomenclature together and then calculations and tried to clearly introduce why the calculations were necessary, their relevance to a particular data set and the concepts behind them, before moving onto calculations, which I felt was a more natural progression. From my own experiences using statistics, I identified certain areas (e.g. Student T-test) which were either less relevant to my students, or would be more appropriately placed in the other two courses or didn't 'fit' with the logical progression of the course.

I created new content for the course, including some illustrative and quite light-hearted examples of statistics being used very poorly and very well in every day examples, to illustrate their importance. I used them as discussion points to allow students to express their

(Continued)

thoughts, debate the topics and think through the importance of using statistics well in their own work, which was a good form of active learning. This additionally served to cut up quite dry slides from the previous course and helped compensate for what may have been quite heavy mathematics, where a torrent of information would soon become difficult to continue to process.

I did also try to incorporate active learning by producing a worksheet in which the learners could analyse a data set gradually using techniques they'd learnt during the course. However, time restraints caused by lively discussions actually limited this, so for my next course I'll either limit the discussion time or perhaps set these as work to be done outside of the lesson.

One difficulty I had foreseen whilst designing the course is the unknown backgrounds of the students. Without meeting the students before the course, I was unable to plan for their academic backgrounds. I now know that they were primarily not of mathematical backgrounds; however, we did have some students who had greater mathematical knowledge and might have benefitted from more detailed analytical solutions to certain areas of statistics. To mitigate this, I plan to deliver further information on the Graduate School website detailing that the course might be best suited for those from biological backgrounds and directing those with previous statistics knowledge to the other new courses. This should allow me to tailor the sessions more uniquely to this particular group

---

Over to you

One of the learning outcomes of this chapter was that you would be able to identify the key components of any course. If you are involved in only one aspect of the teaching process, say leading seminars or marking, you may wish to find out more about the other aspects to ensure that you understand the wider context within which your students are learning.

The other learning outcomes related to being able to define what you want students to learn and to plan a teaching session. If you are given the freedom to plan your own teaching sessions, you can use the process described in this chapter to do so in a structured way. There is further guidance on teaching and learning methods appropriate for different contexts and disciplines in the following chapters.

You may also, either now or in the future, have opportunities to redesign sessions or even design your own short courses and you can use this same structure for that purpose. The three elements of the teaching process – the intended learning outcomes, teaching/learning methods and assessment tasks – are relevant whether you are looking at a whole programme, a smaller module/course or a single teaching session.

Further resources

This book gives a detailed and accessible explanation of the teaching process and of constructive alignment.

Biggs, J. and Tang, C. (2011) *Teaching for Quality Learning at University*, 4th edn. Maidenhead: Open University Press.

A comprehensive resource which applies evidence-based educational principles and cognitive science to online learning design.

Nilson, Linda B. and Goodson, Ludwika A. (2017) *Online Teaching at Its Best: Merging Instructional Design with Teaching and Learning Research*. San Francisco: Jossey-Bass.

This paper provides an overview of debates about the value of learning outcomes.

Hussey, Trevor and Smith, Patrick (2008) Learning outcomes: a conceptual analysis. *Teaching in Higher Education*, 13 (1): 107–15.

References

Anderson, L. W. and Krathwohl, D. R. (eds) (2001) *A Taxonomy for Learning, Teaching, and Assessing: A Revision of Bloom's Taxonomy of Educational Objectives*. Boston, MA: Allyn & Bacon.

Biggs, J. and Tang, C. (2011) *Teaching for Quality Learning at University*, 4th edn. Maidenhead: Open University Press.

Bloom, B. S., Engelhart, M. D., Furst, E. J., Hill, W. H., Krathwohl, D. R. (1956) *Taxonomy of Educational Objectives: The Classification of Educational Goals. Handbook I: Cognitive Domain*. New York: David McKay Company.

Brabazon, T. (2007) *The University of Google: Education in the (Post) Information Age*. Farnham: Ashgate.

Meyer, J. H. F. and Land, R. (2003) *Threshold Concepts and Troublesome Knowledge: Linkages to Ways of Thinking and Practising within the Disciplines*. Enhancing Teaching–Learning Environments in Undergraduate Courses Project, Occasional Report 42003. www.etl.tla.ed.ac.uk/docs/ETLreport4.pdf

Middendorf, J. and Pace, D. (2004) Decoding the disciplines: a model for helping students learn disciplinary ways of thinking. *New Directions for Teaching and Learning*, 2004 (98): 1–12.

4

FACILITATING LEARNING IN SMALL GROUPS

Learning outcomes

After reading this chapter you should be able to:

- Articulate what constitutes small group teaching in your context
- Prepare for small group teaching sessions
- Use a variety of active learning and questioning techniques to engage learners and manage group dynamics.

Introduction

Teaching in small groups is a core activity for many of us who teach and support learning. This chapter provides you with an opportunity to reflect on this form of teaching and on how it relates to your own context. Following on from the discussion about designing learning activities in Chapter 3, we now look more specifically at what you can do to prepare for small group interactions, including agreeing ground rules with your students. One of the main purposes of learning in small groups is to give students opportunities to interact with each other, with you and with the course material, so the focus is on enabling students to participate in the group environment. We suggest a variety of active learning techniques that you can try with your students, and highlight the importance of planned, targeted questioning strategies, which can help to engage students and manage group dynamics.

What is your small group teaching context?

Teaching in small groups can take many forms, from tutorials and seminars to working with a group of students in a laboratory. Depending on your context and discipline, your small group teaching – and ideas about what constitutes a 'small group' – might take different forms.

Reflection

How many students constitute a 'small group' in your context? When does a small group become a large group?

Discussion

Some would say a small group consists of between five and eight students (e.g. Exley and Dennick, 2004); or you might consider one student to form a small group, though this means the 'group' is made up only of the teacher and the (one) student. In our conversations with GTAs and other colleagues who teach small groups, 20 is often cited as a magic number at which a small group becomes a large group. In practice, it does not matter, and is perhaps even unhelpful, to think about small groups in terms of numbers of students. More useful is to think about what we are trying to achieve, or what we want our learners to achieve, in a small group. As a general rule, a small group can be considered small enough if the teacher is able to engage in interaction with each student during the learning session. If you have ever taught many students at once – a large lecture would be an obvious example – it is very unlikely that you were able to interact with each student during the session, or that each student was able to interact with each other. This is perhaps a more useful dividing line between how we define small group and large group teaching. This takes our attention away from numbers and instead enables us to focus on the purposes and aims of small group teaching.

What are the purposes and aims of small group teaching?

The main purpose of teaching in small groups is to enable students to engage actively with the material, with each other and with you. There might be some opportunities to do this in larger groups, but it is much easier to facilitate these interactions in a small group. In small group teaching, we are aiming to promote collaboration, dialogue and interaction. This means we are focused on the students' learning and knowledge construction – the learning is student-centred – and we are aiming to facilitate active learning. We introduced the concept of active learning in Chapter 2, and we return to this later in this chapter where we suggest some active learning techniques that can be used with small groups.

So if the purpose of small group teaching is to encourage students to collaborate, communicate and interact, what are our aims when facilitating a small group session? Here are some ideas:

- To facilitate communication
- To stimulate exchange of ideas and discussion
- To provide opportunities for students to ask questions
- To provide immediate formative feedback
- To develop group cohesion
- To establish a sense of community and cohort among students
- To develop students' team-working skills
- To promote a collaborative approach to learning.

This short list of aims is by no means exhaustive, but it illustrates that small group sessions, if planned and facilitated well, can help students not only to make sense of the content and material, but also develop a variety of useful skills that are not linked to the discipline, such as working with others, solving conflict and collaborating in a team.

Preparing for small group teaching: agreeing ground rules

In Chapter 3, we explored how we can design and plan learning sessions focused around clear and measurable intended learning outcomes. Now we will think about some of the practical steps to take when planning a small group teaching session. The focus here is on what your students will be doing and how they will be learning. The aims of small group teaching listed above mean that we will be encouraging active learning, where students are actively engaged in activities and discussions rather than listening to a lecture. Some questions to begin with are:

1   What are the intended learning outcomes for the module or session? How do your small group sessions fit within the module/programme; how do they relate to the lectures (if there are any)?
2   Is it appropriate or useful to write your own session-level learning outcomes?

Before the very first session, it is important to gather as much information about your learners as possible. This information should be given to you by the course lead or a departmental administrator, but you may have to ask. Information you might need is:

• Number of students in the group
• Previous learning – from other modules and from lectures within the module you are teaching
• Any existing group dynamics – do any students already work well together; are there any problems between particular students?
• Have any of the students declared any specific learning differences?
• The venue for your sessions – is the room conducive to discussion-based work and small group learning? Is the furniture in the room moveable? Is there a whiteboard, a flipchart, a PC and projector? What facilities will you need?

To facilitate small group learning effectively, you will also need to do some work to enable the group to work together, both with you and with each other. An important part of this is agreeing ground rules and expectations. As we have already said, there is an implicit expectation that students participate actively in small group sessions, which may not always be the case in lectures. So your expectations may need to be made explicit. In your first session with your students, it is useful to spend a few minutes agreeing ground rules, as this can help to prevent problems arising in the future. You can avoid an author-itarian tone by involving your students in creating the ground rules and expectations. A structured way of agreeing ground rules could work as follows:

1   Give students a few minutes to think about a group they have enjoyed working with and a group they found unenjoyable.
2   For each scenario, ask students to note down what they would take from the group that worked well and what they would avoid replicating from the group that did not work well.
3   Then give students a few minutes to draft some ground rules based on their reflections on working in 'good' and 'bad' groups.
4   Produce a version of the ground rules once they have been agreed and post them on the virtual learning environment (if you use one) and/or send them to the group by email.

(Adapted from Brookfield and Preskill, 2005)

Activity 4.1

Establishing ground rules

Imagine you are in your first session with a new group of students. What ground rules would you like to agree with the group? If you already have experience of establishing ground rules with a group of students, what did you and your students come up with?

Discussion

From our experience, students tend to have similar ideas to teachers about how members of the group should behave and interact. Here are some examples:

- Inform the tutor in advance if you are unable to attend class.
- Listen respectfully and actively when others are speaking.
- Debate and disagree with peers in a respectful manner.
- Challenge others' ideas and opinions rather than criticise the person.
- Complete pre-session tasks.
- Be prepared to participate actively in discussions and activities.
- Arrive on time, where possible.
- Use electronic devices only for work-related reasons or during breaks.
- Treat class discussions as confidential.

Case Study 4.1

Setting ground rules: Kasim Khorasanee, GTA in Political Theory

My teaching has primarily been seminar-based, and so my teaching philosophy has been informed by – and adapted to – this format in particular. I believe that students engaging in discussions – actively listening to others, practising formulating their own ideas, and learning to receive and accept feedback – is critical to students' development. At the outset I explain that speaking and discussing is a crucial part of the seminar learning experience, not just listening and note-taking. I have all students make themselves name cards. The aim is for them to address one another (as opposed to me) when speaking, and it also assists me with remembering names and avoiding biases towards students with memorable names. The impact of this is facilitating dialogue between students, so that they learn in a collaborative manner with peers and not just a top-down or bilateral manner with me as GTA.

(Continued)

I premise my seminars on three principles – openness, respect and critical thinking – which I discuss with my classes when I first meet them.

(i) Openness means that everyone should feel comfortable expressing themselves – and in particular should not be worried about appearing 'silly' for asking certain questions or expressing their views. 'Having a go' is encouraged – students are often under-confident because they are not sure of having the right answer. The point of the seminars is not to impress myself or their peers, but to help build their knowledge in a collaborative way. Even if they only have 'half' an answer, one of their peers may be able to build on their contribution in a productive way. (ii) Critical thinking means students are encouraged to put forward their views even when they disagree (including with me). The point is for students to feel empowered to disagree, so long as it is done in a respectful manner. (iii) Respect is the most important of the three principles, and is mutual between myself and the students, as well as between each other. This has a variety of aspects, but includes speaking – and in particular disagreeing – with one another in a polite and respectful manner. This is particularly relevant in moral and political theory as students can have sincere and deeply held commitments which they may struggle to discuss in a courteous manner. It also includes keeping phones away during class, not whispering while others are speaking, taking turns to speak, etc.

Although I don't expect all students to contribute equally, I do require them all to participate. I achieve this without cold-calling or 'picking on' students. When small groups feed back their conclusions to the whole class I often ask quieter group members to summarise the group's discussions – they often feel more confident doing this than presenting their own views in a debate-style format. The impact of this is that more uncertain students build confidence and feel included in seminars without feeling stress-inducing pressure to participate. They also understand why I teach the way I do to widen participation.

Preparing for small group teaching online

When working with students online, you can generally do this in two ways: synchronously and asynchronously. In synchronous learning, you and your students are online and working together at the same time. This is the type of online interaction that is relevant in the context of this chapter. In asynchronous learning, students (and you) are online at different times, perhaps working through some exercises, doing some pre-reading, or posting ideas on a discussion forum. If you are teaching online, it is likely that you will use a mix of synchronous and asynchronous learning. We will discuss this more in Chapter 8.

Just as with face-to-face teaching, you will need to prepare your students to interact with you and with each other when working online. This means gathering similar information about the number of students and previous learning, as mentioned above, but there are also some other considerations when teaching online. First, it is important to consider to what extent your students are used to working online for educational purposes. We all have online lives and personas, such as on social media and through online shopping, so it is important to be sensitive to the possibility that some students might feel like there is an element of intrusion on their, otherwise private, online lives. One very tangible point to consider is the space that students use to engage in online learning. Do your students have a quiet space to work when participating in a synchronous online session with you? Do they have reliable access to the internet and a PC? In the face-to-face format, you know your students in a professional context, but in the online world, you could be almost literally beaming into a student's living room or bedroom if that is the only quiet space in which they are able to work. Being mindful of these issues, and perhaps asking students about their online set-up at home, will help you to plan your sessions and, perhaps more importantly, it will help to show that you care.

As with face-to-face teaching, it is a good idea to agree some ground rules when working online, and many of those mentioned above will be applicable. In addition, here are some others to consider specifically when leading a small group session online:

- Ask students to mute their microphone when they join the session. It is also helpful to keep microphones muted whenever the student is not speaking, as this reduces background noise.
- Check if there is departmental guidance on whether students should have their cameras turned on or off. It can be helpful to see students' faces, but some students may be reluctant to be on camera for various reasons. For example, they may not have a dedicated space for studying, and may not want to show this on camera. It can also be helpful to ask students to switch off their camera if they are not speaking in order to save bandwidth.
- If you aim to encourage students to turn their cameras on, you can tell them about the use of different backgrounds and the option to blur their background. This may help students to feel less 'exposed' and maintain privacy.
- Agree when the chat area will be used. You might decide that this is an open area for students to post questions and comments throughout the session, or you might decide that students should use the chat function at particular times. For example, if there is a short segment of the session where you or a student is presenting something, you might all agree that the chat area should not be used at this time.
- Many of the benefits of body language and subtle cues are more difficult to discern online, so turn-taking in discussions can be more complicated. You could agree that students use the 'raise hand' function (available on most platforms) before interrupting another student. Alternatively, you could use the chat function to enable students to pose questions and to indicate that they would like to add something to the discussion.

Some other practical points to consider when teaching online include:

- Make sure students are aware of the features on the platform, such as 'raise hand' function, screen sharing, chat function and so on. These features should be explained at the beginning of your first session and you may need to repeat this information at other times during the course.

- We have already said that small group sessions aim to engage students actively in their learning. However, this can be even more difficult online, particularly if students cannot see all of their peers. Discussions therefore need to be planned even more carefully. One possibility is to ask students to submit ideas and questions before the session.
- Another way of engaging students when teaching online is by breaking into smaller groups, particularly if your small group is on the larger side. This can be done on most platforms using breakout rooms, where you send sub-divided groups into separate online rooms to work on a task, before bringing them all back for a whole-group debrief.

Structuring a small group teaching session

In Chapter 3, we explored how you can design your teaching sessions and we introduced the concept of constructive alignment, which refers to the extent to which the core elements of the course are aligned. That is to say, to what extent do the learning activities help students to meet the intended learning outcomes and to what extent do the assessment methods adequately assess whether students have met these outcomes? You should keep the principles outlined in Chapter 3 in mind when structuring any of your sessions, but it can also be helpful to think through how you will structure individual sessions and how the activities in small group teaching will help your students to learn. A simple structure might be as follows:

1   Introductions, settling down, any course notices and housekeeping.
2   Review previous class, perhaps a lecture, which relates to your session; pose questions to review existing knowledge (see questioning techniques below).
3   Review any preparatory work for the session; don't be tempted to summarise this yourself as this sends the message that preparatory work does not need to be completed.
4   Small group activity aligned with module or session-level intended learning outcomes (see Chapter 3).
5   Feedback and discussion.
6   Plenary; review of learning in the session; preparation required for next session.

When deciding on activities, it can initially be overwhelming because you could ask your students to explore a particular topic in any number of ways. It is helpful to return to the principles of design explored in Chapter 3, particularly the intended learning outcomes for the module or session. It can also be useful to ask yourself some questions to help decide what kind of activity to do with your students. Here are some example questions:

1   What skills, knowledge or concept do I want my students to learn? What is the intended learning outcome I am targeting with this activity?

2   What kind of activity will help my students to learn this for themselves, with their peers? What, in concrete terms, will they be doing during the activity?

3   How will this activity help my students to learn?

4   What size group will be appropriate for this activity? Will I need to divide the students into breakout groups?

5   What resources do I need to provide (if any)? What materials do my students need to bring with them (if any)?

6   How will I know my students have learned what I intended them to learn? How will I assess the students' learning? How will they assess their own learning?

The structure of the session and the activities you use will depend on the subject matter and how your small group session fits in with the rest of the module or programme of study. Regardless of the subject, however, you will need to think about how you will facilitate students' learning and interactions with each other.

Facilitation skills

We have already established that small group teaching aims to engage students and to promote participation, discussion and collaboration. This means the teacher needs to facilitate learning through activities that students work on together, rather than provide a lecture on content. This also means there is a range of skills required when facilitating learning in small groups.

Reflection

Think back to a time when you have worked in a small group. This could be as a student or in a work context, where you have been guided by a teacher or a facilitator to complete a particular task with your group peers. How did the teacher or facilitator guide the group to learn or work together? What skills of facilitation did they use?

Discussion

In Chapter 2, we considered how we conceptualise teaching and discussed the role(s) of the teacher. When facilitating learning in small groups, the very traditional view of a teacher as a didactic disseminator of knowledge is not very helpful, not least because the focus is on what the students are doing rather than what the teacher is doing. This is why we talk about *facilitating* learning, and there are many skills that good facilitators use to help students learn. Arguably the most important skill when facilitating learning is good questioning. Good questions have a variety of purposes, such as enabling the teacher to stimulate discussion, to prompt quieter students to respond, or to prevent a more vocal student from dominating the discussion. So leading a small group session also requires the skill of managing group dynamics and ensuring all voices are heard. We return to the important topics of questioning and managing group dynamics below. It is also essential to develop active listening skills. This means being present in the moment, listening to what the student is actually saying, rather than thinking ahead to how you will respond. You also have an important moderator role, helping to highlight links between different students' ideas as well as between your module and other topics of study in the degree programme. Beyond this, you also need to be able to move discussions forward and bring them to a close, ensuring students have had an opportunity to summarise their learning. Finally, on a practical level, you have to manage time. Time is never your friend when teaching, especially when leading students through activities, where there is potential for plans to go awry, so time management is an important practical skill to develop as a teacher in general, but particularly in small group sessions.

Practical strategies to promote active learning

As we saw in Chapter 2, active learning is an umbrella term for a range of approaches which focus on what students are doing, rather than what the teacher is doing. This means we include activities, time to practise practical skills, space for reflection, and time for students to think about *how* they are learning as well as *what* they are learning. Small group teaching sessions tend to include less didactic teaching and lecturing and more active learning. Having said this, lectures can also include active learning. We will return to this point in Chapter 5.

Reflection

Think about your own teaching or your own experiences as a student. In sessions where you asked students to *do something* or where you as a student were asked to *do something*, what kinds of activities were included? Do you think there are any active learning approaches specific to your discipline?

Discussion

There are many different ways of engaging students actively in their learning, and you probably use many of these in your own teaching and/or experienced many of these as a student. This could be a simple process of asking students to discuss a case or a problem in pairs before feeding back to the group, or asking students to think quietly about their responses to a question. Active learning does not have to be literally active; thinking and reflecting are also forms of active learning, where students are given time and space to think through problems and to reflect on how and why they arrived at their answer or solution. You may have also thought about active learning approaches that are particularly relevant in your discipline. In essence, a wide variety of activities can work well in most, if not all, disciplines. However, depending on your subject area, some activities may be more prevalent, such as making, creating and producing something in arts-based disciplines. Another example is team-based learning (TBL), which seems to be particularly prevalent in medical education. TBL is a structured way of facilitating learning in small groups over a longer period of time, such as a whole semester. You may not be involved in redesigning whole courses, so we will not go into detail about TBL here, but you will find further reading at the end of this chapter if this method is of interest to you.

The important thing to remember when designing any active learning activity is to think about why you are using that particular technique and what skills active learning can help to develop in your students. In general, active learning in small groups can help to develop the following:

- Team working skills
- Negotiation skills
- Communication skills
- Organisation and time management skills
- Leadership skills
- Presentation skills
- Summarising skills
- Conflict management.

These are all transferable skills that go beyond the individual discipline. When planning your sessions, think about how your activities are helping to hone any of these skills. Here are just some of the active learning techniques you might have used, or could use in the future.

Think–Pair–Share

This is a very common way of giving students time to think about their own response to a question individually, then to exchange ideas with a partner, before sharing with the wider group. This is a useful method for encouraging all students to think about the question at hand. The 'pairing' part also removes the pressure of having to commit to an answer individually, so students who are less vocal in the group can feel supported.

Rounds

If you are teaching a relatively small group, say fewer than 20 students, you can pose a question and go round the group collecting a response from each student. This is useful when there are lots of potential answers, opinions or experiences in response to a question. Rounds can be very time-consuming, however, so it often works best with a small group. You also need to beware that you do not always start with the same student. This will mean that the 'last' student always has the most difficult task of trying to think of an answer or an idea that has not already been said.

Pass the pen

This is a modified version of 'rounds', in which students are asked to compile a collaborative list of responses by writing an answer before passing the pen to the next student. This can be particularly useful if you have several students in the group who are initially reluctant to speak.

Line of (dis)agreement (value line)

Pose a question or provide a statement, and assign 'values' at either ends of an imaginary line (e.g. 'A pandemic is the biggest threat to global public health' – agree or disagree?). Students literally take a position by standing at the end of the line – or at a point along the line – which best represents their view. This works well for complex ethical questions. Thoughts and opinions can then be exchanged as students justify their positions. This is a good way of getting students out of their seats and matching their physical movement (moving to a different part of the room) with their answer.

Four corners

This is a variation of the value line. The four corners of the room each represent a different opinion, value or answer. Students move to the corner that best represents their response. This version works well when you want to 'force' students to commit to a particular answer, whereas the 'line of agreement' might encourage greater fluidity in students' answers.

Crossovers

This can be used to assign students to groups for activities. You could ask students to line up in order of their date of birth, from 1 January to 31 December, or ask them to line up alphabetically. This can be particularly useful as an ice breaker, as students have to introduce themselves to each other and start to get to know each other. Once the students have formed a line, you can assign a number to each student. You will need to think about how many groups you would like so that you know how many numbers to assign. Then ask all students assigned number 1 to form a group, all students assigned number 2 to form a group, all 3s form a group and so on.

Buzz groups

This is a way of working with several subgroups or breakout groups at once. Give small groups (pairs, threes or fours) a short, timed task and then collate responses, perhaps using a flipchart. Then one group joins another group to share and exchange answers and views. This creates a 'buzz' of noise and activity in the room.

Snowball/Pyramid

This is a continuation of buzz groups. Once breakout groups have exchanged ideas, groups are combined to form larger groups in order to facilitate further exchange of ideas. As the groups become larger, the task can also be made more complex in order to prevent students from becoming bored.

Jigsaw

This is another way of working with several breakout groups. This technique is highly collaborative as students are dependent on each other to find answers to the whole problem. Figure 4.1 shows how this technique works. Each student in the group has one piece of the 'jigsaw' and they can only find the answers to the whole problem or question by working together. Assign students to small groups of 4–6. Each student is assigned a particular part of a problem, a particular segment of text, or a particular aspect of a topic. This is represented by topics A, B and C in Figure 4.1. The students spend some time individually learning about their assigned part of the problem and share their ideas to consolidate their learning. Then students form mixed groups to discuss and teach each other about the different topics. At this point, the groups have information about all three topics and have therefore put all pieces of the puzzle together.

Polling

You can encourage students to answer questions or share their thoughts on a particular topic anonymously using polling software (see Case Study 4.2). There are many free platforms that you can use to set questions and enable students to submit responses in real time using their own devices – mobile phone, laptop or tablet. There are also several question types, such as multiple choice, sliding scales, word clouds, free text responses and so on.

Fishbowl

This is a technique that encourages active participation as well as observation. Volunteers sit in the middle of a larger circle and work on a task that involves discussion, problem solving or decision making, with the group outside acting as observers. Swap students in and out of the inner circle and ask the observers to provide feedback.

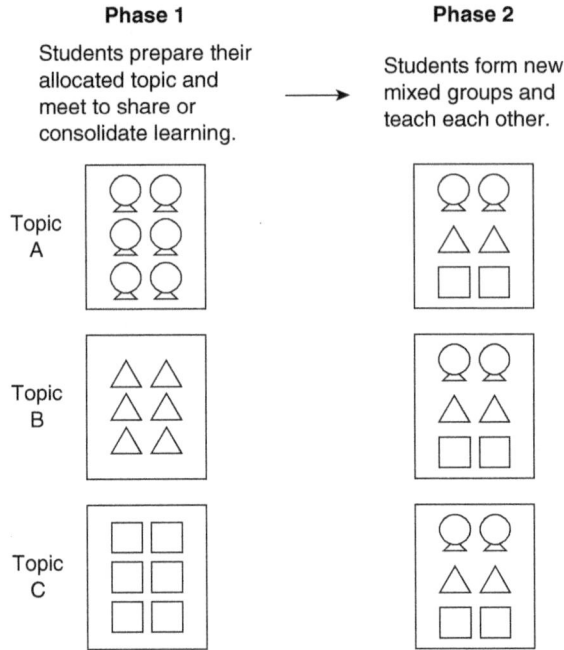

Figure 4.1 The jigsaw method

These are just some of the active learning techniques you could use when teaching small groups. Most important is to keep in mind what you want your students to learn (what are the intended learning outcomes?) and then choose an activity that will help to engage students in their learning. You can find many more techniques in the Further Resources at the end of this chapter (see Howell Major et al., 2016). You should also feel empowered to try different techniques and then reflect on how your students reacted, to what extent they learned and what you might change in future small group sessions. Regardless of which techniques you use, one skill in particular is important when facilitating learning in small groups – questioning. We will explore this next.

Reflection

Consider briefly how any of the active learning techniques presented above might be used in online learning environments. Are any of the techniques more difficult to use in online teaching?

Discussion

Many of the techniques listed above can be used, sometimes in an adapted way, in online sessions. For example, you can replicate a simple round by asking students in turn to post an idea or a response in the chat box. You could also use polling to create a value line or a four corners activity. The difference here is that students will be anonymous. Assigning students to groups – such as crossovers and buzz groups – can be done using breakout groups on most platforms. You can either assign students to groups manually, or you can decide how many groups you would like and then allow the platform to create the groups automatically. After some time, you could replicate the snowball by reducing the number of groups and asking the platform to reassign students, so that there are more students allocated across fewer groups. A similar process could be used with the jigsaw method by assigning different topics – or pieces of the puzzle – to different breakout rooms, and asking students to carousel around the various rooms. The key point is to maintain the engagement that comes from active learning. We should not stop engaging students actively simply because we are teaching online. We explore this further in Chapter 8.

Case Study 4.2

Active learning in seminars: Beatriz Caballero Martin, Learning Technologist

First, I divided the students into two small groups so they could develop their interpersonal skills and the ability to work with a group of peers. Then, I ran a brainstorming session to encourage group discussions on the different research methodologies they could apply to their research. In groups, I made them build a mind map using an A3 paper, Post-Its and colour marker pens to think about the different methods they were aware of. I also used the board to note down the relevant key concepts they were coming up with and we could discuss further later. This exercise helped them to have a clearer idea of the methods they could use, but it also got them talking about the benefits of using certain social research methodologies and not others, as well as being able to manage their expectations regarding the short time scale of the project and the resources available to them. It also allowed me to test their existing knowledge and challenge their assumptions about the most effective and appropriate ways of collecting, analysing and presenting data in a user-friendly and accessible way.

At first, I noticed I needed to promote participation as students seemed reluctant to talk, mostly because they didn't feel confident about how they could contribute and whether their existing knowledge was relevant. The brainstorming exercise gave them a safe space within the group to articulate their current knowledge about the different research methodologies, feedback collection and data analysis without feeling too exposed. Working as a Learning Technologist I was also aware of the value of using appropriate learning technologies and I could apply these technologies to make the session more interactive and allow students to participate anonymously. I used Mentimeter to gather more information on their different views and preferences. I used it to allow them to feel their answers were anonymous and they could contribute more honestly with their answers.

Questioning techniques

Questions are arguably one of the most powerful tools at a teacher's disposal when trying to stimulate discussion and engage students during a small group session. We often ask questions in response to answers given by others, but it can be helpful to plan some of your questions in advance. The purposes of planned, targeted questions are (Exley and Dennick, 2004: 39):

- To arouse students' interest
- To activate prior learning
- To identify strengths and weaknesses and check students' progress
- To influence group dynamics and encourage participation
- To encourage deep-level thinking and active learning
- To review and summarise.

Arousing interest

Planning a 'trigger' question at the beginning of the session can help to pique your students' interest. You could also ask a question that invites learners to relate the topic to their own context or lives.

Activating prior learning

As we have mentioned, small group teaching enables us to take a student-centred approach, where learners are actively engaged rather than passively receiving a lecture. This also means that students can share their knowledge within the group. It follows, therefore, that we are interested in using questions at the beginning of the session to activate and verify students' prior learning and existing knowledge.

Identifying strengths and weaknesses

After activating prior knowledge, you can use your students' responses to decide how to proceed. There may be particular areas of the curriculum that require further explanation or further activities, and equally there may be areas of strength that require no or little further input.

Influencing group dynamics

As mentioned earlier in this chapter, one of the main aims of small group teaching is to encourage students to communicate and to interact. It is the role of the facilitator to employ a variety of questioning techniques to create a learning environment in which all students feel comfortable to express their views and to answer questions. We will look at this in more detail later in this chapter.

Encouraging deep-level thinking

When planning questions during the session, it is important to consider how complex the questions are. If you are aware of this, you can target different levels of Bloom's taxonomy (see Chapter 3). Different types of questions will encourage thinking at lower or higher cognitive levels, such as demonstrating comprehension or, at a higher level, demonstrating analytical and evaluative skills.

Reviewing and summarising

Questions can be used at any point during the session to review students' understanding of key concepts and progress towards meeting the learning outcomes. Reviewing and summarising also provides students with an opportunity to receive formative feedback and to identify areas for development.

Types of questions

There are different types of question that you can use depending on what you are trying to achieve. The main question types are:

- Open (divergent) questions
- Closed (convergent) questions
- Probing questions
- Questions aimed at different levels of the learning hierarchy.

Open questions

Also referred to as divergent questions, open questions usually have several possible responses and encourage deep-level thinking (see deep vs surface learning in Chapter 2). Students may be required to apply their knowledge to new contexts and problems, analysing situations and evaluating evidence in order to respond to the question. The answer is unlikely to be simple or very brief. Open questions are often used later in a small group teaching session in order to encourage deeper thinking and engagement after an initial warm-up.

Examples: What evidence is there to suggest that time travel is possible? How can we design future cities to tackle current housing and transport problems?

Closed questions

Closed questions are also referred to as convergent questions, as they are concerned with factual information and ask the learner to come to (converge on) a specific answer. Closed questions usually have a short, relatively simple answer, even including 'yes' and 'no'.

Questions of this type can be useful for checking prior knowledge and for warming students up at the beginning of a session.

Examples: What is the name of that bone/method/theory? Who developed the theory of evolution by natural selection?

Probing questions

As well as planning specific questions at different times in the session, there may be a need to add additional, probing questions, which encourage students to elaborate on and clarify their responses. Probing questions are particularly useful when students give incorrect or incomplete responses. There are several types of probing question:

- Prompting – used when a student does not respond or gives an incorrect or incomplete answer.

Examples: Remember last session when we talked about ...? That's along the right lines; have you also considered ...?

- Justifying – used when a student gives a correct answer but with no rationale or justification.

Examples: OK, and what is the evidence for that? Why is it so important to do it that way? How did you get to your answer?

- Clarifying – used when a student gives an incomplete response or the response is unclear.

Examples: Can you be more specific? Can you explain what that means in practice? Can you give an example?

- Extending – used when a student demonstrates superficial understanding, but you would like to encourage deeper-level thinking.

Examples: Interesting. How would you modify that treatment if the patient were a baby? How would that be applied in your context?

- Redirecting – used to generate further responses to the same question.

Examples: What do you think? Can you add anything to student X's response?

Questions aimed at different levels of learning

In Chapter 3, we looked at Bloom's taxonomy in the context of writing intended learning outcomes. We can also encourage students to think in different ways by using questions that promote thinking at different levels of the learning hierarchy, from relatively simple recall of facts through to applying knowledge to different problems and scenarios, and questions that require the student to show skills of analysis and evaluation. If we are targeting the knowledge or comprehension domain of Bloom's taxonomy, we might ask a question like: In what year was the European Union formed? This requires (simple) recall of a fact. On the other hand, if we are encouraging higher-order thinking skills, we might ask a question like: To what extent has the European Union been successful at maintaining peace and security? This requires analysis, synthesis and evaluation, and an answer that does not depend purely on recall of facts.

Activity 4.2

Planning questions

Think of a session or topic that you have taught or might teach in the future. Think of at least two questions that you could ask your students, covering at least two of the different types of questions (open, closed, probing, targeting different levels of learning). Consider your choice of questions. What is your rationale?

Discussion

By thinking through your questioning strategies in this way, you will be better prepared to lead discussions and facilitate students' learning. You will also be more aware of how your questions – and the learning activities in general – are aligned with the intended learning outcomes, as you will be thinking consciously about higher- and lower-order thinking skills at appropriate times.

Top tips for effective questioning

- Use ice-breakers and warm-up questions to create a 'safe' questioning environment.
- Use a range of open and closed questions depending on the subject matter.
- Plan questions that target different levels of thinking (Bloom's taxonomy).
- Embrace the silence; allow thinking time.
- Use prompt questions if silence persists.
- Alternatively, give students an opportunity to express their thoughts in writing or to discuss their ideas in pairs.
- Use questions and responses as an opportunity to provide positive and formative feedback.
- Include all students in your questioning but make it safe by including an option to 'pass'.

Managing group dynamics in small groups

When teaching a small group, it is inevitable that, at some point, issues may arise within the group. This is not something to be afraid of; you simply need to be prepared to deal with some of the common scenarios that can arise.

Activity 4.3

Potential challenges of small group teaching

Here are some of the most common challenges that you might encounter when facilitating learning in small groups. Reflect on whether you have experienced these scenarios, either as a teacher or as a student, and note down some strategies that you could use to influence the group dynamics:

- Disengaged or silent group member: You notice that one group member does not contribute during discussions within the group. What do you do? How do you engage this student?
- Disengaged or silent group: The group as a whole seems rather disengaged and you find that you are doing most of the talking during the session. What do you do?
- Dominant group member: One group member in particular dominates discussions, and the other students are rather quiet as a result. What do you do?
- Disruptive group member: One of the students in the group is often disruptive, sometimes even challenging your knowledge and authority. What do you do?
- Unprepared group member: One of your students frequently attends your sessions unprepared and does not complete pre-course reading and activities, which means they are unable to contribute during class. What do you do?

Are there any other challenges you have experienced that do not fall into any of these scenarios?

Here are some suggested strategies to help influence group dynamics in each scenario in Activity 4.3.

Disengaged or silent group member

You notice that one group member does not contribute during discussions within the group. What do you do? How do you engage this student?

- Make clear to the group that you expect students to come to your sessions well prepared, and that you expect students to contribute.

- Explain your teaching approaches to your students. For some students, perhaps from other countries, active learning will be unfamiliar, so it is helpful to explain your rationale for expecting participation.
- Speak to the student one-to-one to explore the reasons for the lack of engagement.
- Use a variety of questioning techniques to encourage different levels of thinking.
- Use a variety of active learning methods to give students the chance to contribute in different ways; e.g. use pass the pen rather than rounds to enable students to respond in writing rather than having to always speak.
- Make it less 'risky' for students to contribute by asking them to work in pairs initially, before sharing responses with the wider group.
- Give the student a low-stakes task to prepare for the next session, so that they can contribute in a prepared way.

Disengaged or silent group

The group as a whole seems rather disengaged and you find that you are doing most of the talking during the session. What do you do?

- If you find you are doing most of the talking, take steps to change this immediately.
- Try setting a clear task and divide students into pairs or small breakout groups.
- Embrace silence. It may be the case that your students need more thinking time. Avoid the temptation to keep talking as soon as there is silence.
- If the disengagement persists, you could try to find out why they do not contribute. You could do this verbally, or you could ask for brief written feedback anonymously on paper or using polling software.
- Try giving small, different tasks for each student to prepare. It will then be the responsibility of each individual student to speak about their personalised task.
- You could ask a colleague to observe one of your sessions. Your colleague may be able to suggest some practical changes that will help to engage your students.
- Review your session plans. What activities do you plan? Which active learning methods do you use? Which questioning techniques do you use? By taking a step back and planning the interactions carefully, you are likely to start engaging your students.
- Reiterate your expectation that students contribute during your sessions.

Dominant group member

One group member in particular dominates discussions, and the other students are rather quiet as a result. What do you do?

- Address students by name in order to encourage responses from different members of the group.
- If the issue persists, meet with the dominant group member one-to-one. The student's dominance in the group may be well intentioned and a result of enthusiasm and motivation. If this is the case, you need to be clear that you welcome their contributions, but that other students need to be given an opportunity to speak.

- Use your planning of questions to decide which individual student you would like to answer. You can deviate from this in the session, but this plan will help you to be consciously aware that you need to engage other students.
- You could experiment with asking different group members to lead short portions of the session, giving responsibility – for leading and contributing – to different students.
- If the issue persists, and you do not think the student's dominance is well intentioned, contact the module lead or a colleague for support.

Disruptive group member

One of the students in the group is often disruptive, sometimes even challenging your knowledge and authority. What do you do?

- Set clear ground rules and expectations at the start of term about mutual respect.
- Meet with the student one-to-one to explore the reasons for the disruptiveness. There may be an underlying issue, or the student may be bored. If the latter is the case, you can address this in your planning by using a greater variety of active learning methods to engage all students.
- Give the student greater responsibility; ask them to conduct background research to inform discussions in the next session. You could also ask the student to lead part of the session.
- Be humble and make it clear that, whilst you are in the teacher role, you do not know everything, and you are not expected to know everything. Most students are reasonable and would agree with this.
- If the problem persists, speak to the module lead or a senior colleague. You are not expected to tolerate rudeness or unacceptable behaviour from students.

Unprepared group member

One of your students frequently attends your sessions unprepared and does not complete pre-course reading and activities, which means they are unable to contribute during class. What do you do?

- Help the student, and all students in fact, to structure their preparation. For example, rather than asking students to 'read chapter 4', you could design a short activity, perhaps online, or set a few questions to guide their reading.
- You could ask your students to prepare a brief summary of their preparatory work, which acts as an 'entry ticket' to your session.
- You could also ask students to prepare a short summary of their preparatory work in small groups, which they present briefly at the start of the session.
- Make it clear that the preparatory task(s) will be used and reviewed in class. You could even go as far as explaining how the tasks will be used in class. Students sometimes do not prepare because they do not think it is necessary, or because the teacher summarises the preparatory work her/himself.

- You could give the student in question responsibility for a particular part of the session, either to research a given topic beforehand and/or to lead part of the session.
- Try starting each session with a quick quiz based on material that students needed to prepare. This will encourage all learners to prepare, not just the student who frequently arrives unprepared.
- You could occasionally ask students to submit their preparatory work before the session. This enables you to give some formative feedback and adds further encouragement for the student to come prepared.
- Alternatively, you could ask students to peer assess their prepared work sometimes.
- Meet with the student one-to-one to explore whether there are any reasons for the lack of preparation.

Depending on the subject matter, there may be specific challenges related to the content of your sessions. This is particularly the case where you are discussing controversial or sensitive topics with your students. We explore this in Chapter 9. In all of the scenarios, we have looked at how the teacher can 'manage' the situation. As you are the facilitator, it is of course important to think about how you can influence group dynamics, but for each situation above – and any others you might have encountered – it can be useful to highlight the students' own responsibility for their learning and interactions within the group. You could ask your students to self-assess (and/or peer assess depending on group relationships) their own contributions during group work. If this is done honestly and with good intentions, students will feel empowered and will probably identify for themselves where they could improve their performance during group work. Table 4.1 shows some sample questions that could be used for a self-assessment exercise.

Table 4.1 Sample questions for student self-assessment of group work contributions

	Frequently	Sometimes	Never
How often did you give an opinion during the discussion?			
How often did you justify your answers with reasons and evidence?			
How often did you listen actively to others?			
How often did you respond respectfully to others during the discussion?			
How often did you express agreement or disagreement in an appropriate way?			
How often did you refer to the preparatory work during the discussion?			
How often did you encourage other group members to contribute?			

Over to you

Small group teaching is an important part of most people's roles in teaching and supporting learning. This chapter has given you an opportunity to explore what small group teaching means, particularly in your context and discipline, and highlighted some of the important points to consider when preparing to facilitate learning in small groups, focusing in particular on agreeing ground rules with your students and managing group dynamics. You can use the activities in this chapter, along with the suggestions about active learning techniques and questioning strategies, to reflect on your own practice, both for your ongoing professional development and in preparation for an Advance HE fellowship application.

Further resources

This book outlines how to facilitate learning in small groups, including how to form groups, group dynamics, and a range of techniques and activities to help students to learn.

Barkley, E. F., Howell Major, C. and Cross, K. P. (2014) *Collaborative Learning Techniques. A Handbook for College Faculty*, 2nd edn. San Francisco: Jossey-Bass.

This book explains succinctly 101 activities that can be used to encourage active learning in a range of teaching scenarios.

Howell Major, C., Harris, M. S. and Zakrajsek, T. (2016) *Teaching for Learning: 101 Intentionally Designed Educational Activities to Put Students on the Path to Success*. New York: Routledge.

This book provides an accessible overview of the team-based learning (TBL) approach.

Sibley, J. and Ostafichuk, P. (2015) *Getting Started with Team-Based Learning*. Virginia: Stylus.

References

Brookfield, S. D. and Preskill, S. (2005) *Discussion as a Way of Teaching: Tools and Techniques for Democratic Classrooms*, 2nd edn. San Francisco: Jossey-Bass.
Exley, K. and Dennick, R. (2004) *Small Group Teaching. Tutorials, Seminars and Beyond*. Abingdon: Routledge.

5

TEACHING LARGE GROUPS AND GIVING LECTURES

Learning outcomes

After reading this chapter you should be able to:

- Critically reflect on the role of lectures in higher education
- Plan a lecture and use active learning techniques to engage students in large groups
- Identify performance aspects of your role and employ techniques to manage nerves, to use the voice effectively, and to deal with the unexpected.

Introduction

In Chapter 4, we looked at your role in facilitating learning in small groups. Depending on the nature of your work in teaching and supporting learning, you may also be involved in large group teaching. When we think of large groups, perhaps the first word that comes to mind is 'lecture', as this has been, and remains, one of the most common teaching approaches in university education. However, as we saw in Chapter 4 in relation to small group teaching, a group might be considered to be large when it becomes difficult to interact meaningfully with each individual student. This means that a large group does not necessarily consist of a lecture theatre packed with hundreds of students. It is important to identify what you consider to be a large group, regardless of whether you are teaching in a lecture format or not. In this chapter, we will take the lecture method as an example of large group teaching and explore the transferable skills you can take from other aspects of your life, such as public speaking and presenting at conferences. We will also discuss how lectures can be made more student-centred and interactive, and explore characteristics of 'performance' when teaching large groups, such as deliberate and careful use of the voice, use of the body, and managing nerves and 'stage fright'.

The lecture

Lectures are one of the most common methods of teaching in universities. Perhaps with the exception of a small number of very practical subjects, it is unlikely that any student has completed a degree programme that did not include lectures. Lectures have a long history, as far back as the ancient Greeks, when the lecturer – from the Latin, *lectitare*, meaning to be in the habit of reading – would transmit knowledge to the audience by reading a text aloud. The use of the word 'transmit' is deliberate here. In Chapter 2, we looked at various theories of learning, including a characterisation of teaching as a process of transmitting knowledge from teacher to student. This is what is at the heart of the original meaning of the lecture method. The idea of 'reading' and transmitting knowledge is also captured in job titles. In the UK, academics are often referred to as 'lecturers' and experienced academics may even be called 'readers'.

Reflection

Think back to your own experiences of learning in lectures. Roughly how much of your degree programme was taught using lectures? To what extent did your lectures align with the characterisation of lectures above as a process of transmission from teacher to students? Did you enjoy learning in lectures?

Discussion

The extent to which your degree programme was taught using lectures will depend partly on the subject you studied. However, we are willing to bet that most people have experienced at least some lectures across the various modules in their programme of study. For you personally, it may not have been the case that your lecturers simply read texts aloud, as was the case in ancient times. Your lectures may have been largely didactic, with the lecturer talking all or most of the time, perhaps using visuals on slides, or there may have been some activities or interactions between you and the lecturer. What is probably true, however, is that there was generally less interactivity in your lectures than in the small group sessions you attended – or have taught yourself. There is now a wealth of research evidence that teaching students in a didactic, passive way results in poorer learning outcomes than methods that promote active, engaged learning (Freeman et al., 2014; Theobold et al., 2020; see also Howell Major et al., 2016 in the Further Resources). Nevertheless, as is probably the case in your own institution, lectures retain an important role in how students are taught in universities. We will explore why this is next. It is also important to remember that some students enjoy lectures and learn well in this format. Perhaps you are one of these people. So, we should consider how to make our lectures and other large group sessions more student-centred so that we can ensure that learning is actually happening.

Why do we still lecture?

Particularly in the context of the recent global coronavirus pandemic, universities have had to rethink quickly how students learn and how teachers teach, which includes considerations around what it means to lecture. It is important to acknowledge the potential pitfalls of lectures whilst also appreciating that this method is likely to remain a part of how we teach in universities for the foreseeable future. Perhaps one reason for this is that lectures are simply part of the language we use in higher education, and it is part of common experience for anyone who has attended university. When you were at school, you might have said you were going to a 'class' or a 'lesson'. Then when you moved on to university, 'lecture' probably became a part of your everyday lexicon. Lectures are also culturally embedded in our psyche, as they feature in countless fictional stories in books and films, and we to some extent come to expect lectures to be a part of university education. Of course, there are also practical and financial reasons: it is more economical and less time consuming to have one teacher deliver a lecture to a large number of students at once than several teachers leading tutorials with multiple small groups of students. There is also existing infrastructure in most universities, where classrooms and lecture theatres are already set up with static tables and chairs arranged in such a way that students are situated as passive learners watching the lecturer at the front of the room. Finally, as mentioned above, some students enjoy lectures, and even expect to be lectured, as this feels like a mark of higher education as distinct from previous experiences in primary and secondary school. So we would not argue that lectures have no place in university teaching, but we should consider how can retain key pedagogic principles when teaching large groups, such as engaging students in active learning, enabling students to construct their own knowledge and make their own meaning, both individually and with their peers (see Chapter 2). We will explore ways of making lectures more interactive later in this chapter.

Preparing a lecture

Much of the preparation we looked at in Chapter 4 is applicable when preparing lectures. If you think back to the discussion of learning outcomes and constructive alignment in Chapter 3, you will see that it is important to consider what you actually intend your students to learn and how your teaching methods and learning activities will help your students to achieve these learning outcomes. This is the case regardless of whether you are teaching a small or a large group. So as in Chapter 4, you could start by asking yourself the following questions:

1   What are the intended learning outcomes for the module? How do your lectures fit within the module; how do they relate to small group sessions (if there are any)?
2   Is it appropriate or useful to write your own session-level learning outcomes for each lecture?

You should also try to find out as much information about the students and the venue as possible, much of which is similar to what we discussed in Chapter 4:

- Number of students
- Number of lectures in the series
- Length of time for each lecture
- Previous learning – from other modules
- Other study hours in the module, such as small group sessions
- Have any of the students declared any specific learning differences?
- The venue for your sessions – will you be teaching in a 'traditional' lecture theatre? Is any of the furniture in the room moveable? Is there a whiteboard, a flipchart, a PC and projector? Is there a microphone? Is there software installed for the lecture to be recorded? What facilities will you need?
- Is all teaching face to face? Are there any online components?

Once you have this information, you can start to think about the content of the lecture and how to structure the time you have with your students. In terms of content, perhaps the most important thing is to decide on the main points you wish to address in the lecture. This should be a small number of key points, no more than five, as this will help to ensure you do not overwhelm your students with content. This is also where it can be useful to write session-level learning outcomes for the individual lecture, as this will help you to focus on what you want your students to take away from the lecture, and then help you to structure the session.

Drawing on your existing presentation skills

When planning a lecture, you will need to consider not only the content and the intended learning outcomes, but also how you will 'present' the lecture. This can be rather daunting, especially if you are new to lecturing. We will explore some of the performance aspects of lecturing later in this chapter, but here we invite you to think about the skills you have already honed in other areas of your work and life, such as public speaking and presenting, and to consider how these skills can be transferred to your lecturing context.

Activity 5.1

Reflecting on existing skills and experiences of presenting

Think about a time when you have had to speak in front of an audience and present information. This could be in a meeting in front of colleagues, at a professional or an academic conference, or perhaps an event or a family occasion such as a wedding. In what ways was this experience similar to the lecturing context? How might you adapt your presenting and public speaking skills from this previous context to the teaching context?

The good news is that you already have many skills from other aspects of your life that can be very helpful when planning lectures. Here are some points from presentations and other public speaking experiences that might be useful, in adapted form, when preparing to give a lecture:

- *Storytelling*: presenting and public speaking are all about storytelling and leading the audience through a (compelling) narrative. You can think of lectures in a similar way, as this will help you to think about how you can speak engagingly about the subject.
- *Interactivity*: perhaps a key difference between the 'stories' told in presentations and in lectures is in the level of interaction between you and the audience or students. A presentation may involve some interactivity, but you are likely to be doing most of the talking. In the lecturing context, you have a different focus so you are unlikely to talk for an hour without interacting with your students. So what is this difference in focus?
- *Focus*: in a presentation, your main focus is on 'telling' your audience something. In a lecture, there will be elements of presenting information to your students but, as with all teaching encounters, your main focus should be on your students' learning.

Returning to our previous point, it follows that there needs to be some interaction (between you and your students and between students themselves) in order to see whether learning is happening.

- *Repetition*: as a rhetorical device, repetition is important to ensure the key message(s) are understood and remembered by the audience. In a presentation, you probably mention your key points at the beginning and at the end. In a lecture, your key messages are (related to) the learning outcomes, so they are likely to be raised several times during the lecture. This will help to motivate your students and communicate the relevance of the material to the learning outcomes (constructive alignment).

- *Level*: in a presentation, you may have audience members with very different levels of knowledge on the topic, and you may not have the opportunity to gauge these different levels beforehand. In a lecturing context, you can plan for this much more thoroughly by asking the questions above about the students who will be attending, about their prior learning, and so on. You might also decide to plan a short pre-lecture task, such as an online quiz on the topic, in order to gauge your students' level before they arrive.

- *Structure*: in any talk, whether it is a formal presentation, an informal talk at a family gathering or a lecture, it is important to consider how you will structure the content and the time you apportion to each part of the session. In a presentation, a good structure helps with your storytelling. Similarly, in a lecture, a clear structure helps you to create an engaging narrative, and it also helps your students to follow the lecture.

Structuring a lecture

One of the influencing factors on the structure of your lectures is your university's timetabling and scheduling. In most institutions, lectures are timetabled in hour-long slots. In practice, this means you have around 50 minutes to plan for your lecture structure, as you will need to leave five minutes or so at the beginning and end to account for students' arrival and for leaving the room in a safe and orderly way, particularly if the group is very large. If the room is vacant before your lecture, it is useful to arrive a few

Table 5.1 Suggested lecture structure

5 minutes	Arrivals, settling down, setting up equipment (if early entry into the room is not possible)
5 minutes	Beginning: introduce yourself (if first lecture), present aims and learning outcomes, signpost the structure of the lecture, perhaps use a stimulus as a 'hook'
35	Middle: main part of the lecture, including activities
10	End: Summarise key points, summarise learning, formative assessment, link to next lecture
5	Exit

minutes early so that you can set up, switch on the computer and projector, and test the microphone (if you are using one). However, this may not always be possible if there is a lecture in the same room immediately before your session. An approximate lecture structure is shown in Table 5.1.

In Table 5.1, there is around 50 minutes of time for teaching and learning and around five minutes planned at the beginning and end to start and finish the session in a relaxed way. The time at the end is particularly important as you may go over time anyway, so the last five minutes act as a useful 'buffer'. On a practical level, you will also need time to gather your materials and leave the room. It is important, and respectful to other colleagues, to do this in a timely manner as the lecture theatre may be used again immediately after you have finished. Let's take a closer look at what to put in the beginning, middle and end of the lecture.

Beginnings

The beginning – the first five minutes or so – are important for setting the scene, tone and expectations. If this is the first lecture with a new cohort, you might outline some expectations or ground rules (see Chapter 4) and introduce yourself. Think about how you want to introduce yourself and what you want to tell your students. Whilst you should not spend too long and tell them your life story, a good, brief introduction can help to set the tone and establish your credibility. You could plan the following in your introduction:

- Your name (this sounds obvious but have you ever attended a lecture or any other session and realised you had no idea who the teacher was?).
- Your role at the university.
- A brief overview of your expertise in the subject – to establish credibility.
- A note about why you find the subject interesting – to show your enthusiasm and passion, as this is infectious.

Then, it is important to contextualise the lecture within the degree programme. How does the lecture fit within a series of lectures? How does it fit within the module, or even the degree programme as a whole? This is where you share your aims for the session as well as your intended learning outcomes (ILOs). These might be the module learning outcomes and an explanation of how the lecture is addressing any or all of the outcomes, or you may have written some session-level ILOs for the individual lecture. Share the structure of the lecture by giving an overview of the session. This will help to give a sense of mutual ownership of the lecture rather than you as the teacher holding all the power and secrets. For some lectures, you might also decide to use some form of stimulus to hook your students; to grab their attention from the start. This could be an image, a shocking or intriguing statistic, a provocative question, a storytelling technique (what if I were to tell you that ...; Imagine if we ...), or possibly a joke – but use with caution as one person's idea of humour is another's idea of offence. You could also give a specific, real-life case, example or problem that illustrates the topic of the lecture. Finally, in this part of the lecture, you want to find out a bit about the students' existing knowledge of the topic. You could do this with a short task prior to the lecture or with a quick question using a simple show of hands, or you could use a poll where students can select an answer anonymously (see Case Study 5.1).

Middles

This is where the bulk of the teaching and learning takes place. In the suggested structure in Table 5.1 we have allocated 35 minutes of a one-hour lecture to this part. These 35 minutes could be used as follows:

10 minutes   Mini-lecture

5 minutes   Activity

2.5 minutes   Debrief, summary and transition to next stage

10 minutes   Mini-lecture

5 minutes   Activity

2.5 minutes   Debrief, summary and transition to 'wrap up'

A common issue when lecturing is the temptation to try to cover too much content. This structure moves away from a purely didactic transmission of knowledge from teacher to students by incorporating activities after input from the lecturer. It is widely cited that our students' attention in lectures starts to decrease after 10–15 minutes. Some dispute this, saying the key factor is how engagingly the teacher presents the material (e.g. Bradbury, 2016), but it is nevertheless useful to change the dynamic in the room regularly. The middle part of the lecture could be structured in any number of ways, perhaps starting with a problem or a case study, followed by input from the teacher. The key point here is that a lecture does not have to abandon the principles of active learning and student-centredness that would be present in your small group teaching. We will explore some ways of making your lectures interactive later in this chapter.

Ends

In Table 5.1, we allocated 10 minutes to this part of the lecture. This may seem like a lot of time, but this is a vital part of the session, both for students' learning and to show an organised, structured approach to your teaching. You might also find that the middle part of the lecture overruns, so deliberate planning of a slightly longer ending will help to absorb a minute or two if the middle section takes longer than planned. In this last part of the lecture you can summarise the key points from the session and return to the learning outcomes that were presented at the beginning of the session. You could either explain briefly how each learning outcome has been addressed or, better still, you could give students a couple of minutes to self-assess their own learning against the ILOs. Depending on time and group dynamics, you could ask a few students to share what they have learned as well as any points that remain unclear. You could also ask students to share their learning with each other as a form of self- and peer assessment. Alternatively, you could ask students to submit their thoughts anonymously using a poll (see the next section, on promoting active learning). You can then use this as a form of formative assessment, and address any areas of common misunderstanding in the next lecture. Finally, you can give a brief overview of the next lecture and provide instructions for any activities that need to be completed before the next session.

Promoting active learning in lectures

In Chapter 2, we introduced the pedagogic principle of active learning, which is an umbrella term for a range of approaches aimed at engaging students in their learning. We then looked in Chapter 4 at just some of the possible activities that you could try when teaching small groups. However, when teaching a much larger group, such as in a lecture theatre, it can be daunting to consider introducing active learning techniques. This is mainly because it is generally more difficult to facilitate activities in a larger group. For example, how can you be sure all students are completing the activity? How will you regain the students' attention when the activity is finished? Questions like this can make active learning in lectures seem (too) difficult, but with careful planning, it is possible to make lectures interactive and engaging. As shown in the suggested structure in Table 5.1 and the sample sequence for the middle section of the lecture, a one-hour lecture is really quite short with only a small amount of time where activities might be incorporated. Recognising this should make the task of engaging a large group in active learning a far less daunting prospect. So how can you promote active learning in your lectures? The ideas in Chapter 4 tend to work well with smaller groups, although some can also be used with larger groups, such as think–pair–share and polling. Here are some other ideas specifically for larger groups.

Reflection and silence

Not all activities have to be literally active. Active learning is about giving students opportunities to engage with the materials, with their peers and with you. This could be in the form of silent thoughts and reflection. An activity like this changes the energy in the room, not least because the teacher stops talking and leaves mental space for students to think about what they have just heard and seen in the lecture. The activity could consist just of silent reflection, or you could transition into think–pair–share, where students then share their thoughts with a partner, before you take some responses from a few pairs around the room. Alternatively, you could ask students to make notes, make a mindmap or draw a sketch of their main learning points. By having a range of activities such as these, you can help to motivate all students to participate.

Problem solving

This is an activity that runs throughout the whole lecture. The teacher presents a problem at the beginning of the lecture. This could be a deliberate mistake, perhaps in an equation or a piece of code, or you might describe a scenario or a case related to the topic of the lecture with a problem or question embedded. The lecture then provides clues and information to solve the problem. The teacher returns to the problem at the end of the lecture to see if the students have solved it. This activity can create a sense of excitement and mystery throughout the whole lecture.

Quizzes and polling

After a mini-lecture, the teacher can pose a few questions and give students a few minutes to answer them. The questions could be shown on the screen and students write their answers or discuss with a partner. Alternatively, polling can be used to allow students to submit their responses anonymously. This is a form of formative assessment, and the benefit of this is that the teacher gains immediate feedback about the extent to which the students have understood the content presented in the preceding mini lecture. Another way of gauging the students' understanding is with a simple traffic lights system. The teacher can include pieces of red, green and yellow card (or other symbols such as a tick, a cross and a question mark) in the module handbook and students hold up cards in response to the teacher's questions – green for fully understood, red for confused, yellow for partial understanding. A simple method like this gives the teacher real-time feedback about the students' understanding of the key content of the lecture.

Handouts and scaffolded notes

Some teachers provide handouts in lectures. This can be turned into an activity by involving students in co-creation of the handout. This can be done by leaving gaps where key points need to be filled in, or there might just be headings with the handout left blank for the students to complete their own notes. An activity like this spans the whole lecture and provides scaffolding (see Chapter 2) to help students to take notes.

Video or audio stimulus

Play a brief video or audio clip and ask students to respond to one or two questions related to the stimulus material. Depending on the nature of the questions, students' responses can then be elicited in an online poll, or students can discuss their answers in pairs or small groups before taking responses from a few groups.

This is just a small number of ways in which you can engage your students in active learning during lectures. Some of the techniques for small group teaching (see Chapter 4) could also be used, such as buzz groups for example, but it might be better to build up to noisier group activities once you have become familiar with the class. Regardless of the activities you use, the size of the group means you need to plan carefully how you will transition into and out of the activity. First, it is vital to give very clear instructions before setting students off on an activity. If it becomes clear that some students did not hear or understand the instructions, it is difficult to stop the whole group to repeat the instructions. Similarly, it is important to plan how you will bring the activity to a close and communicate this to the students. With a larger group, there will naturally be more noise than when working with a small group. If you have access to a microphone, you can use it to gain the group's attention at the end of the activity. Alternatively, you could set a timer and project this on the screen. There are lots of free stopwatches online which can be set to ring an alarm after a set time. This can be used to pace the activity and to regain the group's attention when needed.

Case Study 5.1

Using polling and paired discussions to check understanding in a lecture: Nicolas Newell, Research Fellow in Mechanical Engineering

During my lectures there is a certain part of the teaching that lends itself to using Mentimeter polling when going through example questions. I have used this tool to give students immediate feedback on their understanding. I do this by running a Mentimeter at a certain step of a solution where there are one or two correct answers but I make it multiple choice with a couple of incorrect answers as well. I get them to do the Mentimeter with a small amount of teaching first, so I can see what percentage of the class find this obvious. Inevitably, not many get the correct answers, so I then explain a bit further for two minutes without giving away the answers and I give the students two minutes to discuss the question with the person sat next to them. I then run the Mentimeter again to see if the number of people who get the correct answer has changed. If it has, I am happy that they have understood; if not, I can give some more feedback. I feel this approach allows students to get a deeper understanding of why the answers are correct, rather than them just learning the correct answers.

Performance aspects of lecturing

Teaching can sometimes feel like a performance. Particularly in lectures, where there is a large 'audience' and the teacher is, sometimes literally, on stage, we can feel vulnerable, nervous and pressured to put on a performance. Of course, a teacher is not a performer in the sense of entertaining an audience. Particularly if we are employing active learning techniques and adopting a student-centred approach, we are not the centre of attention. Nevertheless, we know from our own experience, as well as from talking to colleagues who are relatively new to teaching, that there are some common concerns about teaching large groups, all of which relate to performance. These are issues to do with nerves and anxiety, the voice and breathing, and dealing with the unexpected. We will look at each of these concerns here, but you can find more detailed input on performance and teaching in Bale (2020) in the Further Resources.

Dealing with nerves and 'stage fright'

When we talk to colleagues in workshops, one of the most frequently mentioned issues, particularly among relatively new teachers, is 'stage fright' and dealing with nerves. To a large extent, feeling nervous is good for our performance as it helps to focus our attention, keeps us alert and motivates us to 'perform'. The problem comes when nerves are controlling us rather than the other way round. In your day-to-day teaching practice, you may feel nervous about any type of teaching. In fact, even after many years of teaching and working in universities, we still experience some nervousness at the beginning of the academic year or at the beginning of a semester before meeting a new cohort of students. This is important to bear in mind as it shows you that almost everyone gets nervous. It is entirely normal. We are looking at this issue in this chapter because lectures are often where we feel most exposed, as we are in front of a large group of people. It is also important to remember that any form of stage fright does not begin when you are in front of the audience – or students. In the music performance context, Nagel (2017) draws our attention to the fact that nervousness begins long before we start the 'performance', perhaps when we are preparing materials for the lecture and start to imagine things going wrong. This shows that we can act to mitigate the effects of stage fright, both by preparing well and by ensuring we do not allow negative thoughts to take over.

Whilst preparation is important, and we have whole chapters in this book about designing learning and preparing classes, it is important to strike a balance between being well prepared and being so rehearsed that you immediately become nervous if something does not go completely according to plan. We will come back to this later when we discuss improvisation. Something that is important to avoid, however, is allowing yourself to create negative, destructive narratives about yourself as a teacher and about your teaching practice. Nagel (2017) highlights three ways in which nervousness and performance anxiety can arise and become visible:

- psychological – such as fear of looking 'stupid' or feeling embarrassed in front of other people
- physical – such as sweating, shaking, erratic breathing, etc.
- cognitive – such as unhelpful inner thoughts, e.g. what if my students think I'm stupid? My colleagues will hear about how bad I am as a lecturer. I'm an awful teacher.

Reflection

Think about your own experiences of nerves and stage fright, preferably in a teaching context. What do you think are the sources of this nervousness? Do you recognise any of the 'symptoms' of stage fright above in yourself? What do you 'fear' about teaching or speaking in front of others, if anything? How does nervousness manifest itself physically in you? Can you identify any negative, unhelpful thought patterns that you engage in when you are feeling nervous?

Discussion

You may be one of the fortunate people who does not really experience nervousness or stage fright. However, most people experience this to some degree. In a teaching context, the sources of this nervousness could be varied, as summarised by Exley and Dennick (2009): lack of confidence in your own teaching ability or knowledge of the subject matter; lack of experience, particularly with public speaking and lecturing; feeling self-conscious and judged by others; fear of making mistakes or doing a 'bad job'. It is useful to spend a few moments to identify the sources of your own nervousness when teaching and how this manifests itself. Once you identify the source – the trigger – you are able to take action to mitigate this. The cognitive aspect mentioned above is particularly prevalent, not just in teaching but in everyday life. How often have you caught yourself listening to your negative inner voice telling you how bad you are at something or predicting how badly something will turn out? This is something we all tend to do at some point, to greater and lesser extents. Once you become aware of this, you can start to take steps to reframe those inner thoughts to make them more positive and rational.

Another source of nervousness, which is related to feeling self-conscious and judged, is the impact of students' body language and facial expressions while you are teaching. From our own teaching experience, it is all too easy to focus on one or two students who look bored, disinterested or have their arms crossed with closed body language. The first point here is that these are assumptions. A student may look outwardly bored but may be listening and engaged. Similarly, it is a cliché to interpret body language in the same way for each individual person. For some people, closed body language and crossed arms may indicate hostility or a lack of interest, but perhaps the student in front of you simply finds it comfortable to sit with crossed arms. The point here is to avoid immediately arriving at a negative conclusion. The second point is to shift your attention to someone who does not make you feel nervous. Rather than engaging in negative thought patterns ('that student looks really bored and probably thinks I'm a really bad teacher'), look for a student who is smiling and nodding along. There will almost certainly be several students doing this. If you are looking at a student who is smiling and who is outwardly engaged in what you are saying, you are likely to feel far more at ease. It is also interesting how infectious smiling can be. If a student is smiling at you, you are likely to mirror this, almost intuitively, and your smile is likely to make other students smile, too.

The final point we would like to make about nervousness is about breathing. Being conscious of how you are breathing and practising good breathing technique is one of the most important ways to mitigate the effects of nervousness. We will look at this next in relation to the voice.

The voice and breathing

Perhaps the most important tool in any teacher's toolkit is the voice. Particularly in lectures, where we teach in larger spaces, it is important to use the voice correctly in order to protect it from damage. Whilst it is not necessary to study vocal anatomy in depth, it is useful to understand how you produce sound and how you can adapt the sounds that you make. The voice is essentially made up of three components:

- *Respiration*: this is what powers our voice – breathing. The breathing technique we use will affect the quality of the sound produced. We can breathe without producing sound.
- *Phonation*: this is where voiced sounds are created. Breathing combined with vibrations in the vocal folds produces sounds, such as humming.
- *Articulation*: this is where speech and sounds that we can understand are produced, such as letters and words. We achieve this by using a variety of 'articulators', such as the lips and the tongue.

Let us return to the power behind our voice: breathing. This is something we do involuntarily thousands of times a day so we should all be very good at it. But how much do we know about our own breathing?

— Activity 5.2 —

Getting in touch with your breathing

How many breaths do you take per minute when you are at rest? Sit quietly with a stopwatch and count your breaths over one minute. Notice how it feels to breathe in this relaxed state. Notice where each breath originates. Does it start in your diaphragm, in your stomach, or higher up in your chest? If you are feeling particularly energetic, try this again when you are exercising, perhaps by running on the spot and counting your breaths again over one minute.

Of course, we all have different rates of breathing, but most adults breathe between 12 and 20 times a minute at rest. This rate is likely to double or even triple when we are exercising or if we are feeling nervous. This is not a problem during exercise as you are not usually required to project your voice. However, if we breathe in a shallow, nervous way while we are teaching, this will affect the quality of the voice. The first step is to become aware of your own breathing, which we have started to do in Activity 5.2. Then it is important to check your breathing technique. You may have heard people talk about breathing from the diaphragm, but what does this mean? Activity 5.3 should help to demonstrate this.

Activity 5.3

Diaphragmatic breathing

The diaphragm is a large muscle beneath the lungs. When people say something like 'take deep breaths', they probably mean breathe from the diaphragm. By doing this, you inhale more air into your lungs and therefore have more power for the voice. Try the following to check where your breathing originates.

1   Lie on your back on a comfortable surface and breathe for a few seconds. Focus on your breathing. Become aware of it. Are you aware of either your chest or your stomach moving outwards and inwards as you breathe?
2   Now put one hand on your chest and the other over your diaphragm – just below the rib cage on your stomach. Breathe in through your nose, noticing whether your stomach is moving outwards against your hand. The other hand on your chest should remain relatively still.
3   Then breathe out, tensing your stomach muscles as you do so, and feel the hand on your stomach move down as you exhale.

If you noticed that the hand on your chest was rising and falling as you inhaled and exhaled, this means you are breathing in a shallow way from your chest. Many of us do this as a matter of habit, and this tends to happen even more when we are nervous. This means we inhale less air per breath and therefore have less power (respiration) in our voice, which is why some people's voices start to shake or sound weak. By practising this exercise regularly, also in a standing position, you will be able to ensure you breathe more often from the diaphragm and, perhaps more importantly, recognise when you are starting to breathe from your chest and take steps to change it. Good breathing technique will help you to project your voice, which will mean you reduce the risk of damaging your voice, and you will also present a more confident self. Having said this, if you are teaching in a large lecture theatre, there should be a microphone and you should use this where possible.

Dealing with the unexpected

The final aspect of performance that we will explore here is what to do when things 'go wrong' or not according to plan. This is where the skill of improvisation can be useful. Improvisation is a form of theatre where there is no script and the audience creates the story with the performers. This collaboration lends itself to student-centred teaching and active learning, where students are active partners in creating the learning and teaching experience along with the teacher (Berk and Trieber, 2009). In some ways, this perspective helps to allay some of the teaching anxieties mentioned earlier, as the teacher is no longer the centre of attention in a large lecture theatre; instead, the students are partly responsible for how the session plays out. Of course, this does not mean we should be unprepared or unplanned, but if we focus exclusively on what we have planned, there is a risk of becoming anxious when things 'go wrong', or off plan. Sawyer (2011) uses the helpful term 'disciplined improvisation' in relation to teaching, because we always have a plan but we need to be able to react to whatever happens in the room, such as technical problems, discrepancies between the students' level of knowledge and what you have planned, or not knowing the answer to a student's question.

There are lots of improvisation games and techniques, many of which are helpful for teachers to develop a sense of being able to respond to circumstances as they unfold, but they can also be used as activities to engage students in class. You can find some of these in the Further Resources or by searching online. In terms of practical steps to develop your spontaneous reactions in class, it is useful to think about how you would deal with a variety of situations, such as the projector bulb dying halfway through your lecture, or not knowing the answer to a student's question. It is unlikely that any imagined scenario will play out exactly as rehearsed in your head, but the act of thinking through different scenarios and placing yourself in 'challenging' situations, albeit hypothetically, is a good way to hone skills of improvisation. We will do this for one very common scenario in Activity 5.4.

— Activity 5.4 —

Developing skills of improvisation by thinking through possible scenarios

Imagine you have planned a lecture very thoroughly by reviewing your materials and the content and incorporating a paired activity to enable your students to apply some of the content to a particular case. You are feeling confident and well prepared but during the debrief after the paired activity, a student asks a question to which you do not know the answer. Note down how you would respond in this situation. If it helps, you could start by noting down how this situation makes you feel.

The scenario in Activity 5.4 is by far one of the most frequent 'fears' reported by teaching colleagues in our experience. Depending on your outlook, this situation may make you feel anxious, embarrassed, or maybe you are quite comfortable with not knowing the answer to every possible question that might arise. Here, we come back to an earlier point about preparation. It is clearly important to prepare well-structured and engaging lectures, tutorials and so on, but in this scenario there may be a degree of inflexibility. If we try to plan for every possible eventuality, we can become dependent on this plan and feel lost if, or more likely when, the session does not run according to our plan. This reminds us again of Sawyer's (2011) disciplined improvisation, where we are able to respond to events within a looser, overarching plan.

Another useful perspective on this scenario in particular, but also on other scenarios where things go 'off script', is about how you see your role as a teacher. If you present yourself as the expert and authority on the subject, much like in a very didactic, transmission form of teaching (see Chapter 2), this leaves very little room to say 'I don't know the answer to that question'. On the other hand, a teacher who is facilitating activities so that students can learn with and from each other (in addition to the teacher) has already established a more collaborative learning environment, in which it is not necessary for the teacher to have all the answers. So, in this case, the teacher could acknowledge the question and be honest about not knowing the answer, and then invite other students to contribute their own thoughts. If no other students know the answer, the teacher can offer to find out for the next session, or ask the students to find out

Over to you

In this chapter, we have thought about the role of lectures as a teaching method in higher education. For your ongoing practice and professional development, you could write down your thoughts on lectures in general and, more specifically, about what role lectures play in your own practice. We have also discussed some possible ways of moving from didactic lectures, where students are rather passive, to more interactive and engaging lectures. Now you could start to think about the active learning methods you use in different aspects of your teaching practice, such as in tutorials, in laboratories or in lectures, and reflect on how any of these techniques might be adapted to the different contexts in which you teach. Finally, we explored some of the aspects of performance that are present when teaching, particularly when lecturing. Reflect on your own performance, particularly when lecturing, and identify one or two aspects to improve. This could be related to your breathing and voice projection, or how you manage your nerves and feelings of stage fright, for example. In order to see how you look and sound when you are lecturing, you might find it useful to record yourself in order to help identify aspects of your lecturing performance that can be improved further.

Further resources

This book explores the parallels between teaching and performance, and suggests a variety of exercises to help improve the performance aspects of teaching, all of which are inspired by the performing arts.

Bale, R. (2020) *Teaching with Confidence in Higher Education: Applying Strategies from the Performing Arts*. Abingdon: Routledge.

This book provides a detailed overview of 101 ways to make teaching more interactive. Chapter 1 looks at lecturing and suggests a variety of active learning techniques that can be incorporated into lectures.

Howell Major, C., Harris, M. S. and Zakrajsek, T. (2016) *Teaching for Learning: 101 Intentionally Designed Educational Activities to Put Students on the Path to Success*. New York: Routledge.

References

Berk, R. A. and Trieber, R. H. (2009) Whose classroom is it, anyway? Improvisation as a teaching tool. *Journal on Excellence in College Teaching*, 20 (3): 29–60.

Bradbury, N. A. (2016) Attention span during lectures: 8 seconds, 10 minutes, or more? *Advances in Physiology Education*, 40: 509–13.

Exley, K. and Dennick, R. (2009) *Giving a Lecture: From Presenting to Teaching*, 2nd edn. Abingdon: Routledge.

Freeman, S., Eddy, S. L., McDonough, M., Smith, M. K., Okoroafor, N., Jordt, H. and Wenderoth, M. P. (2014) Active learning increases student performance in science, engineering and mathematics. *Proceedings of the National Academy of Sciences*, 111 (23): 8410–15.

Nagel, J. J (2017) *Managing Stage Fright: A Guide for Musicians and Music Teachers*. New York: Oxford University Press.

Sawyer, R. K. (2011) What makes good teachers great? The artful balance of structure and improvisation. In R. K. Sawyer (ed.), *Structure and Improvisation in Creative Teaching*. Cambridge: Cambridge University Press.

Theobold, E. J., Hill, M. J., Tran, E., Agrawal, S., Arroyo, E. N., Behling, S., Chambwe, N., Cintron, D. L., Cooper, J. D., Dunster, G. et al. (2020) Active learning narrows achievement gaps for underrepresented students in undergraduate science, technology, engineering and math. *Proceedings of the National Academy of Sciences*, 117 (12): 6476–83.

6

SUPPORTING STUDENTS IN LABORATORIES AND DURING FIELDWORK

Learning outcomes

After reading this chapter you should be able to:

- Explain the role of practical work in learning at university
- Facilitate learning through the use of questioning
- Plan how to minimise risk and maximise learning in practical settings.

Introduction

Postgraduate students and support staff in many disciplines are involved in supervising elements of practical work in laboratories (for example, scientific, engineering or computer laboratories) or natural environments (such as fieldwork or visits). Sometimes called demonstrators or teaching assistants, they typically assist more senior colleagues by providing individual support for students within the wider group setting.

In this chapter we focus primarily on supporting learning in laboratories (which may be science or computer labs) and during fieldwork, but parts of the chapter will also be relevant to others involved in teaching any kind of practical skill. We first discuss the role and value of practical and experiential settings for learning, and then how you can effectively support student learning. This incorporates relevant theoretical models and discussion of challenges that may typically be encountered in these settings.

The role and value of practical work

We start by asking you to consider the role and value of practical work in Activity 6.1.

— Activity 6.1 —

Benefits of practical work

What do you think students can gain from experience in laboratories, work placements or fieldwork? Consider both the stated learning outcomes and other less obvious benefits. What are the limitations and challenges of learning in these settings?

Discussion

Various studies have explored the value of practical experience within specific disciplines. For example, Davies (2008: 2) described the benefits of practical work in the engineering curricula as to:

- motivate students and stimulate their interest in the subject;
- help them to deepen their understanding through relating theory to practice;
- provide opportunities for students to work together on analysing and solving engineering problems;
- develop skills and attitudes that will enable graduates to operate effectively and professionally in an engineering workplace.

So students can learn not only specific skills and techniques relevant to the discipline but also more generic skills such as problem solving and teamwork that will be valued by future employers.

Croucher (2008), investigating staff and student views of fieldwork in archaeology, found that social skills were seen as the primary benefit, with a better understanding of the subject and the motivating effect of a different environment also considered important.

You may have thought of other benefits and it is worth discussing with senior colleagues what they expect students to gain from the experience and how it contributes to the overall learning programme. You may notice that certain students thrive in a more practical, work-focused setting, and providing a range of different types of learning activities helps to make teaching more inclusive. We will now consider how to support students effectively in these settings.

Effective teaching in practical settings

Although there are doubtless some differences across the disciplines, the following list of attributes of effective teachers, identified by students and teaching assistants in chemistry laboratories, seems quite widely applicable:

1   Knowledge: this comprises disciplinary knowledge (of the procedure, techniques and concepts) and educational knowledge (of how students learn and how to teach).
2   Communication skills, for example the ability to explain complex material in plain English.
3   The affective domain – being friendly and wanting to help, getting to know students and giving individual attention.

(Herrington and Nakhleh, 2003)

Knowledge

Elaborating on point (1), *knowledge*, a key element of preparation is ensuring that you are fully conversant with the content – be it lab procedures, fieldwork techniques, coding principles or clinical protocols – and the theory underlying these. Ideally, you would be well briefed and provided with relevant written information ahead of the session. You may want to seek advice from more senior staff, including opportunities to try out procedures that you are not already familiar with. You can also draw on the wealth of online information available, such as videos of techniques.

Secondly, you need to be aware of how students learn and how to teach, including effective *communication*. We have addressed general learning theories in Chapter 2 and there is additional literature relating to how students learn in specific disciplines and topics, which you may find useful to research. You can also learn much from watching and listening to students: this will help you to assess their levels of skill and understanding.

In addition, you can ask whoever is leading the teaching about common problems and misunderstandings that students have with the topics and procedures.

Finally, the importance of the *affective domain* should not be underestimated: showing a personal interest in student learning and being available and enthusiastic is highly valued by and motivating for students.

Health and safety

When supporting learning, you share the responsibility of ensuring safe practice. You may be able to see a risk assessment document to familiarise yourself with potential risks and the correct safety procedures. If not, you can think ahead about potential health and safety issues and ask your tutor for guidance. You can assist by reminding students about necessary precautions, being observant and noticing if protocols are breached. Setting a good example yourself is important – both for safety and to avoid undermining the requirements, and seek advice if you have concerns.

Now try Activity 6.2 to evaluate different approaches to supporting students.

Activity 6.2

Contrasting approaches

Identify the differences in approach of Michelle and Bogdan, who are PhD students who assist during laboratory sessions. Evaluate the strengths and weaknesses of each.

Michelle likes to read up on the practicals ahead of time so that she is fully prepared to guide the students in the right direction. She arrives early and checks in with the lecturer so that they know who she is. (After all, it's never too soon to start networking.) During the sessions, she makes a point of getting round all the students and directing them as to the next steps. She takes a systematic approach, observing what the students have done, correcting any errors and giving further information. She feels it is important for her to take the lead in giving information so that it is accurate.

Bogdan tends to go to the practicals with the minimum of preparation as he is familiar with most of them from his previous experience. He constantly surveys the group to see who is looking for help and focuses on the students who have their hands up as he feels his time is best spent responding to those who need or want help. In response to their questions, he usually asks further questions to elicit their understanding and what they think might be the answer. He has noticed that students can often find the answers for themselves, given the right prompts, and he thinks they will learn more this way.

Discussion

You may have noticed the following differences:

Preparation: Michelle spends more time on preparation than Bogdan. How much preparation is required depends on your prior knowledge and experience. Making contact with the supervisor before the session starts is a good idea as they can answer questions you may have and may want to alert you to focus on certain things. It also demonstrates a professional approach which contributes to your academic reputation.

Proactive vs responsive approach: Bogdan responds to those requesting help whereas Michelle checks all the students. Ideally you may want a balance – some students may be reluctant to seek help for various reasons (e.g. shyness, not wanting to appear incompetent, lacking confidence) or may not realise that they have made mistakes or misunderstood something. So it is useful to try to check in with everyone in the group whilst also being responsive to individuals who visibly need assistance. Try to avoid one or two students dominating your time: if this starts to happen, encourage them to think about how they can find out things for themselves or give them something to practise or work out while you see others.

Teaching style: Michelle is more authoritative and didactic whilst Bogdan is more student-centred. There are contexts in which each approach is appropriate; however, generally it is better to encourage students to think through and work out answers for themselves, as we will discuss in the next section.

Teaching strategies

We will now look at strategies and principles you can use to promote learning. You are invited to start by reviewing your current practice in Activity 6.3.

Activity 6.3

Your role

Consider your role in a specific practical setting (laboratory, fieldwork, etc.) and:

1   Underline the roles that you fulfil most often.
2   Circle those that you think are most helpful for students.
3   Put a tick by those you would like to do more.
4   Add any additional roles not shown here.

Observe   Correct

                                                     Answer questions

                    Check students' knowledge

Guide

                                                     Challenge

(Continued)

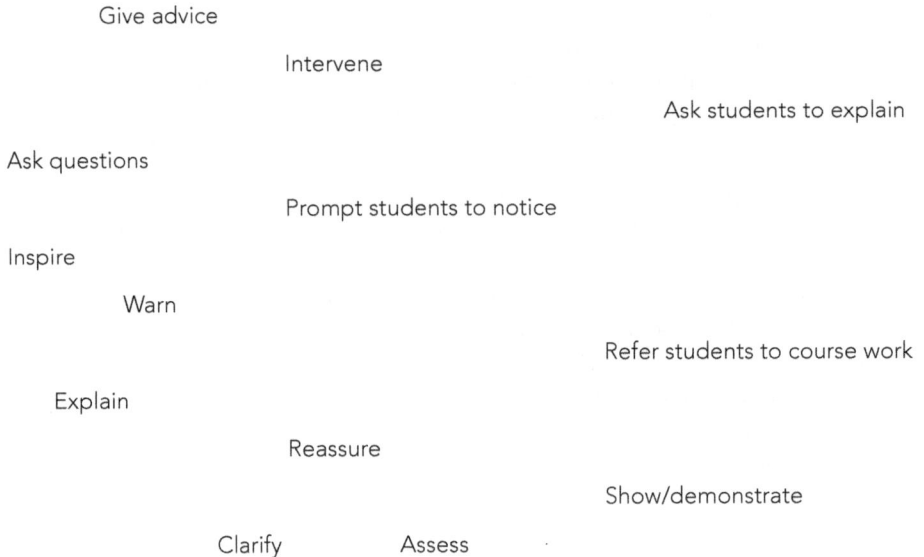

Give advice

Intervene

Ask students to explain

Ask questions

Prompt students to notice

Inspire

Warn

Refer students to course work

Explain

Reassure

Show/demonstrate

Clarify   Assess

Discussion

You may have noticed a difference between what you do most frequently and what you think is most effective. We know that students learn best through active engagement with the topic (Freeman et al., 2014), so it is useful to pose questions more often than you give answers. Other helpful behaviours identified by Davies (2008: 13) included:

- Being proactive as well as reactive – recognising those having difficulties and those who are coasting.
- Giving students opportunities to practise skills and learn from their successes and failures.
- Encouraging students to integrate their learning with other aspects of their studies.
- Having a positive attitude to the subject material, class and students – being a good role model.
- Drawing comparisons and parallels between laboratory work [or fieldwork] and professional practice.

The latter may involve relating your own experience to help students appreciate the relevance of what they are doing, for example talking about your own research or work experience, where appropriate. This may help students start to develop their own interests and identity within the discipline.

Questioning

An important aspect of supporting students is how to engage them in thinking more deeply about their work, reviewing and reflecting on their experience and linking theory with practice. Activity 6.4 prompts you to identify how different strategies may develop different types and levels of learning.

Activity 6.4

Questioning strategies

Consider what is required of students when a teaching assistant says each of the following:

1 'You need to do it this way.'
2 'How have you gone about it?'
3 'What might the next step be?'
4 'How could you learn more about this …?'

When might each be appropriate and what are its inherent benefits and limitations?

Discussion

1 'You need to do it this way.' As you will have noticed, this is not a question but a direction that requires students to follow instructions. It may be appropriate when safety is at risk or time is limited. It provides clarity but does not facilitate thinking by the student.
2 'How have you gone about it?' This requires students to describe their approach, which often leads them to evaluate or re-evaluate their actions. It can be a useful strategy if students have made mistakes as they will often realise it themselves and self-correct.
3 'What might the next step be?' This requires students to plan. It can be helpful when they need to remember a certain sequence or when there are a variety of potential options. It can encourage them to evaluate options and develop a rationale for their plan.
4 'How could you learn more about this …?' This encourages students to consider useful resources (which may include course materials, external resources and people) and to think about practical steps they could take to develop their knowledge and skills. It encourages self-reliance and metacognition (learning how to learn), which are useful skills for ongoing development.

A general principle of teaching is to 'draw out' rather than 'put in'. Simon (quoted by Ambrose et al., 2010) says that:

'Learning results from what the student does and thinks and only from what the student does and thinks. The teacher can advance learning only by influencing what the student does to learn.' (2010: 1)

Teaching practical skills

The principle of ensuring the active engagement of students in learning applies equally to practical skills, when providing opportunities for hands on practice is important. Watching others perform can be a useful precursor to, but is not a substitute for, personal experience. Although there may be constraints within the university in terms of limited resources or large classes, students do need opportunities for individual practice. We know that developing expertise, or 'mastery' requires many hours of practice. The quality of practice is also important as practising doing something poorly will only ingrain bad habits. Ambrose et al. (2010) highlight various ways in which you can help students to acquire and hone their skills by:

- establishing clear goals and standards
- breaking complex skills down into small steps
- providing opportunities to practise these steps in isolation and integrated into a whole
- giving feedback to correct errors and improve performance.

Interestingly, less experienced teachers are often better able to break skills down into their component parts than their more experienced colleagues. This is because, at a certain point, skills become automatic and it is hard for experts to unpick what they are doing. This applies equally to recognising patterns, such as how patients present with certain conditions, and is sometimes known as the stage of 'unconscious competence'.

Learning new skills can be a struggle and students need to feel that they are in a safe environment. You can contribute to this, for example by telling students about things you found difficult or making it clear that you're not expecting them to do everything right first time.

Case Study 6.1 shows how some of the principles from this chapter can be applied and there is further discussion of questioning strategies in Chapter 4.

— Case Study 6.1 —

Camilla Gladstone, GTA and doctoral researcher in infectious disease

One of my main roles as a graduate teaching assistant is to support learning in the laboratory for undergraduates, where the students work in groups of six. The majority of my lab teaching involves teaching students techniques and analysing their results, which can lead to troubleshooting with them if their results are unexpected.

A technique that I often use is trying not to directly answer their questions where possible, instead prompting them either with other questions or with a few hints, leading them to the correct answer themselves rather than just giving them the final answer. I have found that if I had a problem and a teacher made me come to the correct answer myself

I was more likely to remember than if I had just been told the answer straight out. I find that this develops deeper thought in the students, and this results in a better understanding of the *why* behind the answer and allows them to apply it to future problems themselves.

Having spent approximately half of my Master's course doing practical laboratory learning, I feel I have a good grasp of the material necessary to teach others. I tend to take the aforementioned approach, particularly in the laboratory, because I found them helpful myself when I was undertaking my Master's. I believe that they gave me a more solid understanding of the processes and their applications, rather than just learning the theory in lectures. This is also supported by literature, which suggests that students can obtain a deeper learning when they have high 'self-efficacy' (Fry et al., 2014). This is equivalent to being confident in their own knowledge, and by encouraging them to be more self-sufficient in their learning, whilst still being supported, I believe they will become better learners.

The students work in small groups in the laboratory and I have also found it beneficial to give them time to try to come to the right answer together, rather than intervening too soon. Group work is particularly important in the sciences, as research groups are often composed of various different specialists who need to work together to identify the overall picture. One investigation found that interpersonal abilities, as well as teamwork and problem solving, were all key skills desired by employers. By allowing groups to troubleshoot together before stepping in, you prepare them for work in both academia and industry where you would be expected to troubleshoot your problems first, before taking them to your supervisor to discuss the best course of action. This is a key element in higher education, as we want students to be employable, graduating with the necessary skills desired by employers, which include the techniques themselves, but also skills such as critical thinking (Fry et al., 2014).

Challenges

In this section we present some common challenges that GTAs encounter in laboratories or fieldwork and invite you to consider how you would approach each situation:

Scenario 1: A student takes over

You have students working in groups to learn an important procedure. You notice one of the students (Kim) keeps stepping in to assist the others when they experience difficulties, and the others seem happy to accept this. Which of the following options (or another of your own) do you think would be likely to help?

1   Explain to the group why it is important for everyone to learn this procedure.
2   Take Kim out of the group and quietly ask her not to step in to help the others.
3   Let the students know that you will pick one person at random to demonstrate the procedure after the break.

4   Ask the students to watch each other and give feedback and advice.
5   Give Kim the responsibility of ensuring that everyone can perform the procedure.

Discussion

Group dynamics are at play here and different groups will respond in differing ways. Each of the options has pros and cons and all could potentially be useful: one of the skills of teaching is to be sensitive to the atmosphere within a group and the overall context, and judge which approach is most likely to be effective. This may depend on the individual personalities, as well as the importance of the procedure and whether there will be other opportunities to learn it.

Scenario 2: Students are distracted

You are a GTA supervising in a lab of 30 students who are working their way through a manual of materials and tasks. You notice that a few students are distracted; one has headphones on and seems to be just resting, a couple are on social media and two are discussing plans for the weekend.

What should you do?

1   Stop the students and remind them that they need to complete the tasks, otherwise they will do badly in their exams.
2   Leave them to act as they wish: they are adults after all.
3   Approach them individually and ask them to demonstrate and talk through what they have done.
4   Let them know you remember it being a tough task and that you are available to support them.
5   Tell students you've noticed that not everyone is engaged, and ask them how they think the session could be made more productive.

Discussion

The best approach may depend on the reasons for the student disengagement, so you could consider and check with students: Is the material at the right level? Do they understand why they need to learn it? Are they distracted for any reason (which could be nothing to do with the work but something more personal)?

If students are finding the material too easy, you could suggest something more advanced. If too hard, you might invite those who want help with a certain element to come together so that you can explain it to them as a group. If they don't understand its value, you could explain why it is relevant or ask them to work it out for themselves. If they are distracted, you could invite them to take a short break and come back when they are ready to continue, especially if their disengagement is affecting other students.

This scenario raises questions about who is responsible for learning: to what extent are you and to what extent the students? Trying to threaten, belittle or ignore students is unlikely to be effective in motivating them and can negatively impact on all students. Showing respect for students and concern for their learning helps to establish a productive learning environment. There may be occasions on which a more serious problem surfaces (for example, if a student is unwell or has personal issues) and you need to direct them to the course convenor or a student support service.

Scenario 3: You spot a mistake

You are supervising students in a work setting and you notice that one of them has made a mistake that could be quite important. What do you do?

1   Stop the student and point out the error.
2   Ask the student how they are getting on and hope that they will notice the mistake.
3   Ask the student to talk you through what they have done.
4   Ask if the student would like some feedback.

Discussion

Students need to be made aware of mistakes and given the opportunity to put them right. Option (1) might be good if time is short, but you need to make sure that the student understands why they made the mistake and how to prevent it in future. Options (2) and (3) encourage reflection and may lead to the student discovering the error for themselves which can be more effective for long-term learning. Option (3) can help you to understand the student's reasoning (if reasoning is involved) and allow you to tailor your advice to their misunderstanding. Option (4) gives control to the student: if they decline, they may recognise that they have done something wrong but not be ready to hear feedback. Sometimes students are more ready to accept feedback from their peers so it may be helpful to pair them up with a colleague and ask them to compare their strategies and come back to you if they have questions.

Assessment in practical settings

There are some bespoke modes of assessment for practical subjects, such as lab reports, projects and direct observations. If you are involved in marking or providing feedback on any of these, you need to be clear about the purpose of the assessment and what it can and can't measure. For example, laboratory reports can assess understanding of the rationale, methodology, findings and implications of laboratory work but not competence in laboratory skills: that would require a direct observation, or possibly a video recording, of a student undertaking such skills.

When assessing students in practical settings, the same principles of assessment that are discussed in Chapter 10 apply – for example the need to provide clear guidance about expectations (including marking criteria), the importance of being consistent in your marking and of providing helpful feedback. When supervising students in practical settings, you have an excellent opportunity to see students' work at first hand and provide timely and supportive feedback to help them develop.

Over to you

This chapter has highlighted some of the ways in which you can help students to learn practical skills, both for their own sake and to illuminate and consolidate theoretical learning and develop personal attributes. Observing and noticing how students are conducting practical work and prompting them to further thought and action can enhance learning. You may like to trial different types of questions and prompts to see how well they work in your context as well as considering how best to share your relevant knowledge and experience. Helping students to understand the relevance of the work can improve motivation.

Further resources

Chapter 4, 'How do students develop mastery?' (pp. 91–120) provides a review of the literature on how students develop competence and discusses practical ways in which teachers can help them to develop, apply and integrate skills to improve practice.

Ambrose, S. A., Bridges, M. W., Dipietro, M., Lovett, M. C. and Norman, M. K. (2010) *How Learning Works: 7 Research-Based Principles for Smart Teaching*. San Francisco: Jossey-Bass.

References

Ambrose, S. A., Bridges, M. W., Dipietro, M., Lovett, M. C. and Norman, M. K. (2010) *How Learning Works: 7 Research-Based Principles for Smart Teaching*. San Francisco: Jossey-Bass.

Croucher, K., Cobb, H. and Brennan, A. (2008) *Investigating the Role of Fieldwork in Teaching and Learning Archaeology*. The Higher Education Academy. Subject Centre for History, Classics and Archaeology. Available at: www.heacademy.ac.uk/knowledge-hub/investigating-role-fieldwork-teaching-and-learning-archaeology (accessed 30 November 2018).

Davies, C. (2008) *Learning and Teaching in Laboratories*. The Higher Education Academy. Engineering Subject Centre. Available at www.heacademy.ac.uk/system/files/learning-teaching-labs.pdf (accessed 30 November 2018).

Freeman, S., Eddy, S. L., McDonough, M., Smith, M. K., Okoroafor, N., Jordt, H. and Wenderoth, M. P. (2014) Active learning increases student performance in science, engineering, and mathematics. *Proceedings of the National Academy of Sciences*, 111: 8410–15.

Fry, H., Ketteridge, S. and Marshall, S. (eds) (2014) *A Handbook for Teaching and Learning in Higher Education: Enhancing Academic Practice*, 4th edn. Abingdon: Routledge.

Herrington, D. G. and Nakhleh, M. B. (2003) What defines effective chemistry laboratory instruction? Teaching assistant and student perspectives. *Journal of Chemical Education*, 80 (10): 1197.

7

WORKING WITH INDIVIDUAL STUDENTS AND SUPERVISING PROJECTS

Learning outcomes

After reading this chapter you should be able to:

- Define your role(s) in teaching individual students
- Apply skills from mentoring and coaching to facilitate active, student-centred one-to-one meetings
- Decide on appropriate approaches to one-to-one teaching and supervision.

Introduction

Depending on your teaching role, you may be involved in working with students individually. The contexts in which one-to-one teaching takes place vary widely, from supervising projects, to providing academic skills and information literacy tutorials, to supporting students with specific learning differences.

Reflection

Think about the contexts in which you meet with students individually. What kind of teaching does this involve? Are one-to-one sessions about your particular discipline or subject matter? Do you support students with other aspects of their studies, or perhaps offer pastoral advice? Do you meet students as a one-off encounter or meet them several times over a period of time?

Discussion

Regardless of the contexts, there are certain principles to consider when working with students individually. A useful distinction to make is whether you are working with individual students on one occasion – as a one-off – or whether you are engaging in one-to-one sessions over a longer period of time. Depending on your role, you might meet students as a one-off encounter for various purposes, including:

- to help with a student's academic writing
- to help with academic literacy and referencing
- to train a student to use a particular piece of software
- to help a student to use services and resources in the library
- to discuss interview procedures or to provide feedback on a student's CV
- to give feedback on an assignment.

In all cases, the student has a specific need and a limited amount of time in one session to fulfil this need. It is therefore important to engage the student in a collaborative dialogue as soon as possible in order to avoid one-to-one sessions becoming a one-way transmission of information from teacher to student. In the context of individual academic writing tutorials, Wingate (2019) surveyed the literature and found that collaboration and dialogue in one-to-one sessions facilitate more effective learning than didactic, information-heavy teaching. This means we should aim to encourage students to engage actively to help them to find their own solutions, with our support, rather than simply telling them what to do. Some practical strategies for doing this include:

- Gaining a clear idea about why the student has booked to see you and what they would like to achieve. This could be done by email beforehand. Encourage the student to be specific. For example, if they would like feedback, ask them to be specific; what aspect of their work would they like feedback on? Narrowing down the purpose of the meeting will make it more productive.
- Asking the student what they already know about the problem, software, question at hand. Depending on the context, you might do this before or during the meeting.
- Asking the student to bring something concrete to show you, if appropriate. For example, this could be a piece of their writing, their CV, etc.
- Encouraging the student to do the majority of the talking. You can do this by asking well-prepared questions; open questions can help to stimulate thoughts and ideas, and help the student to express themselves and articulate their problems and questions (see questioning techniques in Chapter 4).
- At the end of the meeting, asking the student what they will do next; what will be their next steps after meeting with you. This encourages action on the student's part and prompts them to think about whether they need further support or meetings.

These strategies will help to maximise the use of one-off meetings with students. Perhaps more importantly, these strategies will encourage students to engage actively and dialogically, rather than attending one-to-one meetings with the expectation that you will have all the solutions and answers to their problems and questions. Case Study 7.1 shows how some of these strategies have been used in one-off sessions about literature searches using library databases.

Case Study 7.1

Facilitating one-to-one sessions on information retrieval skills: Kirsten Elliott, Senior Library Assistant

A key element of my role is teaching information retrieval skills, particularly literature searching using database platforms such as Ovid and HDAS (Healthcare Databases Advanced Search). Literature searching is a technical skill requiring usage of specific software, which can change over time, and an area in which there is ongoing methodological debate about best practice, especially with regard to searching which will contribute to systematic reviews (see, for example, Gusenbauer and Haddaway, 2020). The library users I work with have varied levels of pre-existing knowledge and experience, and have a range of different aims for how they will utilise these skills, including for specific academic assignments, general current awareness and publication of research.

(Continued)

I teach information retrieval skills on a one-to-one basis to library users who have asked for help with a particular project. In these circumstances I talk to them in as much detail as possible about their research interests and goals; for example, where they would like to have their research published and what software they are using for different parts of the process. I can therefore show them the most appropriate tools and signpost them to further useful sources of information. In individual sessions I will explain and demonstrate relevant techniques, and then get the student to try out using them. For instance, when delivering sessions remotely via Microsoft Teams I have shared my screen whilst demonstrating, and then asked them to share theirs with me. This means that I can see what they are trying to do, assess what they have understood and offer guidance if necessary. The impact of this is that as a teacher I can be very flexible to their needs, and facilitate both deep and instrumental learning as students develop understanding of the concepts and how to apply them for their own goals.

In addition to one-off meetings with students, some teachers work with students individually in several sessions over a longer period of time. As well as using the strategies above, teachers working with students over the course of several weeks or months also need to develop and manage the teacher–student relationship. In the rest of this chapter, we take project supervision as a common example of one-to-one working over an extended period of time, but the principles will apply to other one-to-one teaching scenarios, such as when working with students with specific learning differences, or when providing office hours (see Case Study 9.2). Project supervision might include working with a final-year undergraduate dissertation student, over-seeing a project in a laboratory or perhaps co-supervising a Master's or a final-year undergraduate project. This kind of teaching involves working closely with a student in a one-to-one context or, sometimes, with a very small group of students. Many of the principles of good teaching discussed in previous chapters, such as taking a student-centred approach and aligning activities and assessment with the learning outcomes, are just as relevant here as in other teaching contexts. However, there are some aspects of practice that we need to consider in relation to one-to-one or small group working.

Your role(s) when supervising student projects

In Chapter 2, you were invited to reflect on your values and beliefs about teaching and learning and to consider how you 'see' yourself in the teacher's role. You might consider yourself a facilitator of learning, a transmitter of knowledge, a manager of classroom processes and behaviour, for example. The way in which you see yourself may also change slightly, or significantly, depending on the type of teaching you are doing.

— Reflection —

If you have experience of supervising student projects or working with students in any one-to-one context, how would you describe your role in that teaching encounter? You may have had multiple roles, in which case you could list all the roles you played. If you have not worked with individual students before, think about your experiences as a student. What role(s) did your teacher or supervisor play?

Discussion

When working in a one-to-one context, the teacher or supervisor is likely to play several different roles at different times. From our experience, these might include:

- Facilitator of learning
- Motivator
- Counsellor
- Mediator
- Time keeper
- Manager
- Mum/Dad
- Friend.

This list is not exhaustive and you may have thought of other roles in addition to these. As this list shows, there is potential for the student–teacher relationship to become quite complex due to both parties working so closely. There may be times when you feel you need to motivate the student to reach the next milestone of the project or piece of work, but there may also be personal or emotional issues which come to the fore, and you may feel you have a supportive, counselling role to play. Or, perhaps due to the one-to-one nature of the teaching encounter, the student may see you as a friend or a mother or father figure. All of these roles are probably legitimate as long as we think about how we would like the student–teacher relationship to proceed. This will help to mitigate potential problems from arising in the future. We will return to this later in the chapter. One role that should be highlighted, however, is the counsellor. As a teacher or a supervisor, a student might become very comfortable with telling you about problems in their personal and/or academic lives. Whilst you can be supportive, it is important not to be led into becoming a counsellor. There are trained counsellors in universities who offer counselling services to students, so any serious cases should be signposted to the appropriate student support services in your university. There may also be times when the student's work is not progressing as required, or the student is struggling with a particular aspect of the project. If the teacher has adopted an exclusively friendly, motherly or fatherly approach, it can be difficult to give constructive feedback on the student's work. Conversely, there is an element of personal development involved when working closely with a student individually, so a nurturing role (e.g. friend/mother) can be useful. The key skill is knowing how to balance these roles and when to bring which role to the fore.

Establishing ground rules: learning contracts

We discussed the importance of agreeing ground rules in Chapter 4 in the context of small group teaching. Some of this might be applicable to the one-to-one and project supervision context, but it is useful to think about particular expectations that need to be discussed in a one-to-one supervision relationship. You are likely to be working more closely with your student(s) as a supervisor than in your other teaching formats, so discussing mutual expectations and boundaries can help to prevent issues from arising during the course of the project.

Some teachers and students use a learning contract as a form of agreement on how to proceed with the project and the student–supervisor relationship (see, e.g., Derounian, 2011). This can be a formal or an informal document setting out the student's expectations of the teacher or supervisor, and vice versa, as well as key milestones in the project. The student should be involved in drafting the contract, or even lead on this, which can have several potential benefits, such as:

- giving the student ownership of the project
- increasing the student's motivation as they have set the agenda for the project
- enabling achievable goals to be set, for which both student and teacher are accountable
- increasing student autonomy and reducing reliance on the teacher.

A learning contract could include anything that you and your student think is relevant for creating the conditions for successful completion of the project or piece of work. The following questions give some ideas about what you and your student could discuss in relation to the work itself:

1 What is the time frame for the project or piece of work?
2 What are the key milestones? Work back from the end of the project. The answers to this question could be written as a series of intended learning outcomes.
3 What are the interim dates for completion of each milestone?
4 What resources are needed to complete the work?
5 Is any training or skills development required in order to enable the student to complete any aspects of the work?

It is also important to discuss patterns of working and expectations. The following questions can be used to help the student and teacher to set out and agree mutual expectations:

1   How often will meetings take place? Where?
2   What will be the primary method of communication between meetings? How quickly can a response be expected (from either party)?
3   Who will keep a record of discussions that take place during meetings?
4   What should each party do to prepare for meetings?
5   Are there any dates when either party will be unavailable (e.g. annual leave)?
6   How often will the teacher provide feedback on the student's work?

There may be other things that arise in your discussions with your student(s), but the importance of reaching agreement on some or all of these questions should not be underestimated. A student–teacher one-to-one working relationship can last several weeks, if not months, and a learning contract can provide an anchor that keeps both parties on track. As time progresses, there are likely to be changes to the timeline, or the needs of the student may change, especially if the work is being carried out over a longer period of time. In this case, the learning contract can be revisited and any changes agreed by the student and the teacher. Finally, as mentioned above, a learning contract can help to give the student a sense of autonomy and independence, which is in itself a key skill that can be developed by the student.

Case Study 7.2

Setting expectations with project students: Kay To, GTA and doctoral researcher in infectious disease

When supervising students, I would initially go through with them the project overview, which consists of what the project is, why we are doing the project, the importance of the piece of research we are doing and how the aims and objectives fit into the wider context of the scientific community. This gives the student an understanding of the purpose of the project and how the results, whether they are positive or negative, will contribute to gaining a deeper knowledge of how research works. I found it is important to emphasise at the beginning that research is not always successful and that negative results are equally important as positive results, as from previous student experience and my own, I know that it can feel de-motivating when experiments do not yield expected results. Furthermore, during the initial project overview meeting, I would set out expectations from both sides in terms of supervisory expectations; for example, there would be more supervision in the lab at the beginning to get them comfortable and confident and then they will develop to be more independent as the project progresses. Having this talk ensures there is an understanding for the student to expect more help at the beginning and then they can see themselves become a more independent researcher by the end of the project.

(Continued)

Furthermore, I often send out background reading material so that they have a grasp of where the research fits in and for the techniques that we will be carrying out in the lab so that they can see themselves applying the theory into practice. It is often helpful being able to see the translation from knowledge learnt from lectures and applying it in the lab as you have a better understanding of the technique and this helps you to troubleshoot when experiments do not work.

What skills do you need for one-to-one working?

Many of the skills developed as a teacher are applicable to the one-to-one context, such as time management, good use of questions and clear communication. However, when you are working with a student individually, there is an additional layer of complexity as you also have to manage the interpersonal relationship with one student over an extended period of time. As discussed above, this includes not only your ability to help the student to learn the subject matter, but also your ability to nurture, guide, mentor and coach the student through the process of an extended project. An important skill for any teacher is the ability to adapt to the needs of different students at different times, or to adapt to the changing needs of one student at different times during the project (Todd and Smith, 2020). The teacher may fulfil all of the roles listed earlier, sometimes providing guidance and expertise and at other times assuming a supporting, nurturing role in the background. Another important skill is to create the conditions for student-centred, active learning (see Chapter 2). We will take a closer look at two potential ways of approaching one-to-one teaching – mentoring and coaching – which can help to make meetings more student-focused and promote independent learning.

Mentoring and coaching skills

The terms mentoring and coaching are often used interchangeably but, though there are similarities, these are different approaches in which the person in the position of coach or mentor plays a slightly different role. What is similar, however, is the skillset involved in being a coach or a mentor. Both approaches require openness and skilful use of open questioning (see Chapter 4) in order to build trust and a productive working relationship with the coachee or mentee. Strictly speaking, mentoring is focused more on relationships and coaching is goal oriented. The mentor aims to stimulate the mentee's development by sharing their own experiences in a forward-looking way. A coach, on the other hand, focuses on the present and asks open questions to help the coachee to improve performance, to solve a problem or to achieve a particular goal (see Parsloe and Leedham, 2017 in the Further Resources at the end of this chapter for further information about coaching and mentoring).

In the supervision context, or in learning and teaching in general, mentoring appears at first glance to be better suited than coaching as an approach to help students to learn. This is because, like a mentor, a teacher is more experienced than the student and has already walked a similar path and learned similar subject matter. A coach, on the other hand, is not necessarily more experienced or more knowledgeable in the particular subject area than the coachee. The skill of the coach is in asking open, probing questions to help the coachee to find their own solutions to problems. Of course, a teacher does not align with this definition, as the teacher does have experience and knowledge of the subject matter and could provide answers to the student's questions if required. However, the attraction of a coaching approach is in its emphasis on student involvement in defining and solving problems. This is an inherently active learning process and encourages reflection and deep learning (see Chapter 2), where the student is not only learning what to do but also reflecting on how and why they are learning during the course of the project. In practice, teachers probably use a combination of mentoring and coaching, sometimes nurturing the relationship with the student and helping to motivate and stimulate academic growth, and at other times focusing on goals and performance and asking intelligent questions to stimulate reflection and to drive problem solving. In our discussion above about learning contracts, we looked at some questions that can help to establish mutual expectations in the student–teacher relationship. We will now look at one way of structuring questions and helping the student to define their own goals using a well-known model – the GROW model (Whitmore, 2017).

The GROW model in supervision meetings

The GROW model is often used, particularly in coaching, to facilitate focused conversations around performance and goals. The acronym stands for:

- **G**oal setting
- **R**eality of the situation and context
- **O**ptions or obstacles
- **W**ill to act.

The coach asks a series of questions aimed at helping the coachee to set their own goals and then to explore how realistic these goals are in the given context and with the given resources and time available. In the next stage, the coach asks questions exploring how the goals will be achieved, including a range of possible options as well as any potential obstacles that the coachee might face. Finally, the coach asks questions aimed at motivating the coachee to take action. Until this point, the discussions are hypothetical so this final step makes it clear that the coachee must take concrete steps in order to achieve their goals.

Activity 7.1

Using the GROW model to plan a one-to-one session

Imagine you are in your first meeting with your student at the beginning of a small-scale project on a topic in your subject area. If you already have experience of one-to-one working, you could think about a real meeting you have had with a student. Work through the GROW model and list potential questions that you could ask at each stage. Remember that the emphasis is on active learning, enabling the student to lead the discussion. Your questions act as a catalyst to help the student to define their own goals and problems.

The questions you have listed will vary depending on the discipline and the project you had in mind. As an example, the following questions are from the project supervision context, and could be used, in adapted form, to lead a structured, student-led discussion in a one-to-one session.

Goal setting: this first stage may be partly completed before the student comes to the meeting. This depends on whether the student already has a good idea about the project or whether the first meeting is used to decide on a topic for the project.

- What do you want to get out of this project?
- How will the project contribute to your personal and professional development?
- How will the project contribute to your wider studies in your programme of study?
- How will you disseminate the results of the project?

Reality of the situation and context: this stage is where the nurturing, more holistic part of the supervisor's role is important. There is little point setting lots of ambitious academic goals without having an understanding of the student's context and situation. At this point, the supervisor's questions aim to check whether anything might prevent the student from achieving the goals.

- How long will you need to complete each of the steps in order to complete this project?
- How much time do you have, realistically, to devote to this project?
- What else do you have to do this semester? Which other modules are you studying? What other coursework assignments or exams do you have coming up?
- Is there anything else at university or outside of university that you need to consider when planning this project?

Options and obstacles: this stage explores how the student will complete the project. The supervisor asks questions aimed at enabling the student to generate several possible options in order to evaluate the most efficient ways of working. The supervisor also encourages the student to foresee potential problems that might arise at each stage of the project and with each option.

- Think about – visualise – project submission day. How will you get to that point?
- Think back to the steps you need to take when we were setting goals earlier. How could you go about achieving these goals? What would be the benefits of starting with the literature review? What would be the benefits of starting with the practical elements of the project?
- How else could you go about completing this project?
- What disadvantages can you foresee with any of the options you have mentioned? Are there any obstacles that might prevent you from progressing if you choose a particular approach?
- How will you go about writing up the project? How often will you write? Will you write from the beginning?

Will to act: this final stage moves the conversation from discussion to action. At this point, the supervisor encourages the student to suggest concrete actions.

- What will you do to get started with this project?
- What have you already read about this topic?
- What do you need to help you get started?
- What will you do between now and our next meeting?

The questions here lend themselves to an initial meeting at the beginning of a project. However, you could also use the GROW model to structure supervision meetings throughout the project, or use adapted questions to help facilitate one-to-one discussions in other contexts. Of course, there will be times when you need to tell the student something and adopt more of a mentoring approach by sharing your own experience and knowledge. A combination of coaching and mentoring techniques will help you to keep meetings student-centred, ensuring that the student is an active participant and encouraging independent working throughout the project.

One-to-one or group meetings?

So far we have used project supervision as an example of teaching practice that takes place in a one-to-one format. There are regular meetings between supervisor and student, with the frequency of meetings agreed upon at the beginning and perhaps logged in a learning contract. Meetings often take place face-to-face but there may be times when online meetings are more efficient. As explored in Chapter 8, much of the work discussed in a supervision meeting can be done online, particularly with the use of platforms that enable document and screen sharing.

It is, of course, important to meet students one-to-one because of the nature of individual working discussed earlier, such as the holistic role that the teacher plays not only in teaching but also in supporting and nurturing the student. However, some teachers recommend meeting students in small groups in order to add a peer element to the process (Baker et al., 2014) and also to relieve pressure on the teacher's time (Guerin et al., 2015).

Activity 7.2

One-to-one or small group meetings?

Imagine you have been allocated four students to work with individually this semester. What benefits, if any, can you see in meeting your four students as a group rather than one-to-one? Are there any particular times when meeting in a group could be beneficial? Can you think of any disadvantages of group meetings?

If you have four students and you spend approximately one hour with each student, there is a clear time saving from meeting your students as a group. Whilst this should not be the main reason for choosing group meetings, it is nevertheless realistic to consider your other commitments and to think about whether your students might in fact benefit from the knowledge and support that can be offered by their peers in a group meeting. Some people advocate for a move away from the traditional one-to-one format, particularly in project supervision contexts (e.g. Del Río et al., 2018; Healey et al., 2013) in order to foreground the student's role as an active, independent learner who is not reliant solely on the teacher. When meeting students in a group, the students can share their experiences of the process of completing their work and gain support from knowing that typical challenges are also experienced by others. You can find more ideas on how to facilitate peer learning in group meetings in Wisker et al. (2008) in the Further Resources at the end of this chapter. There may also be times during a project when the content of the meeting is sufficiently generic to make group meetings an efficient option, such as discussing literature searches and structuring literature reviews, or deciding on appropriate data collection methods. Such sessions could then be complemented with one-to-one meetings in which the student's individual work is discussed. One potential pitfall of group meetings, however, is the perception among students that there is unequal attention on each student, or that one student dominates the discussions in the group (Roberts and Seaman, 2018). Issues arising from group dynamics can be addressed using the techniques discussed in Chapter 4 on small group teaching, such as directing questions to particular students, varying the questioning techniques you use, or asking students to prepare summaries of the work they have completed since the previous meeting.

Structuring and documenting your meetings

The structure of meetings will depend partly on how you agreed to work with your student(s). For example, we discussed above the possibility of creating a learning contract to set out the expectations that you have of your student, and vice versa.

It might be that you agreed on actions to be completed – by the student and/or by you – between meetings, and these action points might then form the basis for discussion in the meeting. The first meeting is likely to be less structured as you get to know each other, and perhaps you will conduct the first meeting with a group of students in order to discuss generic aspects of the work and to create a sense of community among your students.

In subsequent meetings, it is important to have a structure, even if this is quite flexible, as this will help to ensure meetings are as focused and productive as possible. You may only have a small number of meetings with your student, and your department may even stipulate how many meetings each student is permitted to have with the teacher, so the time needs to be spent well. A useful way of planning the structure of meetings is to have a meeting form where key discussion and action points are documented. This can also serve as a useful reminder to you and the student of what was discussed previously and forms the basis for ongoing discussions. An example of a simple form for a supervision meeting is shown below.

In the 'Progress' section, the student can update you on practical work carried out since the last meeting as well as any writing that has been completed. This is a good time to encourage a continuous approach to writing rather than leaving all of the written work until the very end of the project. This part of the meeting might also surface some challenges or problems that the student has experienced since the last meeting. Depending on the approach you are taking, you might offer your own advice and solutions, or you might take a coaching approach, as discussed earlier, where you ask a series of open questions to help the student to find solutions to their own problems. A combination of approaches is likely to be appropriate at different times. A summary of this discussion could then be recorded in the meeting summary section. As a result of the discussion, there will be some concrete actions for the student, and possibly also for you. Examples of actions for the student could be to start writing the Methods section, or to finish transcribing interview data that has been collected. The teacher might agree to read a draft of the Methods before the next meeting or to review a portion of the student's analysis, perhaps checking the codes and themes generated from the data analysis or the statistical methods used. As with any goals, such as learning outcomes, it is most productive if the action points are concrete and specific. At the end of the meeting, you can agree the date of the next meeting and, depending on the level of formality you have adopted, you and your student can sign the form as an official record of the meeting.

Structuring and recording meetings like this is a good way of reflecting on and documenting your own practice. It also sends a clear message to your student(s) that you take your role seriously, which can help to encourage students to take their role in the student–teacher relationship just as seriously. This aligns with our discussion of active learning in Chapter 2 , where the student takes a more active role in their own learning. A practical way of encouraging this in one-to-one meetings is to give the student the responsibility of scheduling and documenting the meetings. In some departments,

Supervision Record: Example 1

Student:

Supervisor:

Project title:

Meeting number:

Date of meeting:

[To be completed by the student before the meeting]

Desired outcomes of the meeting:

Progress since last meeting on [date]:

[To be completed at the meeting]

Summary of key discussion points:

Actions for student:

Actions for supervisor:

Date of next meeting:

Student signature:

Supervisor signature:

students are even expected to submit records of meetings as part of the assessed component of a project or an extended piece of work. A slightly adapted version of the supervision record above is shown below.

Supervision Record: Example 2

Student:

Supervisor:

Project title:

Meeting	Date	Summary of Discussion	Student Signature	Supervisor Signature
1				
2				
3				
4				

This record shows all the meetings in one document and the student has responsibility for filling it in after each meeting. This might then serve just as a record of meetings to remind both the supervisor and the student of action and discussion points and to help structure subsequent meetings, or the record might be submitted with the project as part of the assessment. Either way, the emphasis here is on the student leading, and taking responsibility for, the project and the recording of the meetings. Case Study 7.3 shows how one FHEA applicant reflected on facilitation of student-led supervision meetings.

Case Study 7.3

Student-led supervision meetings: Nicolas Newell, Research Fellow in Mechanical Engineering

When I undertook my own undergraduate final-year project I was always frustrated with the amount of time that I got to interact with my supervisor so I always ensure that I have at least one 30-minute meeting with each student every week. After attending a workshop on supervising students, I developed a better understanding for giving the student space

(Continued)

to drive their own project and importantly make mistakes and for the project to go wrong. I therefore ensure that the students have time within the meeting to tell me what is going wrong with their project. I try to do this by telling the students some of the problems that I'm currently facing with my research. This not only gives them some insight into what research I actually do, hopefully getting them more interested in the subject area, but also shows them that research doesn't always go right first time. I always start the meeting by asking what they want to achieve from the meeting. I find this focuses our discussion, and at the end of the meeting we both reflect on whether we have achieved what we had set out to. I also ask the student to bullet point a couple of aims for the upcoming week so they are focused on what they need to do.

Potential challenges

As we discussed earlier in this chapter, working with students individually is a more intense, often extended relationship between the student and the teacher, and there are potential challenges that can arise. Activity 7.3 invites you to think about challenges for students and for the teacher so that solutions can be found, or issues can be avoided altogether.

Activity 7.3

Reflecting on challenges of one-to-one working

1   Reflect on your own experiences of being a student in a project supervision or other one-to-one learning context. What challenges did you experience during that time? You may have had issues related to the work itself and/or to do with the relationship between you and your teacher.
2   If you have experience as a teacher or a supervisor working with students individually, what challenges have you experienced and how did you deal with these?

From the student perspective, common challenges arise around the (perceived) level of support they receive during an extended piece of work, the time they have available to complete the work and the level of autonomy expected of them by the teacher (Todd et al., 2004). As a teacher, you may have experienced issues such as students not attending or being unprepared for meetings, students not acting on your feedback, feeling that you are leading discussions too much during meetings, or feeling pressured to have all the answers to your students' questions. In practice, all of these issues can potentially be avoided by approaching one-to-one meetings in ways discussed in this chapter. If you discuss early on – in the first meeting – mutual expectations and perhaps formalise these in a learning contract, both you and the student will have a clear idea about the level of support that can be expected from you. Through skilful questioning, perhaps using a coaching approach, you can help the student to identify potential problems and respond to the uncertainties that are inevitable in a complex piece of extended work. A coaching conversation using the GROW model will also help you to encourage the student to explore the realities of their context and the potential obstacles they might encounter, one of which is likely to be a lack of time alongside their other modules and pieces of assessment. This kind of approach is also learner-centred and engages the student as an active participant in discussions so that you become just one potential source of help and information, with the aim of empowering the student to take responsibility for their work and to promote independence. Of course, as we discussed at the beginning of this chapter, the teacher's role is versatile, including a nurturing, pastoral element. If issues arise around the student's attendance at meetings, or if you notice changes in the student's behaviour, it is important to remember that you are not the only person who can help in this situation. Your role here is to signpost the student to the relevant services in the university, such as Student Services, the Counselling Service, or perhaps the student's personal tutor.

Over to you

In this chapter, we have looked at the different roles played by the teacher when working one-to-one with students or with small groups. Reflect on what kind of teacher you would like to be in this context and the extent to which you need to adapt your approaches to individual students. We have also explored the skillset of a good teacher when working with individual students, highlighting in particular skills used by mentors and coaches. The focus here is on promoting active learning and a student-centred approach in meetings. Having read this chapter, you could now think about your own approaches and reflect on the extent to which you promote independent learning and create the conditions for the student to take responsibility for their work. Finally, we have discussed how you might carry out the process of working with individual students over an extended period of time, incorporating a combination of one-to-one meetings and sessions with small groups of students. This should help you to identify when you could employ each of these approaches and decide how you – or the student – will record the meetings and document the student's progress with their project.

Further resources

This book provides a detailed overview of coaching and mentoring, including the similarities and differences between the two approaches and how they can aid learning.

Parsloe, E. and Leedham, L. (2017) *Coaching and Mentoring: Practical Techniques for Developing Learning and Performance*, 3rd edn. London: Kogan Page.

This book provides further detail on different contexts in which teachers work one-to-one with students, such as project and dissertation supervision and personal tutoring.

Wisker, G., Exley, K., Antoniou, M. and Ridley, P. (2008) *Working One-to-One with Students: Supervising, Coaching, Mentoring and Personal Tutoring*. Abingdon: Routledge.

References

Baker, M.J., Cluett, E., Ireland, L., Reading, S. and Rourke, S. (2014) Supervising undergraduate research: a collective approach utilising groupwork and peer support. *Nurse Education Today*, 34 (4): 637–42.

Del Río, M. L., Díaz-Vázquez, R. and Maside Sanfiz, J. M. (2018) Satisfaction with the supervision of undergraduate dissertations. *Active Learning in Higher Education*, 19 (2): 159–72.

Derounian, J. (2011) Shall we dance? The importance of staff–student relationships to undergraduate dissertation preparation. *Active Learning in Higher Education*, 12 (2): 91–100.

Guerin, C., Kerr, H. and Green, I. (2015) Supervision pedagogies: narratives from the field. *Teaching in Higher Education*, 20 (1): 107–18.

Gusenbauer, M. and Haddaway, N. R. (2020) Which academic search systems are suitable for systematic reviews or meta-analyses? Evaluating retrieval qualities of Google Scholar, PubMed and 26 other resources. *Research Synthesis Methods*, 11: 181–217.

Healey, M., Lannin, L., Stibbe, A. and Derounian, J. (2013) *Developing and Enhancing Undergraduate Final-Year Projects and Dissertations*. York: The Higher Education Academy and University of Gloucestershire. Available at: https://s3.eu-west-2.amazonaws.com/assets.creode.advancehe-document-manager/documents/hea/private/resources/ntfs_project_gloucestershire_2010_final_0_1568037223.pdf (accessed 25 January 2021).

Roberts, L. D. and Seaman, K. (2018) Good undergraduate dissertation supervision: perspectives of supervisors and dissertation coordinators. *International Journal for Academic Development*, 23 (1): 28–40.

Todd, M. J. and Smith, K. (2020) Supervising undergraduate dissertations. In S. Marshall (ed.), *A Handbook for Teaching and Learning in Higher Education*, 5th edn. Abingdon: Routledge. pp. 135–44.

Todd, M., Bannister, P. and Clegg, S. (2004) Independent inquiry and the undergraduate dissertation: perceptions and experiences of final-year social science students. *Assessment and Evaluation in Higher Education*, 29 (3): 335–55.

Whitmore, J. (2017) *Coaching for Performance: GROWing People, Performance and Purpose*, 5th edn. Boston, MA: Nicholas Brealey.

Wingate, U. (2019) 'Can you talk me through your argument'? Features of dialogic interaction in academic writing tutorials. *Journal of English for Academic Purposes*, 38: 25–35.

8

USING DIGITAL TECHNOLOGIES IN LEARNING AND TEACHING

Learning outcomes

After reading this chapter you should be able to:

- Select appropriate activities to ensure online learning is active and collaborative
- Use a storyboard to plan and design a sequence of online learning
- Decide when and how to use digital technologies in your face-to-face and online teaching.

Introduction

When we use the term 'technology', we tend to refer to advanced, electronic software and devices that help us to carry out day-to-day tasks. Strictly speaking, however, technology is any kind of equipment developed from scientific knowledge. In this way, a pen or a pencil could be considered a piece of technology. In this chapter, we will focus more on the former use of the term – on digital technology – but it is important to keep in mind that technology can be any equipment, machinery, software and so on that helps us to carry out our roles as teachers, and in turn helps our students to learn. For the purposes of this book, we are discussing technology here in a chapter of its own but, in reality, technology plays an integral part in our day-to-day learning and teaching practice. As such, the ideas presented in this chapter should be read and reflected upon in conjunction with the other topics discussed in this book.

In Chapter 2, we explored some of the key theoretical perspectives on learning which have been proposed over the years. Particularly relevant in the context of technology is connectivism, which aims to help us understand how students learn using digital technologies. From a connectivist perspective, learning is about making connections between and across people and networks. Technology can help with these connections, but it is important to note that we – students and teachers – are still the key players in learning and teaching encounters. This means we must foreground our teaching aims and what we want our students to learn, and then consider how, and which, technologies can aid teaching and learning, if at all. We sometimes hear about a new tool or a piece of technology and can be tempted to wonder how that particular tool can be used in our teaching. In this chapter, a key point to keep in mind is that any use of technology needs to involve a critical decision-making process. Rather than asking how a particular tool can be used, we should start with the teaching and learning scenarios we engage with in our day-to-day lives and then consider whether technologies might enhance our practice. In short: pedagogy first, technology second. We will look at technology from two perspectives: first we will look at how we can use technology to design learning in online spaces, and then we will explore how we can use technology in face-to-face classes to enhance students' learning.

Designing for online, active, collaborative learning

Unless you have already had extensive experience of learning in online spaces, either as a student or as a teacher, the task of designing online learning can seem like a daunting prospect. This is something you may have experienced, either directly or indirectly, during the recent global coronavirus pandemic when, almost overnight, teachers were faced with the task of moving existing face-to-face classes to online spaces. In this situation, there can be a temptation to focus on content, ensuring that subject matter usually discussed in face-to-face lectures and other teaching formats is 'transferred' to an online format. Whether you are designing a new online course, or whether you are transferring face-to-face learning to an online environment, it is important to take a step back and to consider not only how to provide content but also how to encourage students to engage actively in online sessions. We also need to consider whether the course will take place completely online, or in a blended learning format, which combines face-to-face sessions with online learning. Whilst there are differences between teaching online and in physical spaces, the underlying principles that guide your teaching remain the same, so it is important to remind yourself what your key principles are.

Activity 8.1

Identifying your key principles and values when planning teaching

When you are preparing a class in a face-to-face format, what are your key principles and values that guide your planning and subsequent interactions with your students? What will your role be throughout the learning and teaching encounter? What will your students' roles be? Make some notes on your responses to these questions.

The reason for asking these questions is to encourage you to pause and think about what we really value when we are teaching, regardless of whether we are teaching online or face-to-face. The principles that guide us in our day-to-day practice do not change simply because we are teaching online. Some long-standing principles were suggested by Chickering and Gamson, who, in 1987, published their 'seven principles for good practice in undergraduate education' (Chickering and Gamson, 1987). These seven principles posit that good practice:

1   encourages contact between students and faculty
2   develops reciprocity and cooperation among students
3   encourages active learning
4   gives prompt feedback
5   emphasises time on task
6   communicates high expectations
7   respects diverse talents and ways of learning.

You may have written down similar principles, particularly around active learning, collaboration, feedback and inclusivity. Chickering and Gamson published these principles in relation to learning and teaching generally rather than in online teaching specifically. However, they later published some thoughts on how their principles also underpin learning and teaching where technology plays an important role

(Chickering and Gamson, 1996). The key point is that we should not abandon our core values when designing online learning. By thinking through our principles, we give ourselves time and space to ensure our students are at the heart of our design decisions, focusing on activities and interactivity rather than simply uploading content to online platforms.

Making online learning active and engaging

In Chapter 2 and at various points throughout this book, we have highlighted the importance of facilitating engaging learning experiences that promote active learning. If we would not design a wholly teacher-centred face-to-face session with little or no interaction with and among students, why would we do this when designing learning for online spaces? The importance of activity and engagement is just as important, if not even more so, when learning and teaching online, and many of the activities we would do face-to-face, such as quizzes, group work, role plays, simulations, and so on, can also be done in online courses (Nilson and Goodson, 2017). A useful framework to help us to ensure online learning engages students in a variety of activities, rather than passively watching a pre-recorded lecture, for example, is Diana Laurillard's Conversational Framework and her six learning types (Laurillard, 2012). The framework is not exclusively for online learning, but it can be particularly helpful when designing online learning because, as the teacher is not physically present, it is even more important to think carefully about what students will actually do and how they will interact with each other, with the materials and with you. The six learning types in this framework are:

1   Acquisition: this is a common type of learning in which the student learns by listening to a lecture, reading books, papers and other documents, or watching a demonstration.
2   Discussion: learning through discussion requires the student to articulate their ideas and also respond to and challenge the ideas of other students and/or the teacher.
3   Inquiry: in this learning type, the student uses a range of sources to find answers to questions. These questions are often set by the student, which means the student has more autonomy and is able to engage actively in the learning process.
4   Practice: learning through practice requires a dialogue between students and teachers. Students work towards a learning goal, then receive feedback – this could be feedback from the teacher, from peers, or from self-assessment – then interpret and act on the feedback to improve their performance.
5   Collaboration: learning through collaboration encompasses some of the other learning types, such as discussion, practice and production, where students work together to produce a joint output, such as a presentation or a report.
6   Production: in this learning type, the student produces some form of artefact which is evaluated by the teacher. This is a way for the teacher to motivate the student to consolidate their learning, resulting in an output to demonstrate what they have learned.

Reflection

To what extent do you use the range of learning types in your existing teaching? Perhaps think about one course that you teach or co-teach. What proportion of students' time is spent engaging with each of the learning types? How might you incorporate these learning types into the design of an online course?

Discussion

Traditionally in higher education, the most common learning type is acquisition. As we saw in Chapter 5, the lecture has a very long history in university teaching and, overall, learning takes place through acquisition in lectures. It is likely that you use a variety of learning types in other teaching formats. For example, a small group session is likely to include some discussion-based activities, or perhaps some inquiry before and during the session. A lab-based session might include some group work resulting in an output produced collaboratively. The extent to which each of these learning types is used in different disciplines and in different teaching formats is likely to vary widely. It is useful for you to reflect on whether the proportions you have identified are appropriate in your discipline and whether you would make any changes. The key point is to consider what your students are actually doing and how they are engaging with you, with each other and with the course materials.

Designing online learning using a storyboard

A useful tool when designing online learning is a storyboard. This is essentially a visual representation of how students will progress through the course, much like the flow of scenes in a storyboard for a film. As we saw in Chapter 3, the learning activities are one part of the puzzle. We explored the concept of constructive alignment, where we need to consider what we would like our students to learn (the intended learning outcomes), how we will assess students' learning (the assessment methods) and how we help our students to meet the learning outcomes (the learning and teaching activities and materials). So by reflecting on the variety of activities in our courses, we can check that our teaching is constructively aligned whilst also checking that we are creating opportunities for our students to learn actively. We can follow the same process when designing online learning. We start with our intended learning outcomes and the assessment methods for the course, and then select appropriate activities to help our students to meet the outcomes. All of this will also ensure that students are active participants in the course rather than passive recipients of online content, in a purely 'acquisition' format. One way of representing this process is by using a storyboard. This can help you to identify how, and to

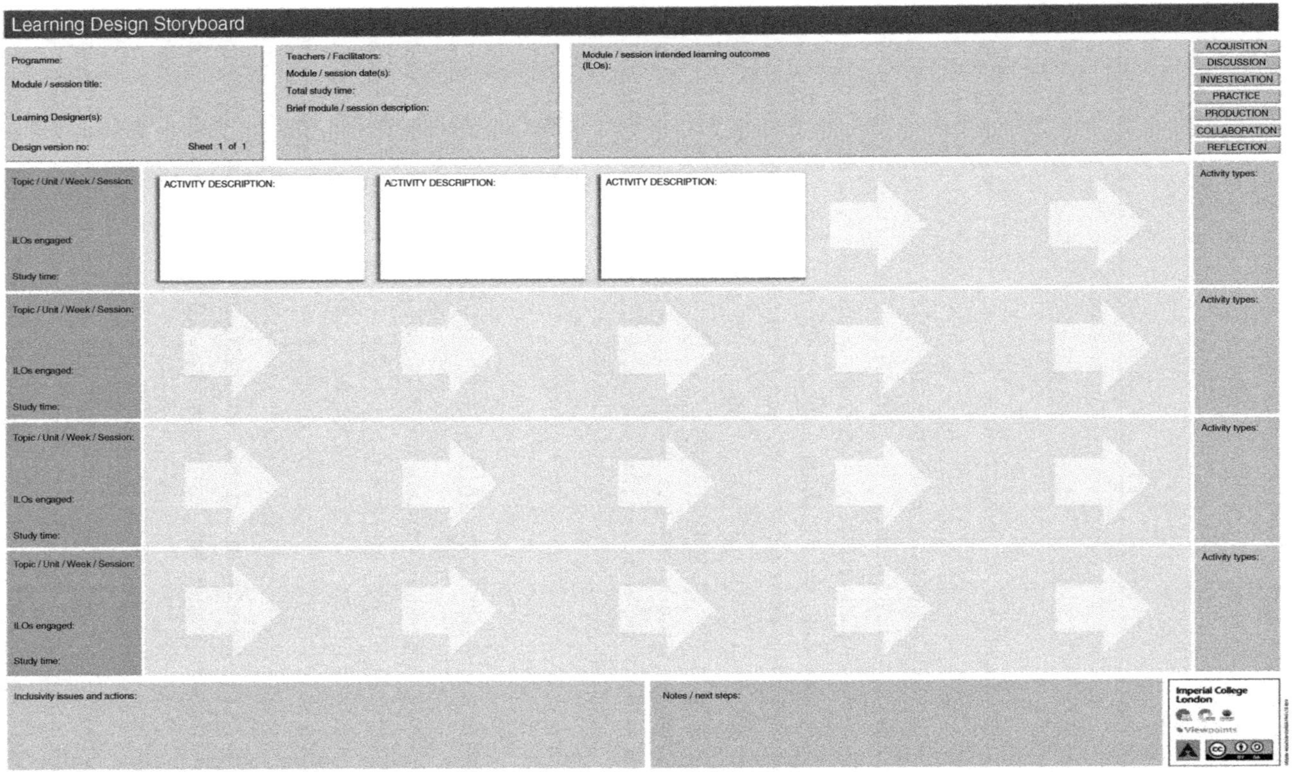

Figure 8.1 Storyboard template (M. Anderson/Akkadium Consulting 2013)

what extent, you have designed interactivity into the course, and whether there is a variety of different learning types. A simple storyboard template for a single session is shown in Figure 8.1. Figure 8.2 shows part of this template with two steps (or scenes) completed for a module about qualitative research methods.

Learning Design Storyboard

Programme: Msc Research Methods Module / session title: Qualitative Research Methods Learning Designer(s): Design version no: Sheet 1 of 1	Teachers / Facilitators: Module / session date(s): Total study time: Brief module / session description:	Module / session intended learning outcomes (ILOs): Evaluate the strengths and weaknesses of key qualitative research methods.

Topic / Unit / Week / Session: ILOs engaged: Study time:	Pre-session activity (asynchronous) 1. Watch the video "Qualitative Research Methods" (20 minutes). 2. Post on the discussion board at least one key characteristic of one of the methods introduced (10 minutes). Learning types: Acquisition/ Discussion	Live session (synchronous) 1. Q&A about pre-session video (10 minutes). 2. Breakout rooms (groups of 4): Review the project description and decide which method to employ. Prepare a brief (5-minute) justification of your approach (20 minutes). 3. Group presentations (30 minutes). Learning types: Discussion / Acquisition / Collaboration
Topic / Unit / Week / Session: ILOs engaged: Study time:		

Figure 8.2 Example of a storyboard for a series of online learning on qualitative research methods. (Adapted from M. Anderson/Akkadium Consulting 2013)

The storyboard draws our attention to activities, which emphasises what students will be doing at each stage during the course. By using a framework like Laurillard's learning types, you are also able to see at a quick glance whether there is a variety of activity types. For example, the two sample activities in Figure 8.2 include acquisition as one of the learning types. As the learning designer, you might decide that there need to be more opportunities for students to engage actively by including other learning types. In the example, this is taken into consideration by introducing aspects of discussion and a group task involving collaboration and a presentation. When designing activities for online courses, it is useful to consider a few questions to guide your thinking and decision making:

- What do you want students to do during this activity?
- Which learning type(s) does this activity involve?
- Is there a variety of learning types across the activities?
- How does each activity help students to meet the intended learning outcomes?

- What support – or scaffolding – will students need in order to complete the activities? Remember that the teacher is not physically present so the additional support requirements need to be considered carefully.
- What learning materials need to be created for each activity (e.g. videos, worksheets, slides)?
- How do the activities flow from a student perspective? Can you see a 'story', a logical progression, in your storyboard?
- How will formative and summative assessment be incorporated into the activities?
- What opportunities will students have to receive feedback?

Case Study 8.1 shows one example of how interactivity was designed into an online course in neuroanatomy.

Case Study 8.1

Designing online learning: Michael Armitage, medical student

I had the opportunity at medical school to aid in designing a neuroanatomy teaching module. I contributed within a team to the design of a set of online modules, each designed in a case-based teaching format that delivered teaching on complicated neuroanatomical topics in an accessible way. I created the course content focused on the anatomy of the cerebellum, which formed the basis for one of the modules. I opted for a case-based approach, with a pre- and post-module exam, as well as interactive visual content throughout. The modules focused on topics that students had reportedly performed poorly on in exams, and met a set of identified needs within the field of neurosurgical teaching. Pilot data on the modules have shown a statistically significant increase in scores from pre- to post-module tests. Polling of participants found that students rated the module highly from 0 to 10 for enjoyment (7.7), usefulness (8.7) and as an aid for learning (9.1). Computer assisted learning has been an important part of medical education since the early 2000s, and with the introduction of more readily accessible design platforms it is easier than ever to create e-learning resources. These modules were designed from the beginning with not only medical students in mind, but also with the goal of providing an accessible learning platform to the broader healthcare team. By making the modules case-based, and incorporating feedback from students in other healthcare professions throughout the design process, I believe the core material was made more relevant to a wider audience.

Another important question when designing online learning is about when and where activities will be completed. Will everything be done live while all students and the teacher are online together, or can some aspects of the course be done offline? This brings us to the concepts of synchronous and asynchronous learning.

Synchronous and asynchronous learning

When planning online learning, and when compiling a storyboard, a key consideration is the time and place when students will be expected to complete the various aspects of the course. We can think about this is two ways: synchronous and asynchronous learning, both of which are included in the example in Figure 8.2. In synchronous learning, students come online together at the same time to work 'live'. Asynchronous learning, on the other hand, involves self-study at a time and a place that is convenient for the student. They do not need to be online at the same time as their peers or the teacher, but can work on an aspect of the course in their own time. Most courses will include synchronous and asynchronous elements, and it is up to the teacher to decide which activities might lend themselves to the live, synchronous format and which ones could be completed more independently in an asynchronous way. To help with this decision making, Table 8.1 shows some considerations about the benefits and potential drawbacks of each format.

Table 8.1 Benefits and potential drawbacks of synchronous and asynchronous learning

	Benefits	Potential drawbacks
Synchronous	• Learning is more social • Creates a sense of belonging to a cohort of learners • Enables live interactions between learners and teachers • Enables real-time responses to questions • Creates opportunities for immediate feedback • Facilitates unplanned learning, including peer-to-peer learning • Enables the teacher to answer common questions for the whole class	• Requires all students and teachers to be available at the same time • Students may be in different time zones • Internet connections may be disrupted during a live session • Technologies may not work on different devices • May be experienced as fast-paced with little time to pause and reflect
Asynchronous	• Lesson content and activities can be accessed online or offline • Students can complete activities at times and in places that suit them • Learning is not constrained by scheduling or different time zones • Learning is less dependent on a stable internet connection • Opportunities for students to work at their own pace and to pause and reflect • These advantages make asynchronous learning more inclusive	• Learning might be perceived as a less social experience • Students may miss contact with the teacher and their peers • Potential loss of sense of belonging • Real-time responses or immediate feedback are more limited • Students need to set time aside to study • Students require a high level of motivation and self-regulation to complete asynchronous learning tasks

As we have said above, whether designing synchronous or asynchronous learning, it is important to enable students to engage actively when learning online. Here are a few suggestions for how this can be done, both in live synchronous classes and in asynchronous sessions:

- Students can contribute thoughts, responses, opinions, etc. on an online canvas or a discussion forum.
- Students can respond to questions in a poll (see Case Study 5.1 and Case Study 8.2).
- Students can work on a collaborative document and provide peer feedback to another group.
- Students can ask questions and make comments in the chat area.
- Each week, one student could be nominated to chair the chat area (it can be difficult for the teacher to keep an eye on the chat area at all times while teaching).

Active learning strategies such as these promote peer-to-peer learning alongside interactions between the teacher and students. In this way, the teacher can still act as a facilitator, as would be the case in a face-to-face session. In an online space, however, it is perhaps even more important for the teacher to show a presence, particularly in asynchronous learning. The teacher can establish a presence by checking in regularly to respond to students' comments and questions and by posing prompt questions or adding additional stimulus material to encourage greater participation. In practical terms, it can be useful to plan time when you will check in on students' engagement with asynchronous activities. Otherwise, it can be easy to spend an unrealistic amount of time moderating an asynchronous learning environment.

Activity 8.2

Using a storyboard to design online learning

Think about a course you teach or co-teach. Use the storyboard template in Figure 8.1 – or a similar document of your choice – to start designing online learning. It might be easier to start by thinking about a single session. Think about the following questions as you complete your storyboard:

- What are the intended learning outcomes?
- How long is the session?
- How much study time will students have? This includes time spent in live, synchronous sessions and time spent studying asynchronously.
- What do you want students to do? Which learning types will you use?
- Which activities can be completed by students asynchronously? Which ones would you like to do together in a synchronous format?
- How will you assess students' learning? Are there any opportunities for self- and peer-assessment?
- What opportunities will students have to receive feedback?

Technology to enhance learning in face-to-face teaching

Aside from designing courses explicitly for learning to take place in online spaces, we also make use of various digital technologies in our face-to-face teaching. As mentioned at the start of the chapter, we should consider how, if at all, technology can enhance our teaching and in turn enhance our students' learning. In the remainder of this chapter, we will explore how digital technologies can help us to facilitate interaction and active learning. We will also look briefly at virtual learning environments (VLEs), as you are likely to be using at least one VLE in your practice. Social media is also gaining increased attention, so we will explore how social media platforms can be harnessed to enhance learning.

Using technology to facilitate interaction

At the beginning of this chapter we attempted to define what we mean by 'technology' by pointing out that any piece of equipment developed from scientific knowledge can be considered to be a piece of technology, including items which, nowadays, are seemingly simple and commonplace, such as pens and pencils. The point here is that technology does not necessarily have to be complex. For the purpose of this chapter, though, we will reflect on the *digital* technologies we already use in our practice, some of which we may not even consider to be 'technology'.

Activity 8.3

Identifying your rationale for using different digital technologies and resources

Think about your day-to-day teaching practice and list the different digital technologies and resources you use in in your face-to-face teaching, particularly those that help to facilitate interactions with and/or between students. Then think about why you use these technologies. What is your rationale?

You almost certainly use a range of technologies, some of which are so commonplace that you may not give them too much thought. The aim of Activity 8.3 is to encourage you to reflect on your use of technology and to ask yourself why you use each piece of equipment, software, etc. This is something we should all do as reflective practitioners, but you will also need to do this if you apply for Fellowship (FHEA) or Associate Fellowship (AFHEA). For example, in your list of technologies, you may have written down PowerPoint (or other presentation software) – or you may not have considered this to be a digital technology at all. It is useful to take a step back to consider how and why you use this. How else could you present information that you usually show your students using PowerPoint? How do you know this technology helps you to achieve your teaching aims? How do you know it helps students to learn? Asking yourself questions like this in relation to any technological resource you use will help to make you a more critically reflective teacher. Here are some others you might use to help facilitate interaction:

- Presentation clickers: if you are presenting information, perhaps in a lecture, you may have experienced the problem of feeling rooted to the front of the room because you have to be near the computer to move to the next slide. This significantly reduces your ability to interact with your students. A simple and commonplace solution is to use a wireless clicker, which enables you to control your presentation from anywhere in the room. Clickers usually also have a button which blanks the screen. This is particularly useful when encouraging students to think or reflect rather than look at the screen. If you are using PowerPoint, the blank screen function can also be initiated simply by pressing the 'B' key when you are in presentation mode.
- Polling and e-voting: particularly when teaching larger groups, it can be difficult to gather responses from all students in order to interact but also to check understanding. There is a range of options available to poll students, whereby they use their own devices (mobile phones, tablets, laptops) to input their answers to questions. Depending on the system you use, there is a range of question and response options, such as multiple choice, free text, graphs, word clouds, etc. Such technologies change fast so we will not explore the various systems currently available, but we have included links to two commonly used voting systems in the Further Resources at the end of this chapter.
- Visualisers: many teaching rooms are now equipped with a visualiser, which is a small camera which points downwards at a flat, white surface where the teacher can show documents and other objects using the projector. Visualisers can be particularly useful for showing a developing process in real-time, such as working out a mathematical problem. The visualiser can also be used to share students' work with the rest of the class, for example by displaying students' notes or thoughts after a group task.

This is clearly not an exhaustive list of ways in which digital technologies can help to facilitate interaction. Your university is likely to have a variety of technologies which are supported at institutional level, so your local digital learning team is a good place to start when thinking about how to incorporate technology into your teaching. There is also a wealth of information and links to publications about learning technologies on the Association for Learning Technology website, which is included in the Further Resources at the end of this chapter.

Virtual learning environments

It is very likely that your institution uses a virtual learning environment (VLE) where content is accessed and assessments are submitted and sometimes marked. Depending on the VLE you use, there are several functionalities that can either accommodate fully online courses or complement face-to-face teaching in a blended learning format. Individual teachers are unlikely to have much or any input into which VLE is used; these decisions are usually taken at institutional level. Some colleagues – and you may be one of them – may also be critical of VLEs on the basis of aesthetics, usability or their general perceived (lack of) value in enhancing students' learning. Nevertheless, it is likely that your teaching will involve the use of a VLE in some way, and there are several features that are worth mentioning here.

First, it is important to find out which VLE your institution uses. Among the most commonly used in UK universities are Blackboard, Moodle and Canvas. Then you will need to find out how your particular department uses the VLE. There might be expectations about the extent to which the VLE is used, or individual teachers may have a certain amount of freedom to use the VLE more extensively, or not to use it at all. One area in particular that will need to be clarified is assessment: students may be expected to submit assignments via the VLE, and teachers may also be asked to mark students' work and provide feedback online. For online assignment submission, your institution is likely to use a form of plagiarism detection software. Most common at UK universities is 'Turnitin', which compares students' work with texts on the internet to detect instances of academic misconduct. Some colleagues criticise the use of tools such as Turnitin on the basis that this shows a lack of trust in students. However, as with the choice of VLE, individual teachers are unlikely to have significant input into whether such software is used. In any case, it is a good idea to check with module leads how the VLE is used by teachers and how students are expected to use the VLE – and submit assignments – before you start planning your teaching.

VLEs are perhaps most commonly used as content repositories where teachers create folders and sub-folders to store materials in a range of file formats, from written documents, to images, to video and audio files. This sometimes attracts criticism as it means the VLE is being used quite passively rather than creating a space for students to engage and interact with each other. Nevertheless, this is one way of using a VLE that you might find useful.

There are also other functions that might be available to you, such as discussion forums, wikis, blogs and quizzes. As well as using in-built functions, you can also integrate external applications into your courses on the VLE in order to facilitate greater interactivity and engagement among students. For example, you could ask students to add their thoughts to an online canvas, such as Padlet (www.padlet.com), where they can start a discussion and comment on their peers' work. Another example is to integrate a poll from an external polling platform (see Case Study 8.2). As mentioned above, polls like this offer different question and answer options, such as word clouds, free text, multiple choice responses and so on.

A final point we will make here is that teachers can track students' progress and engagement with particular aspects of courses on the VLE. This may initially seem intrusive, and it is important that we use this functionality not for surveillance but to enhance our students' learning. Nevertheless, it can be useful to know whether students have accessed a particular document or whether they have completed a particular activity, as this can help to identify aspects of the subject matter that appear to be challenging for students, which in turn can help to inform future teaching. Your institution is likely to run workshops for teachers about the particular VLE used locally, so it is worth finding out about this so that you can learn about the full functionality of the VLE in use at your institution.

Case Study 8.2

Using an online poll as a formative assessment method: Daniel Whittaker, Senior Library Assistant

Mentimeter is a tool I use frequently in sessions to create online quizzes as a method of formative assessment. For example, I have been involved in delivering inductions to larger groups of undergraduates in how to use library facilities and services. I use a Mentimeter quiz to assess the learners' understanding of the material covered in the session. I try to ensure that the questions are targeted around the information I want the students to learn by ensuring the questions closely correspond with the session ILOs. I use Mentimeter as it is informal, accessible and a useful way to incorporate an assessment activity into the 60-minute time frame. It is particularly useful as it helps to identify any areas learners have struggled to understand. I am then able to display the results of the quiz and provide feedback without having to single out individuals. I would like to expand my use of this tool in my future sessions where possible, but it does have drawbacks as an assessment method. Some learners fail to take part and it can be difficult to discern when an individual learner has failed to understand a concept.

Social media

The use of social media is now so widespread that it has become important for students to learn about how they present themselves online (Beckingham, 2019). As well as this, though, various social media platforms are becoming useful tools to enhance teaching and learning. YouTube is perhaps an obvious starting point, as many teachers incorporate videos into their teaching. These may be pre-existing videos or materials created by the teacher and then uploaded to YouTube on a separate channel. Similarly, students may be asked to create their own videos as part of assignments, and then comment on their peers' work.

Other platforms have also started to offer interesting and creative ways for students and teachers to interact in educationally stimulating ways. Perhaps the biggest platforms currently in use are Twitter, Snapchat and Facebook, and all of these have found their way into learning and teaching. Here are some examples:

- Using a Facebook group for a cohort of students where key topics can be debated, documents and links can be shared, and course announcements can be made.
- Using a Twitter poll to gauge students' understanding of a topic or to gather feedback on your teaching.
- Using hashtags to help with research for class preparation or assignments.
- Answering quick questions on Snapchat and/or asking students to respond to their peers' questions.
- Conducting regular Tweetchats about key topics using a unique hashtag created for the module or cohort.
- Using Snapchat stories to present content to your students, which they can view at a time and a place convenient for them.

There are many other ways social media platforms might be used in learning and teaching. As with any technology, the key is to be clear about your rationale for using a particular tool or platform. One advantage of using social media is that we are bringing our teaching into students' spaces – meeting them where they are. Having said this, we also need to be careful that any decisions about using particular platforms are inclusive. If we decide, for example, to use Twitter as a key part of the course, we have to make sure all students are happy to either use their existing account or to create one if they do not already have one. If a social media platform becomes the main site of learning and interaction, and some students do not use this platform, there is the potential for feeling excluded. A more inclusive approach can be to use platforms that do not require students to sign up with an account. It can also be useful to ask students at the beginning of the module which social media platforms they routinely use so that this information can inform your choices. There is already a wealth of examples of how social media can be used in higher education teaching. You can find some case studies on the use of social media in teaching and learning in the Further Resources at the end of this chapter (see Rowell, 2019).

Over to you

Depending on your current role in learning and teaching, you may have greater or lesser involvement in designing online courses. Nevertheless, it is likely that you already incorporate digital technologies into your face-to-face teaching. The key message in this chapter is to keep in mind your pedagogical principles and to let these take the lead when deciding which technologies to use – or whether to use any digital technology at all. Think about what you want your students to achieve and how you engage your students in active learning in your day-to-day practice. Then, if there are any digital technologies that might enhance your practice, and in turn enhance your students' learning, you can start to think about how these tools can be incorporated and look for published evidence of their effectiveness. These are useful reflections if you are applying for Fellowship or Associate Fellowship. Then you can apply a similar reflective process when designing online courses, whether this is part of your current role or whether this becomes part of your practice in the future.

Further resources

The website of the Association for Learning Technology.

www.alt.ac.uk

A Jisc report on developments in technology-enhanced learning.

Phipps, L., Allen, R., Hartland, D. et al. (2018) *Next Generation [Digital] Learning Environments: Present and Future*. Jisc. http://repository.jisc.ac.uk/6797/1/JR0090_NDGLE_REPORT_FINAL.pdf

A guide from Advance HE on starting to use technology in your teaching.

Pickering, J. (2015) *How to Start Using Technology in Your Teaching*. Higher Education Academy. https://s3.eu-west-2.amazonaws.com/assets.creode.advancehe-document-manager/documents/hea/private/how_to_start_using_technology_in_your_teaching_1568037330.pdf

This edited volume provides a series of practical case studies explaining how various social media platforms have been used in the teaching of a range of disciplines in higher education.

Rowell, C. (ed.) (2019) *Social Media in Higher Education: Case Studies, Reflections and Analysis*. Cambridge: Open Book Publishers.

References

Beckingham, S. (2019) Developing a professional online presence and effective network. In C. Rowell (ed.), *Social Media in Higher Education: Case Studies, Reflections and Analysis*. Cambridge: Open Book Publishers. pp. 21–34.

Chickering, A. W. and Gamson, Z. F. (1996) Implementing the seven principles: technology as lever. *AAHE Bulletin*, 49 (2): 3–6.

Chickering, A. W. and Gamson, Z. F. (1987) Seven principles for good practice in undergraduate education. *AAHE Bulletin*, 39 (7): 3–7.

Laurillard, D. (2012) *Teaching as a Design Science: Building Pedagogical Patterns for Learning and Technology*. Abingdon: Routledge.

Nilson, L. B. and Goodson, L. A. (2017) *Online Teaching at Its Best: Merging Instructional Design with Teaching and Learning Research*. San Francisco: Jossey-Bass.

9

DEVELOPING INCLUSIVE TEACHING PRACTICE

Learning outcomes

After reading this chapter you should be able to:

- Identify aspects of student identity or experience that may impact on progress at university
- Recognise some of your own tacit beliefs, biases and assumptions and those of students
- Plan inclusive pedagogies that recognise, value and support all students to succeed.

Introduction

Tracy grew up on a council estate in Leeds and entered university through a 'Widening Participation' scheme (a scheme to raise the aspirations and educational attainment of prospective students who are under-represented at university, especially those from neighbourhoods with traditionally low participation rates). She is from an English, white working-class family and is the first in her family to go to university. She lives with her parents and has epilepsy, which she controls with medication.

Michael is from an English/Afro-Caribbean family living in Surrey. He went to a private school where he experienced bouts of depression due to bullying from other pupils. This affected his studies and although he managed to get the grades for university, he feels a bit of a fraud.

Norazimah is a postgraduate student from Malaysia. She is married, with a daughter who is being looked after by family back home while she is studying. She is a devout Muslim.

Every student has a unique story, and whilst we cannot be expected to know each individual's background, circumstances and experience, we do have a responsibility, enshrined in law, to ensure that our teaching is inclusive. In this chapter, we will explore how we can work towards understanding students' needs and designing our teaching so that all students can benefit.

Inclusive teaching in higher education has been defined as 'the ways in which pedagogy, curricula and assessment are designed and delivered to engage students in learning that is meaningful, relevant and accessible to all' (Hockings, 2010: 1). It seems self-evident that we would want our pedagogy (how we teach), curricula (what we teach) and assessment (how we evaluate learning) to engage all students, but in practice there are real differences in how well students fare at university.

Students from poorer backgrounds are less likely to enter university, particularly the most competitive ones, with so-called 'white working-class boys' the least likely (Social Mobility Commission, 2019). They are also more likely to drop out and less likely to progress to high-skilled jobs. Students from ethnic minorities experience unexplained differences in degree outcomes, with 81.4% of white students obtaining a First or Upper Second Class degree, compared to 76.9% of Chinese, 70.0% of Asian and 58.8% of Black students (Advance HE, 2020). There are differences across subject areas, geographical regions and for students at the intersections of characteristics, such as Black men from poorer backgrounds. Prior attainment on entry to university is the best predictor of success, suggesting that universities perpetuate rather than redress existing societal disadvantage. Student satisfaction, based on National Student Survey scores, also tends to be lower for ethnic minority and disabled students: you may like to check the results for your university.

The duty to provide an inclusive education is enshrined in law via the Equality Act of 2010, which prohibits discrimination, harassment and victimisation against people based on the following 'protected characteristics':

- Age
- Disability
- Gender reassignment
- Pregnancy and maternity
- Marriage and civil partnership
- Race
- Religion or belief
- Sex
- Sexual orientation.

Discrimination can be direct (where you treat a student worse than others because of one of the protected characteristics) or indirect (where a rule or practice has a worse impact on people who share a protected characteristic than on those who don't; for example, holding lectures in a building that is inaccessible to disabled people).

The 'public sector equality duty' of 2011 further requires universities to advance equality of opportunity and foster good relations between people who share a protected characteristic and those who do not, and to take regard of inequalities due to socio-economic disadvantage (which is not on the list). So universities are required not just to remove barriers (preventing exclusion) but to take positive steps to foster inclusive learning environments. To do this we need to understand what causes the current differential outcomes and experiences of students.

Reflection

Consider your own experience of higher education by reflecting on the following questions:

- When you grew up, had any of your close circle been to university?
- Were your parents (or the people closest to you) supportive of your attending university?
- Did you know what to expect?
- Did your school have the relevant experience and expertise to support you?

During your studies:

- Were you constantly worried about money?
- Did you juggle studying with work and/or caring responsibilities?
- Did such responsibilities curtail your opportunity to take part in social or extra-curricular activities?
- Were you often confused about what was expected of you?
- Were you studying in a foreign language and worried about your language skills?
- Did you feel a sense of being different or isolated?
- Did you experience racism, sexism, harassment or other forms of intended or unintended discrimination?
- Did you feel that the subjects you studied were relevant to you?
- Did you have a disability or mental health problem that affected your studies?

(Continued)

- Could you 'be yourself'?
- Were the teaching and learning methods used at university familiar to you?
- Did you mostly understand what the assessments were looking for?

Now think about the students briefly profiled at the start of this chapter. How might they answer the same questions?

Discussion

A review into the causes of differential student outcomes (Mountford-Zimdars et al., 2015) identified four broad categories of contributing factors, encompassing societal, institutional and individual levels:

1   Students' experience of learning, teaching and assessment: for example, how relevant and interesting the curriculum is to them, whether they see role models they can relate to, whether they understand assessment requirements.
2   The relationships that underpin students' experience of HE: for example, whether staff convey high expectations and confidence in them and experiences of racism or sexism from staff or students.
3   Psycho-social and identity factors: for example, whether students feel a sense of belonging and have an expectation that they can achieve.
4   Cultural and social capital: this refers to the resources and contacts that students have to help them navigate and succeed at university; for example, having access to good technology or parents and friends who can help them to find an internship or provide a reference.

Looking at the categories above, you will see that you may be able to influence most of them. In the rest of the chapter we will discuss how to make your teaching inclusive, focusing on areas that are within the control of early career staff, rather than those that need addressing at a higher level. These are:

- applying the principles of universal design when planning teaching
- creating a sense of belonging, including when teaching sensitive topics
- developing greater awareness of yourself and your students.

Before we start, a note on terminology: the language used to describe and classify people often carries hidden assumptions and meaning. Many terms used to describe specific groups are contested and socially acceptable terminology evolves over time: some examples of language and associated critiques are given in Table 9.1.

You may like to think about the range of terms you have heard relating to other areas such as class, gender and sexuality, which are similarly contested. It is helpful for teaching staff to be aware of the debates around language and its implications, whilst

Table 9.1 Issues around terminology

Examples of terms used in the UK	Critiques of the terms
BAME (Black, Asian and minority ethnic groups), people of colour, ethnic minorities, white	BAME, people of colour and white people are very broad categories, comprising varied groups of people who may have little in common. People of colour excludes ethnic groups that may carry disadvantage despite being white, such as Roma people (gypsies). The use of the word 'minority' in 'ethnic minority' may suggest something of lesser importance than the majority
Non-native speakers, second language speakers (L2)	Non-native is a deficit term, highlighting a lack of something which others have. L2 assumes that English is the person's second language whereas it may be their second, third or fourth language. More positive terms might include bilingual or multilingual, although that does not differentiate between native and non-native speakers
Dyslexic (similarly schizophrenic, manic depressive, etc.), suffering from dyslexia	When used as a noun (as in 'he's a dyslexic') these are 'totalising' terms in that they make the condition synonymous with the person, rather than just one facet of their life. 'Suffering from' assumes that dyslexia has a negative impact whereas it could be considered simply a difference in how the brain functions, or even a gift that provides unique abilities as well as limitations. A more general term is neurodiversity, which acknowledges differences in the brain between individuals that may affect learning, attention and mood

also avoiding becoming so wary of opening up discussion that relevant differences in perspective or experience are ignored for fear of causing offence.

A key concept is that of 'othering' – labelling people as different from ('other than') an assumed norm, which is usually white, male, able bodied, heterosexual and middle class. This assumed norm represents the dominant group in society, with other groups holding less powerful positions (even though individuals within the dominant group may not feel powerful).

Who defines the terms is important (e.g. whether it is people within the group or the dominant group in society) and for what purpose. Identifying certain groups can allow us to measure the impact of difference and evaluate efforts to make education more inclusive. However, we all have multiple characteristics that affect us in varied ways and there may be more differences between individuals within a category than between different categories.

In this book, the purpose of discussing difference is to ensure that our teaching is equally accessible and engaging for all students and that our assessments are fair to everyone.

Universal design for learning

The concept of universal design originated in architecture with the idea that buildings could be designed to be accessible to people of all ages and (dis)abilities. The same principle can be applied in educational settings to design courses that are flexible enough to cater to the diverse needs of all students, rather than designing for the majority and then making adaptions for those with particular issues.

The principles of universal design for learning are based on neuroscience research and recognise that there is no single approach that is optimal for all learners (Gordon et al., 2016). Instead, educational planning should accommodate differing needs and preferences through providing:

- Multiple means of *engagement*: this is about using a variety of creative activities and resources to tap into diverse learners' interests and motivate them. It involves optimising individual choice and autonomy which helps learners to become more self-sufficient in their learning.
- Multiple means of *representation* is about giving learners choices in how they acquire and understand information; for example, providing not just articles to read but different types of text, visual or auditory resources or real life experiences. Highlighting critical features, patterns and relationships is also helpful.
- Multiple means of *action and expression is about* allowing students different ways to set and achieve goals and demonstrate progress, for example, orally or in writing, and with access to assistive technologies where appropriate. (If for summative assessment, the options should be equivalent in their demand and assessed with the same marking criteria.)

How can you apply these principles in practical terms? See below for guidance on resources and try Activity 9.1 to consider some specific scenarios.

Guidance on teaching and learning resources

The digital divide – inequalities in ownership of and access to computing devices, broadband, connectivity, digital literacy and online communication competence – became starkly apparent during the COVID-19 crisis. Differences in working environments were also evident, such as those with access to quiet, dedicated office or study space and those sharing with parents, children or peers in multi-functional spaces. Ensuring that both staff and students could access and use appropriate teaching and learning technologies became an urgent priority. Whilst technology offers opportunities to make teaching more inclusive (for example, by allowing students to study flexibly), it requires investment by universities to support staff and students to make teaching fully accessible. Your university will have guidance on requirements; some examples of practical steps you can take are given below.

- Check that you and your resources can be seen and heard by everyone (whether teaching online or face to face).

- If teaching online, ensure that students know how to use the relevant functions.
- Make teaching resources available before the session: this helps students with dyslexia and those for whom English is not their first language, amongst others.
- Provide documents in formats that are accessible across different devices (don't assume people have access to the latest technology).
- Use simple, logical and consistent design.
- Include visual elements to demonstrate or illustrate points (not just for decoration), with 'alternative text' to describe them for blind students (this function can be found in most digital formats).
- If showing videos, include captions/subtitles (this can help international and deaf/hard of hearing students, amongst others).
- Use 'sans serif' fonts such as Arial, Callibri or Helvetica – these are the simplest design and therefore easier to read.
- Similarly lower case letters are easier to read than capitals and should be used for the majority of text.
- If using PowerPoint in classrooms, check that the font size can be read by students sitting at the back.

Activity 9.1

Inclusive design scenarios

Imagine the following scenarios. What are the potential implications and how could you modify your teaching design to build in universality?

Scenario 1: A student asks if they can bring their child to the teaching session as they are having trouble finding childcare that morning. They assure you that the child will be quiet and well behaved.

Scenario 2: You have set up a timetable whereby each of your students will give a 10-minute presentation at some point during the module. A student approaches you afterwards and tells you that they have social anxiety disorder and therefore can't participate.

Scenario 3: You ask the students to discuss a current issue, using a clip from a well-known film to help stimulate discussion. Usually this exercise works well but today the group are silent.

Discussion

Scenario 1

Whilst you may be sympathetic to a parent in this position, the situation is problematic for various reasons: whether or not the child is well behaved, they may distract other students and indeed the parent and teacher. It also sets a precedent so that other parents within the student body may expect the same treatment. Your university may have a policy on this and may offer help with childcare provision.

An inclusive approach might involve recording the teaching and posting it online, and/or making the materials available. These options would accommodate not only parents but other students who are unable to attend through illness, or who could benefit from being able to stop/start the teaching or watch it in slow or quick motion. Of course there can be disadvantages and limitations to this as well which would need to be considered. Depending on numbers, another option might be to repeat lectures at different times of day.

Scenario 2

If the student is registered with the university as having a disability or a mental health problem, you should be given guidance as to any special arrangements that are necessary. Assuming that presenting in class is not specifically excluded, you might want to offer some flexibility to make the experience less stressful. For example, you could allow the student to work with another student and present together, to pre-record a presentation, read from a script or give the presentation to a smaller group of students.

These options assume that improving students' presentation skills is one of the intended learning outcomes for the course. If this is not the case and the presentation is simply a method of assessing understanding or engaging students in the class, then you could allow a written option, such as producing a handout for other students. In either case, it would be fair to build a limited number of acceptable options into the course design and offer them to all students. Of course, you would need to check with the relevant course leader and/or university policy.

Scenario 3

Discussion activities work well for many students but not all. Students on the autistic spectrum, shy students or those with limited English may find them challenging and prefer to listen to others. It is always best to include a range of activities, including individual, reflective activities that allow students to work at their own pace in a quiet environment. The film clip you showed may not be easy to comprehend for those who haven't seen the film and don't understand its cultural context. It might be helpful to provide relevant background information, make it available in advance, ensure it has subtitles and offer a choice of activities to meet the objectives of the session.

An important point about universal design is that all students benefit from the approach as we learn in diverse ways and generally appreciate being able to choose options that suit our personal preferences.

Creating a sense of belonging

Students who leave university without completing their degree generally do so in the first semester or shortly after Christmas. Research exploring student engagement and belonging identified the primary reasons as feelings of isolation and/or not fitting in and worries about achieving future aspirations (Thomas, 2012). This can be particularly acute for working-class, international or ethnic minority students who are usually in a minority and may experience culture shock and the feeling that no one understands them.

So the way in which you engage students with yourself, each other and the institution in the early part of a course is important. Bear in mind that the diversity of students in our universities includes both visible and invisible differences, so even if your classes don't look particularly diverse, further exploration may find a range of socio-economic backgrounds, religions, abilities and so on. There are also an increasing number of students suffering from mental health issues such as anxiety and depression that can impact on their engagement.

So how do students perceive the social and educational climate within classes? A model representing how learning contexts can be perceived, based on a qualitative study of the perceptions of gay and lesbian university students is shown in Figure 9.1.

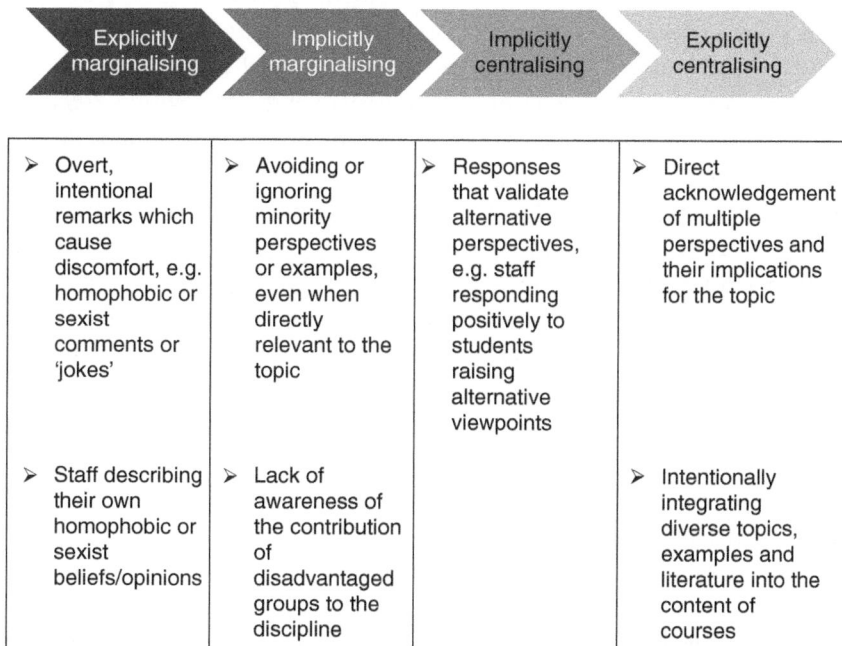

Explicitly marginalising	Implicitly marginalising	Implicitly centralising	Explicitly centralising
➢ Overt, intentional remarks which cause discomfort, e.g. homophobic or sexist comments or 'jokes'	➢ Avoiding or ignoring minority perspectives or examples, even when directly relevant to the topic	➢ Responses that validate alternative perspectives, e.g. staff responding positively to students raising alternative viewpoints	➢ Direct acknowledgement of multiple perspectives and their implications for the topic
➢ Staff describing their own homophobic or sexist beliefs/opinions	➢ Lack of awareness of the contribution of disadvantaged groups to the discipline		➢ Intentionally integrating diverse topics, examples and literature into the content of courses

Figure 9.1 Classroom communication: a continuum. (Adapted from De Surra and Church, 1994)

Classroom communication was classified along a continuum from *marginalising* to *centralising*. Although the study related specifically to homosexuality, the categories in the continuum would be equally relevant to ethnicity, gender, class or other characteristics that may carry cultural disadvantage, and the examples in Figure 9.1 have been adapted to reflect this.

Reflection

Think back to specific classes you took as a student and consider where they would come on the continuum shown in Figure 9.1 – considering all aspects of diversity. What impact did the climate have on you and your experience of higher education?

Discussion

Your response may vary greatly according to your discipline and personal characteristics. You may be more aware of the issues if you come from a group that tends to be less well represented, even ignored, in discussions or the curriculum. DeSurra and Church's model also identified differing ways in which students responded to these class climates depending on how self-conscious or self-assured they were; for example, whether they felt able to be open about their sexuality or to challenge teachers.

An inclusive teaching approach would be consistent with the *explicitly centralising* end of the continuum and is a theme, not just in this chapter, but throughout the book. In Chapter 4, for example, we looked at pedagogical aspects such as how to create a positive environment for learning within the group so that students feel comfortable enough to engage with and learn from each other. This included ways to structure learning activities to facilitate maximum participation and learning.

Inclusion is also important with regards to curricula, and in recent years student activists have put pressure on universities to 'decolonise' their curricula. This involves broadening what are accepted as legitimate contributions to academic knowledge, which has long been the preserve of European and North American literature, dominated by white, male authors.

An 'explicitly centralising' curriculum would include diverse perspectives that rebalance power so that all sections of society and voices from different cultures and traditions are included. Many course teams in universities are now reviewing reading lists and course content to incorporate a wider range of perspectives and resources on a topic. An example of a module that was designed not only to accommodate but also to leverage the educational value of diversity is given in Case Study 9.1.

Case Study 9.1

Inclusive design: Aleksandra Kubica, GTA in Culture, Media and Creative Industries

'Theatre of Discovery': designing the module and planning the individual sessions:

The module that I was involved in developing and delivering for two subsequent academic years was built on an art-based, interdisciplinary and research-led pedagogic model. The group enrolled was very diverse: there were many international students and one student with visual impairment.

The students came from more than 10 different departments. For some of the activities I divided students into groups in which different departments, levels and cultural backgrounds were represented. Especially the disciplinary differences were important for my decisions on how the groups would be divided. This is because I believe that interdisciplinary learning in the university context can encourage students to think critically about the limitations of their own disciplines (Woods, 2007: 854) and practise communicating across disciplines. This was described by students in the feedback forms as a very valuable element of the module. Students wrote: 'Teamwork cross-discipline has been the most important thing for me. I've found that students in each department have different ways of approaching things, and it's been really fascinating to see how we can communicate and bring both approaches to fruition.'

The activities which I prepared for the module encouraged students to use different senses and ways to engage with knowledge. For example, students discussed assigned questions sitting around the table with their eyes blindfolded or they made drawings to illustrate what they were talking about. The groups then summarised their discussions in front of the others. This was done to offer students a chance to find out about how they learn, reflect and communicate with others and to enable them to explore the diversity of stories and backgrounds that each individual brought to the module. It also was meant to give me and other module leaders an opportunity to learn about those. My rationale for this was that it is crucial to not only search for ways to appreciate diversity in the classroom but also to respect and acknowledge all students as individuals, and this includes trying to understand the backgrounds and needs of everyone (Darder, 2012).

Students reported in evaluation surveys that the discussions helped them to become open to other perspectives. For instance, one student wrote: 'the module really helped me to think creatively, out of the box and interpret things differently [...] the guided discussions helped to open my mind to new ideas and perspectives.' And another one: 'expanded the method in which you approach certain problems and how you see the world'.

You may not be in a position to design courses, but you can make a difference in your everyday practice; for example, by ensuring that the examples, case studies and visuals in your teaching materials reflect the diversity within society. This can often be unconsciously overlooked. One of the authors was involved in developing a suite of case studies for use in medical education. A quick count at the end surprised the compilers when it revealed that many more men than women featured, especially in the medical roles, with women primarily included as patients. The case studies were subsequently revised to rectify this.

You can also be aware of including differing voices in discussions with and amongst learners. This may be particularly relevant when discussing sensitive or controversial issues which can provide challenges for the teacher, such as those described in Activity 9.2.

Activity 9.2

Challenging scenarios

Consider what you might do in the following scenarios:

Scenario 1: You are leading a session on Middle Eastern politics. You know that some of your students have very strong views on the subject and are worried that discussion might degenerate into a heated argument. How might you prepare for the session?

Scenario 2: Feedback about your course contains several comments from students that remarks they found racist, sexist or otherwise intolerant did not meet with a timely response from you. They feel that you tend to avoid controversial topics, and fail to challenge inappropriate opinions. How could you respond if you encounter such feedback?

Discussion

Scenario 1

Universities are places where differing views should be debated, but ensuring that this happens in a constructive way can be challenging. There is no single answer, but some strategies for handling sensitive discussions are discussed below:

- In some departments, there is a policy of giving 'trigger warnings' to tell students in advance that certain sessions will touch on sensitive topics so that they can choose whether or how to participate. In others, it is considered impossible to predict which topics students might find sensitive and therefore better simply to outline the content and let students decide for themselves.

- Before starting discussion, whether face to face or online, you could remind students of some ground rules, or invite them to generate their own, e.g. 'How should we conduct these discussions?'
- Structure activities so that students have to consider all sides of an argument. You could have them argue from the opposite view to their own, or from a nominated perspective; for example, allocate groups of students to discuss what might be a feminist/economic/Christian/environmental perspective on the issue.
- Aim to elicit and help students to understand the range of views, rather than to reach consensus.
- Explain the importance of respecting diverse opinions and using neutral language, but recognise that if students speak passionately, it is because these subjects are important to them.
- Remind students that stereotypes and certain language/views can cause offence and if things upset them, encourage them to explain to each other rather than making accusations, e.g. 'When you say X, it makes me feel Y' rather than 'You are transphobic/anti-Semitic/ ...'.
- Separate the comment from the person: focus on challenging different viewpoints, not the individuals that espouse them. For example, ask students to interrogate the assumptions underlying a statement or identify evidence or points from the literature to support a particular claim.
- It is your role to ensure that differing perspectives are addressed: don't expect individual students to speak on behalf of a particular group or to educate others. You could pre-prepare information from the literature highlighting different perspectives that you can use to ensure balanced coverage.
- Tell students that you or any individual can call 'time out' if they feel the conversation is out of hand. At that point, ask for 2 minutes silence during which students can reflect and maybe record their thoughts in writing.

Scenario 2

Firstly, reflect on the comments. Can you recall specific instances where these comments were valid? In retrospect, how could you have responded? What options would you have if the same situation arose again? What situations have you found difficult to handle and why? Sometimes this is due to conversations touching on areas that are personally sensitive, or because you find some personalities difficult to handle. It can be useful to discuss and compare your approach with that of colleagues teaching similar material and consider a range of possible strategies, or to observe someone else leading a discussion on a controversial topic.

Another option would be to summarise the feedback, present it to students and ask them how they would like such situations to be handled. They may appreciate you being open about the challenges of teaching and inviting them to share in the management of the conversation.

Developing awareness

In this section, we consider how a greater awareness of our unconscious assumptions and biases can help you and your students. We will draw on the work of Carol Dweck (2006) to discuss how you can encourage a 'growth mindset' in students.

Fundamental to an inclusive approach is developing a greater awareness of yourself and your students and recognising that students do not all experience university in the same way. Activity 9.3 invites you to consider the people with whom you have close contact. (Depending on your subject discipline, it may be useful to do this activity with your students.)

Activity 9.3

Social network inventory

Step 1: Fill out the first column with details about your background. These are broad categories and there may be other aspects of your identity that are important to you: use the blank rows to include these as well (for example, home town, nationality, marital status, political persuasion, parent/non-parent, cancer survivor).

Step 2: Excluding family members, how many people in your close social groups are from a different background than you? Think about your close friends and other people that you socialise with regularly at university, where you live, through your social networks (e.g. hobbies, parent groups, part-time jobs). In the last two columns, draw a tick for every person who is from a similar background and different background to you.

	You	Your social network	
		Similar	Different
Example: Ethnicity	Chinese	✓✓✓✓✓✓	✓✓
Gender			
Age			
Ethnicity			
Sexual orientation			
Religion			
Highest level of education			

```
┌─────────────┐
┤  Reflection ├─────────────────────────────────────────
└─────────────┘
```

Does anything surprise you about your social network? Why does it matter?

Discussion

Social networks can influence our worldviews and the way we interact with others, including students and colleagues. Several recent studies have found that most people are in social networks made up of like-minded people, whereas only a small minority mix with people with a wider range of views. This can sometimes lead to unconscious bias, misunderstanding or a skewed/polarised view of issues. For example, we may see our own group as 'better' (more interesting, informed, intelligent) and other groups less favourably. Limited exposure to other worldviews may also leave 'blind spots' in our knowledge and understanding of certain issues. While it is difficult to 'know what we don't know', it is useful be aware of these blind spots and actively seek out perspectives that are different from our own.

In recent years there has been a heightened awareness of how the unconscious biases of teachers can hinder learning. We all hold implicit beliefs or assumptions that are below our level of consciousness and which, consciously, we may disagree with. These biases affect our behaviour; for example, numerous studies show that male students frequently control classroom conversation and receive more teacher attention, although teachers think they are being even-handed (Sadker et al., 2019). They can also influence the expectations we have of certain groups of students, and low expectations can lead to low performance. For example, girls are stereotypically considered to be less good at mathematics than boys by parents and teachers although tests show otherwise. However, believing that they are less good can be internalised by girls, resulting in poorer performance: a phenomenon known as stereotype threat (Lindberg et al., 2010). Similarly, boys' interest in the arts and language may be subtly undermined.

You can take online tests to reveal some of your own unconscious biases (see the Further Resources section at the end of the chapter), and the results can be unsettling. However, we should not be unduly self-critical as we all have unconscious biases, and becoming aware of them is a positive step. And people from disadvantaged groups are not immune from these biases, as illustrated in Nelson Mandela's account of how he started to panic the first time he boarded a plane and saw a Black pilot (Mandela, 1995). This made him realise how he had been enculturated into the racial biases of South Africa that assumed that such jobs were just for white people.

Students too have perceptions of their own abilities that can limit their motivation to learn. Research by Dweck (2006) has shown that people have differing views as to whether intelligence is innate (which she terms 'a fixed mindset') or the result of effort and effective study habits ('a growth mindset'). Those with a fixed mindset believe that their intelligence cannot be developed and thus tend to be sensitive to failure as it highlights what they see as inherent weaknesses. In contrast, those with a growth mindset understand that failure can aid learning and persist in tasks for much longer. This research has been very influential in schools, and increasingly in universities, with staff being encouraged and trained to help children/students recognise how achievement is improved by effort and feedback.

Reflection

Which of the following do you think would help students to develop a growth mindset?

1   Giving feedback on assignments before students submit the final version.
2   Telling a student that they are really good at essays.
3   Having students work something out and then praising their effort.
4   Suggesting that some students will never understand this concept.
5   Praising how a student has approached a task; for example, paying attention to detail or using effective literature search strategies.
6   Having students reflect and share ideas on how they have overcome challenges in their study.

Discussion

Anything that helps students to understand that learning improves with application and focused practice is helpful – the analogy of the brain being like a muscle can be useful in this regard. Comments implying that success or failure is due to inherent strengths or weaknesses, such as (b) and (d) encourage a fixed mindset. The other examples encourage a growth mindset by helping students to see how they can and have improved.

The Higher Education Funding Council for England (HEFCE) review quoted earlier found that the actions of individual staff can make a difference and impact on students' motivation, engagement, satisfaction, achievement and retention (Mountford-Zimdars et al., 2015). An example is given in Case Study 9.2. The work was carried out during 'office hours' – an hour a week allocated for students to seek individual support. If you hold office hours, bear in mind that if run on a voluntary drop-in basis, students who could benefit most may never attend. It is worth considering rostering students so that they all receive some individual guidance.

Case Study 9.2

Individual support for students: a GTA in War Studies

I prioritise face-to-face feedback with my students, and generally I prefer this type of feedback as it gives the students an opportunity to engage directly with the assessment of their work and it helps me provide feedback that is specific for the individual student's needs (Sambell, 2013). Moreover, it provides me with an opportunity to engage with the students on their individual level and to get a sense of how they are generally adjusting to university life. Thus, I use the face-to-face feedback sessions to gauge how my students are doing, and to assess if there is anything non-academic I can help them with. Seeing feedback as a process, the face-to-face feedback allows students to close the feedback loop and improve their learning strategies (Carless and Boud, 2018), and I have observed how the encouragement from a seminar leader can make a radical change in student participation and attitudes.

Specifically, I had a student who in the beginning of the second term came to me with the frustration of not being able to follow class discussions and the arguments presented by their peers, and with a general inclination that history as a subject 'just wasn't for them'. They wanted general feedback on their performance in the seminar sessions, specific feedback on their previous essay and presentation, as well as help on how to better make sense of history as a subject and discipline. After meeting with this student over several weeks to help them grasp how to use argumentation in history, the student has gone from never participating in seminar discussions to confidently voicing their opinion in continuous weeks tackling several different historical topics. This particular student was therefore able to close the feedback loop, and actively improve their learning strategies by engaging in face-to-face feedback with me.

Over to you

The diversity of students in higher education requires that teaching is designed to be accessible and inclusive to all. Whether you are teaching one to one, in small or large groups, online or face to face, the climate you create can help students from all backgrounds to feel recognised and valued, which has been shown to have a positive impact on learning. Simple things such as learning students' names, offering different ways for them to contribute and explaining your expectations clearly will all help. Avoid making assumptions about students' background and experience or writing some students off as unlikely to succeed. Explain the standards required and show confidence in all students to succeed.

Developing awareness of our own implicit assumptions and biases is an ongoing project no matter what level of experience you have. Remember the power inherent in your position (even if you don't feel powerful) and be aware of the language you use. When planning teaching, aim to apply the principles of universal design: use a variety of different teaching and learning activities to allow different modes of engaging with the material and encourage everyone to participate. Check that your teaching resources reflect the diversity in society, incorporate diverse perspectives on topics and provide guidance on useful resources. Even if you are not always successful, students will appreciate and respond to your efforts.

Further resources

This paper gives a useful discussion of the nuances of terminology around race and ethnicity (despite not being very recent).

Aspinall, P. J. (2002) Collective terminology to describe the minority ethnic population: the persistence of confusion and ambiguity in usage. *Sociology*, 36 (4): 803–16.

This website provides guidelines on interpreting and using the principles of universal design for learning.

CAST (2018) *Universal Design for Learning Guidelines Version 2.2*. https:// udlguidelines.cast. org

A summary of research around fixed and growth mindsets. See also Dweck's TED talk: 'The Power of Yet'.

Dweck, C. S. (2006) *Mindset: The New Psychology of Success*. New York: Random House.

A teacher describes how she learned to recognise and address some of her hidden biases.

Fiarman, Sarah E. (2016) Unconscious bias: when good intentions aren't enough. *Educational Leadership*, 74 (3): 10–15. www.responsiveclassroom.org/wp-content/ uploads/2017/10/Unconscious-Bias_Ed-Leadership.pdf

Here you can explore your own implicit biases (relating to race, gender, sexuality, etc.) by taking Implicit Association Tests, developed and explained by Mahzarin R. Banaji and Anthony G. Greenwald in *Blindspot: Hidden Biases of Good People* (Delacorte Press, 2013).

Project Implicit. https://implicit.harvard.edu/implicit/education.html

A website established by students to provide diverse reading material that can be used to broaden mainstream curricula.

Project Myopia. https://projectmyopia.com

References

Advance HE (2020) *Equality + Higher Education: Students Statistical Report*. York: Advance HE.

Carless, D. and Boud, D. (2018) The development of student feedback literacy: enabling uptake of feedback. *Assessment & Evaluation in Higher Education*, 43 (8): 1315–25.

Darder, A. (2012) *Culture and Power in the Classroom*. New York: Routledge.

DeSurra, C. and Church, K. A. (1994) Unlocking the classroom closet: privileging the marginalized voices of gay/lesbian college students. Paper presented at the Annual Meeting of the Speech Communication Association. https://files.eric.ed.gov/fulltext/ ED379697.pdf

Dweck, C. S. (2006) *Mindset: The New Psychology of Success*. New York: Random House.

Gordon, D., Meyer, A. and Rose, D. H. (2016) *Universal Design for Learning: Theory and Practice*. Boston: CAST Professional Publishing.

Hockings, C. (2010) Inclusive learning and teaching in higher education: a synthesis of research. EvidenceNet. Available at https://www.advance-he.ac.uk/knowledge-hub/ inclusive-learning-and-teaching-higher-education-synthesis-research

Lindberg, S. M., Hyde, J. S., Petersen, J. L. and Linn, M. C. (2010) New trends in gender and mathematics performance: a meta-analysis. *Psychological Bulletin, 136* (6): 1123–35.

Mandela, N. (1995) *Long Walk to Freedom.* London: Abacus. pp. 347–8.

Mountford-Zimdars, A., Duna S., Moore, J., Sanders J., Jones S. and Higham, L. (2015) *Causes of Differences in Student Outcomes.* London: HEFCE.

Sadker, D., Zittleman, K. and Koch, M. (2019) Gender bias: past, present, and future. In J. Banks and C. Mcgee Banks (eds), *Multicultural Education: Issues and Perspectives,* 10th edn. Hoboken, NJ: John Wiley & Sons.

Sambell, K., McDowell, L. and Montgomery, C. (2013) *Assessment for Learning in Higher Education.* Abingdon: Routledge.

Social Mobility Commission (2019) State of the Nation 2018–19: Social Mobility in Great Britain.

Thomas, L. (2012) Building student engagement and belonging in Higher Education at a time of change: final report from the What Works? Student Retention & Success programme. Paul Hamlyn Foundation. www.heacademy.ac.uk/system/files/what_works_final_report_0.pdf

Woods, C. (2007) Researching and developing interdisciplinary teaching: towards a conceptual framework for classroom communication. *Higher Education, 54* (6): 853–66.

10
ASSESSING AND GIVING FEEDBACK

Learning outcomes

After reading this chapter you should be able to:

- Help students understand how they will be assessed and provide activities that will help them to succeed
- Ensure that your marking is fair and consistent
- Engage in discussions about student work and give helpful feedback.

Introduction

The word *assessment* is often thought to be synonymous with final examinations or other assessments that determine whether students pass or fail, and the grade or mark they achieve. In the educational literature, however, assessment is used in a much broader way to include any activities that help staff to understand the abilities and performance of their students. Below we discuss different types and stages of assessment -- you may or may not be involved in formal, summative assessments but keeping track of your students' development is important for all teachers.

Types/stages of assessment

Assessments may be conducted formally or informally, for various purposes and at different stages of a programme.

Initial assessment (sometimes called *baseline* or *diagnostic assessment*) involves exploring students' existing knowledge and competence in order to plan teaching at the right level. This might be done before teaching starts, for example using a pre-course online quiz, or during sessions, for example by observing students undertaking a task. There is more on this in Chapter 3 and Case Study 3.1.

Formative assessment is the process of gaining information about students' progress during a course; for example, using an online forum to engage students in discussing course themes, having small group exercises in class with feedback to the whole group or reviewing pre-prepared practice exam questions. Formative assessment should be *in*formative in terms of helping you and the students to understand the quality of their work, allowing students to direct future studying and teachers to pitch their teaching accordingly. For this reason, it is also called 'assessment *for* learning'.

Summative assessment is any assignment that counts towards the final marks or grade for a course or programme. It is about formally recognising what has been achieved at a certain stage and may be used to certify performance (e.g. to qualify as a health professional, architect or lawyer) or to allow progression (e.g. to the next year of a programme). Also called 'assessment *of* learning', it can have important consequences and thus is sometimes referred to as 'high stakes assessment'.

It is important to note that these stages of assessment are not always discrete, for example, a mid-course presentation worth 10% of the total is a summative assessment because it contributes to the final result. However, it is hoped that students would use the feedback to improve future presentations; hence it also has a formative element.

Why do the distinctions matter? They are important because the purpose of an assessment affects the way that students approach the activities.

┌─────────────────┐
│ — **Reflection** — │
└─────────────────┘

Imagine that you are a PhD student doing a traditional research project, and that new rules require you to be graded for your performance at every supervision meeting. Or that you are a member of professional services staff that are now graded at regular appraisal/performance reviews. How would this affect your preparation for and experience of the meetings? How might it affect your subsequent work and your relationship with your supervisor or manager?

Discussion

There may be individual differences here; for example, some PhD students might feel that they would be more motivated to prepare for the meeting, and others that they would feel inhibited from raising problems or dilemmas with their supervisor. Professional services staff might become more or less motivated following their appraisal, depending on how they were rated and their individual response to the rating. Most people would probably experience higher levels of stress, which we know, from neurological studies of the brain, can raise the level of stress hormones in the body and inhibit learning. Your relationship with your supervisor or manager would inevitably be affected as the power differential would be increased and their role would become both assessor and guide – which can be an uneasy balance to strike and may create role conflict for them.

There is an ongoing debate about whether assessments can be both formative and summative. Whilst we hope that students will learn from feedback on any piece of work, we do know that if an assignment counts towards the final grade, most students will approach it as summative, however small the percentage. They will aim to present their best work and hide any areas of confusion or inability.

As an analogy, imagine you are a violinist who is strong on interpreting the music but weaker on technical ability. When you go for lessons, you spend much of the time focusing on improving the technical aspects. However, when you play in a concert or competition that can affect your career, you try to choose pieces that showcase your musicality. If you were constantly playing in competitions without opportunities for tuition, you may never improve your technique.

This has implications for course design: too many summative assessments can produce a relentless pressure to perform, leaving little room for learning to take place. A focus on formative assessment (i.e. lots of low stakes practice and feedback) throughout a course, with rigorous but sparing summative assessment, is considered best practice (Sambell et al., 2013). Course design is outside the scope of this book, but there are references at the end of the chapter if you would like to explore this further.

Thus, students need opportunities to make mistakes and learn from them, try out new ideas, admit misunderstandings, discuss difficulties and receive feedback on work without fear of being penalised. The kind of teaching and learning activities discussed in Chapter 4 facilitate this and provide ongoing feedback for tutors. Case Study 10.1 gives an example of a routine classroom activity that provides skills practice and learning from peers and the tutor in a supportive environment. It doubles as a formative assessment as the tutor is able to assess the students' level and provide feedback. Other formative assessments may be more formal, such as submitted assignments, class presentations or mock exams.

Case Study 10.1

Providing feedback to small groups: Federico Castagna, GTA in Informatics

This is the most common kind of feedback during the small group tutorial sessions. Usually, I invite one student at the board to attempt solving an exercise, while the rest of the class (or a good amount of it) supports and interacts with him/her. Often, the resolution of an exercise becomes a common effort where the students exchange comments or ideas. In this context, if the group endeavour results in a mistaken solution, the provided feedback has to be tailored to all the participants. As such, my remarks are general and aimed at helping them spot the errors by themselves through examples or a quick review of the theoretical notions involved. Indeed, generic feedback can sometimes 'work much better than slow and perfect feedback as it has to be fast enough that students are still interested' (Gibbs, 2015). Once the corrections are made, I normally recap the mistake and, where possible, describe some trick that will help to avoid it in the future. I have observed that this approach usually entails an effective enhancement of the class collective engagement.

The summative assessments on any course to which you contribute will already have been set, but you may be able to increase the amount of initial and formative assessment, with positive consequences for learning. Activity 10.1 helps you to consider how you might develop your practice in these areas.

Activity 10.1

Developing your own assessment practice

Think about a course to which you contribute and note (a) what you already do and (b) what else you might do in these areas.

	Initial assessment	Formative assessment
Already do		
Could introduce		

We will now look at good practice in marking and feedback. We will discuss general principles and consider how to respond to various challenging situations.

Marking

A wide variety of assessments are used within higher education, which may be either individual or, less frequently, group assessments. Depending on your discipline, these may involve:

- essays, reports or other written documents
- exams (of various kinds – written, vivas, practicals)
- observations of performance, e.g. practical procedures, dramatic or sports performances
- products, e.g. posters, designs, video recordings, websites, artistic creations, portfolios
- oral presentations.

Whichever type of assessment you are marking, some core principles can be applied to ensure fairness and consistency. Without procedures in place, different teachers can give wildly differing marks for the same piece of work. To illustrate this, try Activity 10.2.

Activity 10.2

Marking exercise

Look at the sum below and give it a mark out of 10.

$$\begin{array}{r} 45 \\ \times\ 23 \\ \hline 135 \\ 800 \\ \hline 935 \end{array}$$

Discussion

This task has been given to many groups of people on teaching courses, and the results are invariably widely spread (Figure 10.1 shows an example of the distribution of marks in one group). Similar exercises in which groups have been asked to mark a painting or a doctor–patient consultation have shown similar divergence.

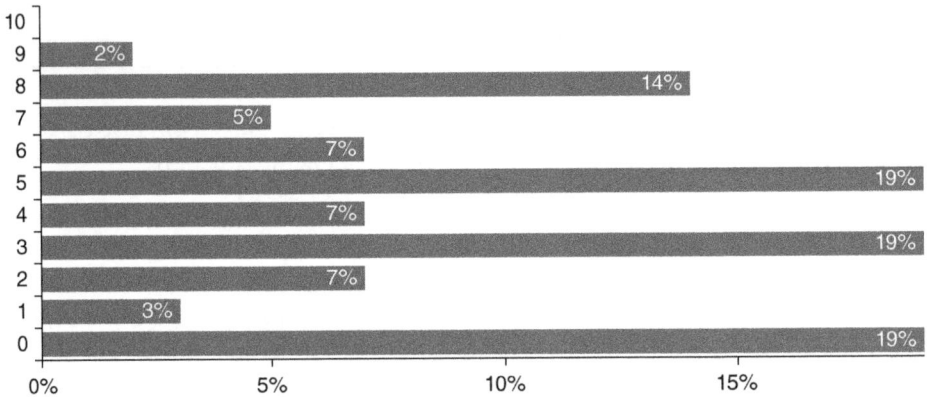

Figure 10.1 Marks out of 10 given to the sum in Activity 10.2 by a group of GTAs

How can marks vary so greatly? When we mark, we are making decisions, often unconsciously, about what we value – and our values differ. So, in the example above, some people give a high mark because the correct process was used to do the sum, even though a small error had been made. Others take the view that the answer was wrong and therefore had to score 0. And many people balance the two views in differing proportions. When deciding on your score, you were not given any information about the context: to mark fairly we need to know what criteria should be used, and this should have been decided by the course team based on the level and discipline of the students, the purpose of the assessment and so on. For example, if it was a pharmacy student, a correct answer could be essential, whereas for a child learning to do long multiplication, using the correct process may be more important. If you were frustrated by not knowing this when marking the sum, then you clearly understand the importance of context.

It is clearly unfair on students if their mark depends too greatly on who has been allocated to mark the work, so universities have processes in place to ensure that consistent standards are applied.

Marking fairly and consistently

If you are marking questions for which there are clear right and wrong answers, then it should be fairly straightforward and in some cases could be done electronically. If the work is more nuanced, then you will need to use your judgement to determine an appropriate mark.

To promote consistency, marking criteria should be available for all assignments: these represent the qualities that teachers have decided are important. They provide a common framework for marking and allow students to see how their work will be evaluated. They might be at a fairly broad level; for example, criteria for any written assignment could include:

- depth of knowledge and understanding
- clarity of argument
- use of relevant literature
- critical evaluation
- structure and organisation
- referencing.

Or they may provide descriptions of different grades, with the marker aiming to find the best fit for the submitted work; for example:

First: An excellent essay showing extensive reading and critical analysis. A clear and well-substantiated argument and engagement with current debates. Excellent expression, style, structure and referencing.

2.1: A competent essay, showing wide reading and understanding of key debates. A clear argument. Well written with appropriate vocabulary, style and structure. References appropriately used and cited.

2.2: A satisfactory essay showing some evidence of reading and understanding. May be more descriptive than analytical. Addresses the question but may lack a clear structure or argument.

Or there may be percentages attached to different elements; for example, assessing an oral presentation according to the following criteria:

- Knowledge and understanding: clear grasp of key concepts, critical thinking, ability to answer questions (60%).
- Presentation skills: audibility, clarity, pace and body language (20%).
- Structure and resources: organisation of material, use of audio visual material (20%).

Such criteria appear to make everything explicit, but in fact there can still be a divergence in the marks due to different interpretations of the criteria between teachers. So, it is a good idea to familiarise yourself with the marking criteria and then check your understanding with the module/programme leader. For example, you could:

- Check the module leader's priorities for the assignment.
- Ask to see good assignments from previous years – it is often easier to understand what constitutes a good assignment from exemplars.

- Ask to see examples of previously marked assignments.
- Clarify the amount and type of feedback that is expected; for example, do you annotate the essay, give comments at the end, or both?
- Ask the module leader to check your marking after the first 2–3 assignments so that any required changes can be identified early on.

New staff often worry about being objective, but perhaps a more useful concern is how to hone your academic judgement. Remember that you are in an assessment role due to your subject expertise which will enable you to make that judgement. In addition, your marking should take place within a framework that promotes fairness through consistency: you should receive local guidance on this. For some general principles, Biggs and Tang (2011: 232–3) recommend the following (with explanatory comments in brackets added by the authors):

- Assessment should be 'blind' – the identity of the student concealed. All second marking should be blind to the first marking. [This is good practice in summative assessments in order to prevent unconscious bias – however, for formative assessments it may not be required. Also, blind or anonymous marking is not always as anonymous as it seems – if you have taught the group, particularly if numbers are small, you can often pick up cues as to whose assignment you are marking.]
- Each question should be assessed across students [i.e. mark all students' answers to the first question before marking all answers to the second question, and so on].
- Between questions, the order of students should be shuffled. [This and the above point are to prevent one answer biasing you when you mark the next one as people tend to mark subsequent answers higher if they've just marked a poor answer or lower if the previous one was good.]
- Recheck borderline cases [it is often useful to ask a colleague or your module leader to double mark these].

Universities should also employ standardisation and moderation procedures designed to make marking more consistent.

Standardisation takes place before you start marking. Typically it involves all the markers on a course assessing a small sample of assignments (which may be from previous years). They then compare and discuss their marks and the judgements they made in an attempt to come to an agreed standard. Hopefully, whoever has set the assignment might organise this for you, or you could request it.

Moderation takes place after the marking has been completed (see Case Study 10.2 for an example). A sample of assignments will be double marked to check that markers are working to similar standards. In some cases, individual markers may be given statistical analyses of their range of marks compared to those of other markers to see if they are broadly comparable; however, this can be misleading unless large numbers are involved, as individual groups' performance may differ.

— Case Study 10.2 —

Assessment moderation: Eleanor Larsson, GTA in History

I attend bi-termly marking moderation meetings with my fellow GTAs and the module convenor. These meetings have helped me to be consistent in my own marking but also calibrate that with my colleagues. I have also been encouraged to reflect on my own practice and, based on our discussions, I have altered my feedback style and now offer more directed and less comprehensive feedback after it was suggested to me that my former method might have been overwhelming for students. I now structure my feedback around three central points – highlighting something they have done well, an aspect that could be improved and how that feedback could be applied to the next assignment (Winstone et al., 2016); for example, by improving the structure or reducing the dependency on secondary literature. I also annotate students work to highlight typical examples and how they correlate to my comments. I think it helps for students to see specific examples of what we mean, but do so sparingly so as to not overwhelm or discourage them.

Common concerns and challenges

Some typical concerns of staff new to marking are given in Activity 10.3.

— Activity 10.3 —

Marking challenges

Consider how you might respond to these common scenarios.

Scenario 1: You have just had your first set of assignments to mark on a module that you haven't taught previously. Despite getting advice from your module leader, you are finding it incredibly time consuming and quite monotonous. You have gone way over the hours for which you are paid, which is impacting on your work and life.

Scenario 2: You have recently marked an in-course presentation worth 15% of the course. When you arrive in class, several students come to see you to complain about their marks. One actually got an A but still thought it wasn't high enough. Another complained that you had failed her (even though she had clearly not met the marking criteria). Another said that he had put in a huge amount of time and effort which wasn't reflected in his mark.

Scenario 3: You are marking an essay containing many small grammatical errors and some unusual phrasing. Apart from that, the essay is quite strong. You are unclear how much to take the standard of English into account as you admire students who can write academic essays in a foreign language.

Discussion

Scenario 1

It is time consuming to mark fairly and consistently and provide helpful feedback. As with any new task, there is a learning curve, so first-time marking tends to take longer as you familiarise yourself with the nature of the assignment and the marking criteria. There are no easy answers and individuals vary in what they find effective, but the following points may be worth considering:

- Aim to mark in small bursts – a few assignments at a time. This can help to maintain energy and focus.
- It can be useful to scan a few assignments before starting to mark to get an idea of the overall standard.
- When marking electronically, take time to invest in learning about features that can help; e.g. ways of storing typical comments that can be copied and adapted to the individual, or giving audio feedback, which is often quicker to provide.
- Focus on key points: what are the key strengths of the assignment? What are the main points for the student to take forward? If there are many areas for correction, you could just comment on the most important ones. This saves time and can prevent the student from becoming overwhelmed or demoralised.
- Recognise that some assignments will take much longer to mark than others. Good assignments often take less time than those that are poorly written or contain multiple misunderstanding. If you are really stuck on one, put it aside and return to it later, or ask your module leader to double mark it.
- Some people like to set a timer as a guide to how much time they should be spending; others find that this adds to their stress. Try to find a system that works for you.
- Remember that marking is not an exact science. It is rarely possible to discriminate to a single percentage point, so don't spend ages trying to decide between a 66% or 67%.
- You may want to consider how marking will fit into your overall schedule and limit the amount you take on.

Scenario 2

Assessment is very important to students and there can be a lot of emotion attached to the results. We can probably all remember the disappointment of receiving a poor mark, especially if unexpected. When this happens, students' immediate reaction may be to challenge you rather than looking at where they went wrong. This can be stressful for the marker. The following strategies may be helpful:

- If possible, leave a gap between students receiving their marks and seeing you so that they have time to come to terms with the results and process the feedback. Release the results some days before you see the students, or advise them that you will take queries next week when they have had a chance to review the feedback. By this time, you should have a more useful discussion.

- Acknowledge students' feelings; for example, tell them that you are sorry that they are disappointed/upset/angry about their mark. Convey to them that you would like to help them understand the reasons so that they can do better next time. Show confidence that they can improve in future assignments.
- Ask students what they understood from the feedback. This will help you to judge if they have read and understood it. If not, go through it with them.
- If someone has done particularly poorly, it may be best to give them the mark in person and make arrangements to meet them to discuss the work.
- If students still want to challenge the mark, refer them to the appropriate appeals procedure (this should be written down somewhere). Students usually have a right to appeal and it does not reflect on you as a marker. Sometimes the process may require you to re-mark the assignment. If so, do not feel obliged to raise the mark. Take a fresh view and mark it again: if you feel you have given the right mark, stick with your decision. If, on reflection, you feel that you undermarked, you can make an adjustment.

Scenario 3

Disciplines and course teams vary in the importance they place on well-written English and this should reflect the learning outcomes of the course. In some disciplines, expressing yourself clearly, using correct grammar, punctuation and vocabulary is vital, whereas in others it is secondary to the correct knowledge or argument. Check whether there is guidance in the marking criteria and, if not, seek advice from your module leader.

Feedback

In this section, we will discuss principles of effective feedback and the concept of student feedback literacy. We will consider how to make feedback part of a wider process in which students give and receive feedback and use it effectively. Before that, we will briefly review the main modes of giving feedback.

Feedback methods

There are various ways in which feedback can be given and you will need to check expectations on your module. If you use formative assessments, you may have more choice over the feedback process. The most common methods are:

Written feedback: this usually includes in-text comments as you go through the assignment and a summary at the end. Check how much of each is expected – students value consistency across markers.

Audio-feedback: most electronic marking systems provide this option, or you can record an audio file. This can be done for individuals or for generic feedback to a whole class/cohort. Students' evaluations of audio-feedback are generally positive as it feels more personal. From the teacher's perspective it is often quicker to give and allows you to say more than you would write. Disadvantages can include technical issues in providing or accessing the feedback.

Face-to-face feedback: this allows discussion so that you can check students' understanding of the feedback and clarify points. It can be particularly useful for students who have performed poorly. If you have office hours, it is often worthwhile scheduling all students to see you individually to discuss their work, particularly after their first assignment.

Automatic feedback: online quizzes can allow students to access bespoke feedback in an anonymous way, which can reduce anxiety. Whilst time consuming to set up, they can save a huge amount of time later. They are limited to questions that can be written with pre-determined answers (such as multiple choice questions) but well-written questions can test application of knowledge, conceptual understanding and data analysis as well as factual information.

Cohort feedback: this is generic feedback to the whole group and can be particularly useful for formative assessments. The common strengths and weaknesses of an assignment can usually be picked up fairly quickly by the marker without having to read every assignment. This makes it quicker to provide general guidance, which can be useful albeit less personalised. In some disciplines, this can be provided in the form of a commentary on what would have made a good assignment; for example, specific legal arguments that should have been referenced or source material that should have been cited. In other disciplines, a video/screencast can be provided showing how the assignment should have been completed (e.g. demonstrating coding or a mathematical proof) that allows students to check their own work against a model.

Principles of feedback

Before we discuss principles of effective feedback, take a couple of minutes to reflect on your own experience.

Reflection

Think about your experience of receiving feedback. Can you remember any feedback that was particularly effective or ineffective? What made it so? How much time did you spend reading feedback? How much did you use it to inform your future assignments?

Discussion

People can often remember examples of feedback from as far back as their childhood, usually due to the high level of emotion associated with it. Feedback can have a long lasting impact – positive or negative – and history is littered with examples of famous people who were told they would never amount to anything. Because feedback is interpreted differently by each individual, it is unlikely that it will always be effective, but we do know a lot about what students do and don't find helpful that can inform us.

Meta-analyses of research have shown feedback to be one of the most important factors contributing to learning (see, e.g., Hattie, 2009). Despite this, it is not always well used and sometimes not even read by students.

Problems with feedback identified by students are that it is often:

- *too late*: marking is time consuming, and there are formal processes that have to be implemented (such as moderation), which mean that by the time students receive it, they have moved on to a different assignment and their interest in the last one has waned
- *overly negative*, which can be demoralising and, for some, can reinforce the feeling that they don't belong at university or won't succeed
- *too generalised*, so that students aren't clear how to improve
- *hard to understand*, for example using terms that students don't fully comprehend such as 'critical analysis' or 'academic' – whilst these terms seem self-evident to academics, students often don't understand how to enact them
- *too focused on the current assignment* rather than on points to improve the next one.

Problems from the teachers' perspective include:

- an insatiable desire from students for ever more feedback
- pressure to provide individual written feedback to increasing numbers of students and the time this takes
- lack of engagement with feedback: for example, students not reading or acting on the feedback.

Another issue is that where marks and feedback are given simultaneously, students will tend to focus on the mark and may ignore the feedback. Feedback given without marks is the most effective in terms of stimulating student thinking so, if you can, build this into formative assessments.

Taking account of these issues, it is effective to:

- provide feedback promptly while it is still relevant
- be constructive and encouraging in tone
- be specific: explain and give examples of how specific aspects of the work do or don't meet the marking criteria
- feedforward: provide constructive suggestions to be taken forward in the next assignment rather than concentrating solely on the current one
- be concise: summarise the most important messages unless there is a good reason to correct every small point.

Bear in mind that your overall goal is to help students understand the standards they need to achieve and how they can improve.

These principles represent current thinking on good practice in the British context. However, there are cultural differences in how feedback is given and received, and in some countries there is a tendency for more direct communication about faults and deficiencies. Colleagues from these countries are sometimes concerned that, without this, students may not recognise problematic aspects of their work. If you know the student to whom you are providing feedback, you may be able to personalise your feedback.

Activity 10.4 is designed to help you evaluate feedback in relation to the principles outlined above.

Activity 10.4

Evaluating feedback

Look at the examples of feedback below, taken from in-text or final comments, and consider how helpful you might find them. As they are out of context, you can only judge on the basis of their clarity and helpfulness, rather than their appropriateness to the assignment. Then read the comments beneath each.

1 'You provide a good discussion of the social causes of anorexia, particularly around the influence of the media and social media. You needed to address all areas of the biopsychosocial model and include more about biological factors (e.g. genetics) and psychological factors (e.g. aspects of personality).'

Comment: This identifies a strong point of the essay although it is not specific on why it was good. It provides guidance on other topics that should have been included, giving specific examples that should help the student understand what has been missed.

2 'Try to summarise Fuller's argument in your own words rather than using extensive quotes. This would show your own understanding better. What do you think are the strengths and weaknesses of her argument? Do you agree with her?'

Comment: This gives a suggestion and explains the rationale. The questions should be useful to prompt further thinking, particularly if the student recognises that these principles of summarising and then critiquing the author's argument will apply to future essays.

3 'You haven't shown your working.'

Comment: This highlights an omission. It could be rephrased as 'Remember always to show your working' or 'I can't see your working and therefore can't credit you for this'. Which would you find most informative?

4 'You need to improve your structure.'

Comment: This is a feedforward point but is too vague to be helpful to most students. It would be better to identify specific problems with the structure or to give guidance on how it could be improved, e.g. 'You should divide your presentation into three parts and outline your structure in the introduction.'

5   'There is some good content, but it needs a more philosophical essay style. You wrote "Descartes felt …": why should we take Descartes' "feelings" seriously? You should rewrite so that you are extracting an argument from Descartes, instead of just reporting what he says. For example: "Descartes argued that he was distinct from his body."'

Comment: This is very specific, with the marker clarifying disciplinary expectations regarding essay style. It includes a principle with a specific example to illustrate it which should help the student with future work.

6   'This is a poor essay, which according to the marking criteria implies "unsystematic, incomplete and/or inaccurate work", with "some knowledge but limited understanding". "Work contains inaccuracies and meaning is unclear." It also uses "limited and/or inappropriate literature".'

Comment: This is a summary comment, which would be supported by annotations within the text giving more detailed feedback. It can be useful to apply phrases from the marking criteria, as shown here, to help students understand how their assignment meets or does not meet them.

In the following section, we will look at ways to help ensure that feedback is understood and acted upon.

Developing students' feedback literacy

Many hours have been spent training academics how to give effective feedback, based on the simple model below. The student submits work (or conducts an observed task) and the teacher provides feedback, with an assumption that the student will learn from it and develop accordingly.

Figure 10.2   A traditional model of feedback

In fact, the picture is more complex than this and more attention is needed to help students benefit from the feedback that academics spend so much time producing.

Carless and Boud (2018) highlight the importance of student feedback literacy which they describe as 'the understandings, capacities and dispositions needed to make sense of information and use it to enhance work or learning strategies'.

So, how can you help students to understand their feedback and use it to inform not only future work, but also how they go about learning? Nicol and McFarlane-Dick (2006) reviewed research on formative assessment and identified seven principles of good practice, which help to develop students' understanding of how they learn (metacognition) and their ability to regulate their own learning. These principles are that the process of assessment:

1 helps clarify what good performance is (goals, criteria, expected standards)
2 facilitates the development of self-assessment (reflection) in learning
3 delivers high-quality information to students about their learning
4 encourages teacher and peer dialogue around learning
5 encourages positive motivational beliefs and self-esteem
6 provides opportunities to close the gap between current and desired performance
7 provides information to teachers that can be used to help shape the teaching.

The principles highlight the importance of students being actively engaged in learning what good performance looks like in their discipline rather than just being the passive recipient of feedback.

Putting these ideas into practice suggests a broader range of activities through which students are prepared for assessments and engage in feedback discussions with colleagues and teachers. So the simple model of teacher to student feedback can be expanded to give a richer context for learning, as illustrated in Figure 10.3 and elaborated below. Some of these activities may already be built into the course(s) on which you teach and you may be able to incorporate others yourself.

Helping students to understand the assignment

Students will often ask about assignments early on and you can help them to understand the requirements. They may take time to understand the expectations of the discipline and the university. Check who is responsible for explaining each assignment to students and try to be present, if possible, so that you can give a consistent message.

Sometimes people worry that it is somehow cheating to tell students what is expected from them; however, remember that students come from very varied backgrounds. As an analogy, imagine you were to organise a game of cricket for your students. Would you expect everyone to know the rules already? Probably not – you would recognise that some students come from countries where cricket is not played, or from schools where it is not taught, not to mention that there are different forms of the game with different rules. However, we tend to assume that because all students have been assessed, they

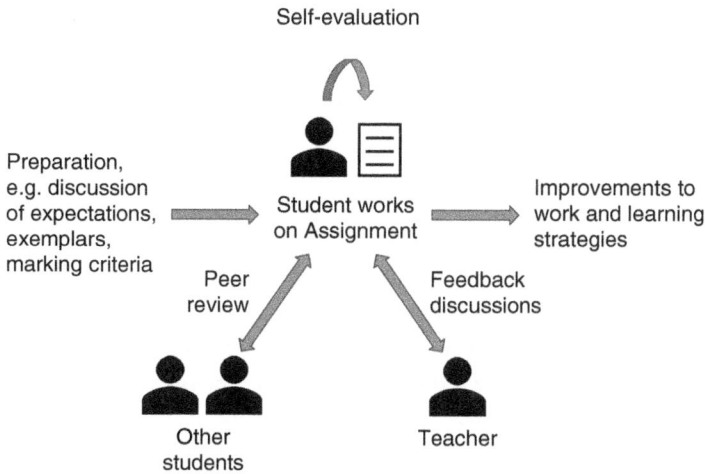

Figure 10.3 A rich context for learning

understand how it works. In fact, they may have dissimilar experiences and expectations; for example, international students' home countries may have different traditions, such as a predominance of oral rather than written assessments or different conventions in essay writing. Home students who sat exams under different exam boards may also have differing expectations. Carless (2006: 24) explains how developing dialogues about assessment 'can help students to clarify "the rules of the game", the assumptions known to lecturers but less transparent to students'.

Explaining what is expected does not, of course, involve giving the answers, but could involve discussing the purpose and format of the assignment. Is the purpose of the assignment, for example, for students to:

- Recall and organise facts?
- Make an argument?
- Critique different authors' perspectives?
- Analyse something, such as a case study, data, text or a visual or musical piece?
- Plan or execute something – a research project, translation, computer program, design, performance or exhibition?
- Reflect on something, such as a work experience, personal performance or group project?

In terms of the format, are there expectations in terms of structure, referencing or other aspects? Ensure that students are clear about what is required and in what areas they have discretion. This is also an opportunity to discuss the concept of academic integrity, helping students to understand why it is important and what they can and can't do to stay within the rules.

Helping students to understand the marking criteria

You can help students understand what constitutes good performance in your discipline by having them actively engage with the marking criteria. Aim to *show rather than tell*, for example by:

- Asking students to mark a couple of past assignments using the marking criteria. (Remember to seek permission from the essay writers and anonymise the essays, and avoid showing ones with exactly the same title that students will be submitting). Include examples of different standards and ask students to identify what makes them strong or weak. It can be useful to do this in small groups so that they can start to articulate and explain the judgements they are making. Then review and discuss their answers as a whole class.
- Doing similar exercises with extracts showing strong and weak examples of referencing, or structure, or argument.
- Asking students to translate the marking criteria into their own language, or get them to design criteria themselves and then compare them with the real criteria. A process to achieve this is described by Race (2007: 27–94).

Encouraging peer review

Encourage and facilitate students to review each other's work and provide comments. This has been shown to be highly informative, with students learning as much (if not more) from seeing how others have tackled the same assignment as from the comments they receive. This can be implemented informally in small classes or for large classes, electronically via the virtual learning environment. It needs careful preparation so that students understand why they are doing it and have an opportunity to review what they have learnt from the process.

Encouraging students to self-review

You could ask students to pre-mark their own work using the marking criteria and submit with their assignment. Alternatively you could provide an interactive cover sheet (see Figure 10.4 for an example): these can take various forms but are essentially a means to prompt students to review their work before submitting and consider what they would like feedback on.

Assignment 1: Interactive Cover Sheet
Interactive cover sheets aim to enhance the dialogue between learners and tutors, support learners to become more active contributors to the feedback process and enable tutors to target their feedback. This cover sheet encourages you to reflect upon your work and identify the feedback that you would like to receive.
Participant name: *Frank Elboni*
Module title: *An Introduction to Theology and Religious Studies*
Assignment title: Discuss the insights which theology and ethics bring to contemporary global issues.
Due date: 10-6-21   Word count: 1,000 words

Self-assessment: What do you think are the strengths of your assignment, and what did you find difficult? What could have been improved?)
I think the assignment has a clear structure and key arguments. I think I have used the relevant literature. The part I found most difficult was choosing which current issues to discuss. I'm not sure if I should have discussed more issues.
Aspects of my assignment on which I would like to receive feedback:
I would like feedback on the general flow of the piece and if my argument is well defined. Also, was there any other literature I should have used? Any general feedback is welcome.
Any other comments?
I enjoyed most of it but wish I'd had more time to develop my ideas.

Figure 10.4 Sample interactive cover sheet

Case Study 10.3 gives an example from an AFHEA application of how some of these strategies can be used.

Case Study 10.3

In-class feedback: Shuang Wu, GTA in History

Often times students do not understand what is involved in a research-based essay. This can easily be circumvented by dedicating time in class to discuss and provide students with good essay examples. The most beneficial activity is through incorporating informal assessment and feedback into normal class activities, and this is where self- and peer-assessment can be valuable. Oral presentations are an effective way to help facilitate this. Like essays, formal presentations are structured, and highlight key concepts and references on historical topics. This assignment trains critical research skills, like articulating an argument about a question, finding evidence to support a position and accounting for possible objections. The Q&A section following group presentation(s) is structured as follows: students who are not presenting will have to think of (i) a compliment; (ii) a question; or (iii) a suggestion for improvement. Students will come up with a compliment, a question or a suggestion for improvement from the module presentation guidelines/rubric. Peer-assessment promotes deep-learning and self-evaluation (Brown et al., 1994). This is because in order to properly assess the work of their peers, students need to have a good understanding of the assessment criteria and the assignment task, both of which promote a deeper approach to learning (Hughes, 1995). Furthermore, informal feedback from peers will help shift the focus of assessment and feedback from being completely teacher-centred to being student- and teacher-centred (Bloxham and Campbell, 2010) Student-centred learning can help improve students' communication and collaboration skills, as well as allow students the ability to think and work independently (Assodeh et al., 2012).

Over to you

This chapter has highlighted a range of purposes for which assessment is used. Establishing your students' prior learning and keeping track of their progress are vital threads underpinning your teaching, and you can use a variety of teaching and assessment processes to achieve this. This initial assessment establishes a baseline and ongoing formative assessment provides feedback to you and the students with the aim of improving teaching and learning. Summative assessment grades achievement and before teaching on a course you need to understand and be able to explain the purpose and format of each assessment to students. In a well-structured course, students do not have to wait until the end to find out how they are doing, but have multiple opportunities for informal feedback throughout. Remember that giving feedback is just one part of a wider endeavour to help students understand disciplinary expectations which may encompass engagement with marking criteria and peer and self-assessment. A rich environment for feedback encourages students to be actively involved in interpreting and applying marking criteria, reviewing their own work and that of other students, as well as interpreting and taking action following teacher feedback to improve future work and learning strategies.

It is likely that you will have plenty of opportunity to practise your marking and feedback skills and we have discussed various processes that will help you to mark fairly and consistently. Providing opportunities for students to seek clarification of your feedback is helpful as this will shed light on their interpretation of your comments and help you to learn what is effective. It can also be informative to review examples of other colleagues' feedback and learn from differing approaches.

Further resources

A concise summary of the evidence about feedback in higher education and guidance on how to make it effective (part of a suite of resources from the TESTA project: Transforming the Experience of Students through Assessment).

Feedback Guide for Lecturers. http://testa.ac.uk/index.php/resources/best-practice-guides

This outlines a framework to understand the concept of student feedback literacy, with practical examples of how it can be applied using exemplars and peer feedback.

Carless, D. and Boud, D. (2018) The development of student feedback literacy: enabling uptake of feedback. *Assessment & Evaluation in Higher Education*, 43: 8.

If you are interested in assessment design, the following are useful:

These are further succinct, evidence-based guides from the TESTA project.

'Principles of assessment' and 'Revised assessment patterns that work'. http://testa.ac.uk/index.php/resources/best-practice-guides

References

Assodeh, M. H., Assodeh, M. B.and Zarepour, M. (2012) The impact of student-centred learning on academic achievement on social skills. *Procedia – Social and Behavioural Sciences*, 46: 560–4.

Biggs, J. and Tang, C. (2011) *Teaching for Quality Learning at University*. Maidenhead: McGraw-Hill Education.

Bloxham, S. and Campbell, L. (2010) Generating dialogue in assessment feedback: exploring the use of interactive cover sheets. *Assessment and Evaluation in Higher Education*, 35 (3): 291–300.

Brown, S., Rust, C. and Gibbs, G. (1994) *Strategies for Diversifying Assessments in Higher Education*. Oxford Centre for Staff Development, Oxford: Oxonian Rewley Press.

Carless, D. and Boud, D. (2018) The development of student feedback literacy: enabling uptake of feedback. *Assessment & Evaluation in Higher Education*, 43 (8): 1315–25.

Carless, D. (2006) Differing perceptions in the feedback process. *Studies in Higher Education*, 31 (2): 219–33.

Gibbs, G. (2015) *53 Powerful Ideas All Teachers Should Know About*. London: SEDA. https://www.seda.ac.uk/53-powerful-ideas/

Hattie, J. (2009) *Visible Learning*. Abingdon: Routledge.

Hughes, I. E. (1995) Peer assessment of student practical reports and its influence on learning and skill acquisition. *Capability*, 1: 39–43.

Nicol, D. J. and Macfarlane-Dick, D. (2006) Formative assessment and self-regulated learning: a model and seven principles of good feedback practice. *Studies in Higher Education*, 31 (2): 199–218.

Race, P. (2007) *The Lecturer's Toolkit: a Practical Guide to Assessment, Learning and Teaching*. Abingdon: Routledge.

Sambell, K., McDowell, L. and Montgomery, C. (2013) *Assessment for Learning in Higher Education*. Abingdon: Routledge.

Winstone, N. E., Nash, R. A., Rowntree, J. and Menezes, R. (2016). What do students want most from written feedback information? Distinguishing necessities from luxuries using a budgeting methodology. *Assessment & Evaluation in Higher Education*, 41 (8): 1237–53.

11
OVERCOMING CHALLENGES OF THE TEACHING ROLE

Learning outcomes

After reading this chapter you should be able to:

- Identify aspects of the role that you find challenging
- Apply strategies to address common concerns
- Develop personal support mechanisms.

Introduction

Starting to teach at university can be a sharp learning curve, particularly for those without prior teaching experience. Studies exploring teachers' early experiences suggest that they typically go through a number of developmental stages, during which they have particular concerns.

In this chapter, we briefly review research evidence of the experiences of those new to teaching before giving examples of typically encountered challenges, with suggestions as to how to address them. Some of these challenges are specific to the context within which professional services staff or GTAs work and you may have other challenges that are best discussed with colleagues in your discipline. Finally, we discuss ways to help promote confidence and credibility and suggest potential sources of support as you develop your teaching practice and identity.

Stages of teaching development

Below is a summary of typical stages through which new teachers tend to progress, based on research in general teacher education as well as studies exploring the particular experiences, concerns and development of GTAs and professional services staff by Biggs (1999), Cho et al. (2011), Fuller (1969), Graham and Regan (2016), Nyquist and Wulff (1996), Raaper (2018), Sharpe (2000), Van Lankveld et al. (2017) and Winstone and Moore (2017). The stages are not discrete and will vary according to individuals and their circumstances.

First stage: Survival

In the initial 'Survival' stage, staff new to teaching are often enthusiastic but feel vulnerable and may respond emotionally to situations. They have concerns about classroom management (whether they will look the part, have sufficient knowledge to answer questions and be able to keep discipline) and their relationship with students (how they are perceived and whether their students will like them). They may have polarised views about students, viewing them as 'good' or 'bad' and attributing the blame to students if they don't understand.

Postgraduate students taking on a teaching role find particular challenges as they negotiate the liminal space they occupy as both teacher and student. A liminal space is a kind of half-way house where you are not one thing or the other, like teenagers who are no longer children but not yet adults. GTAs may find themselves in an uncomfortable position between overworked academic staff (on whose evaluations their future careers may depend) and demanding students expecting more from a course for which they are paying. However GTAs also have the ability to understand the students' position and relate to them. They may face challenges communicating effectively with both students and course leaders and often experience difficulties with time management due to conflicting research and teaching priorities. Professional services staff may face similar challenges, having to navigate across professional boundaries to share their expertise with academic staff and students. Both groups may feel that their contribution to student learning is undervalued and unappreciated.

The early phase of teaching is often stressful, characterised by uncertainty and self-doubt and concerns about receiving favourable evaluations from supervisors. The context in which the teaching takes place can constrain or enhance the development of a teaching identity. It is supported in environments where teaching is highly valued, there are good role models and colleagues provide practical and emotional support. It is constrained in departments that appear competitive and hierarchical and by a general perception within universities that research is more highly valued than teaching.

Second stage: Learning to teach

As teachers gain experience and start to develop more confidence, they move to a stage where they think more about how they teach – finding effective ways to talk about their discipline and explain concepts. They may become more interested in professional development that can improve their teaching strategies, provide access to like-minded colleagues and help them to develop an educational vocabulary.

Third stage: Focus on impact

At this stage, teachers start to feel like credible and legitimate professionals, and are better able to handle classroom situations. They focus more on what the students are doing and learning, evaluating the effectiveness of their teaching and taking greater responsibility for student learning. Recognition of their teaching role by others is important and may influence how they envisage their future career.

Reflection

Do you recognise yourself in any of these descriptions?

Discussion

Individuals approach teaching with differing levels of confidence and competence depending on their prior experience, personality and the context in which they are operating. As with many areas of endeavour, there is often a sharp learning curve at the start. This book is designed to help you with all aspects of teaching and in this chapter we focus primarily on the 'Survival' stage, as the second and third stages are addressed in other chapters. Here we will consider the more generic concerns and dilemmas such as navigating the student–teacher boundary and developing confidence and credibility.

Navigating the student–teacher boundary

Activity 11.1 provides some examples of challenges encountered by GTAs to help you consider how best to prevent or manage them.

Activity 11.1

What would you do?

Consider the following scenarios: What are the risks? What would you do in a similar situation?

Scenario 1: Jasmine has just started as a Graduate Teaching Assistant. Although she holds weekly office hours, students rarely come but instead she receives messages at all times of the day and night asking for information and advice, much of which has already been provided. She is finding this quite disruptive and time consuming. Often students seem to be very informal, use text speak and seem to expect an immediate answer.

Scenario 2: Asmah has developed a good relationship with her class and is pleased that they seem to like her. Recently she met one of them in the university café and he bought her a coffee and later asked for her mobile number so he could send her a link. He also asked if he could send her a draft of his essay to proofread.

Scenario 3: Matt noticed that one of his students has been very quiet recently. After class, he asked him if he was okay and the student told him that he has been very down recently since splitting up with his partner. Also, he is finding the class difficult and is getting a bit behind.

Discussion

These cases all relate to boundaries of various kinds.

Scenario 1

Jasmine could prevent some of these out-of-hours demands by setting clear expectations from the start. It can be useful to clarify with students when you will be available (e.g. during normal weekday work hours), the time frame in which you will respond to messages (e.g. 'I'll aim to get back to you within 48 hours') and what is/isn't acceptable (e.g. 'Please check the guidance before you send me a query'). Other options might include:

- Providing an online forum for general queries that all students can access, whilst allowing students to contact you directly with more personal queries.
- Referring students back to previous guidance rather than providing it again. This may encourage them to check before asking you in future
- Setting aside a specific time or times in the week when you work on teaching-related matters and communicating this to students.
- Using a separate work/university email address which you direct students to use.
- If you are using social media, having similar guidance in place that provides clear expectations and limits as to its use and how you will engage.

Scenario 2

Asmah is in danger of swapping friendliness (which is important in developing a good relationship with students) with being friends (which is inappropriate in a teacher–student relationship). Whilst it is fine to chat informally in this situation, now that the student has bought her a coffee, Asmah may feel an implicit sense of obligation, which could lead her, perhaps unconsciously, to favour the student when marking or in class. As a teacher, it is wise to keep to official channels of communication (such as your staff e-mail or meetings during office hours) so that students understand that you are in a professional, not personal, relationship. Asmah also needs to avoid taking on excessive extra work such as proofreading or helping one student in a way that she could not replicate for all students. It is important to be approachable whilst maintaining a professional persona and being seen to treat all students equally.

Scenario 3

Matt has acted appropriately in showing concern for the student. He now needs to help the student without getting drawn into a counselling role. Universities and Student Unions provide a range of support: this usually starts with an academic or personal tutor system and is supplemented by a variety of services that can assist students with practical and emotional issues, such as housing, visas, disability support and mental health problems. Matt can help the student by listening, showing understanding and helping him to find support ('Have you got anyone you can talk to about this?' 'Are you aware that there is support available through the Student Union/specific university service?'). Alerting (or 'signposting') students to relevant services or resources allows them, if they wish, to access people with the appropriate expertise and the teacher to stay within the limits of their teaching role.

Confidentiality is important and such conversations should remain private, unless you are concerned that students are at risk of harming themselves or others. In this case, confidentiality can be broken and the student referred to an appropriate colleague. If a student asks to speak to you in confidence, it can be useful to explain this. If in doubt or if you have an ongoing concern about a student, ask a senior member of staff for advice, initially without giving the student's name.

These three cases highlight boundaries with regard to your relationship with students and in terms of managing your time and workload. Trying to maintain time for your research/work whilst fulfilling teaching duties can be difficult as teaching often has an urgency, such as a seminar that needs to be prepared before tomorrow, whereas other work may have a longer timeline. It is important to balance the urgency of a task against its importance: sometimes you will need to settle for good enough rather than doing everything perfectly.

Developing confidence and credibility

It is normal to be anxious about a new role, and many experienced teachers still feel nervous before they teach. This can be positive in motivating you to prepare well but can be inhibiting if it impairs your enjoyment and engagement with students.

In Chapter 5, we explored how you might reduce the impact of nerves and anxiety when teaching large groups. Here we will explore other ways to develop your confidence and credibility as a teacher. We start by asking you to consider what you bring to the teaching role.

Reflection

Think about what you bring to the teaching role that can benefit students. This may be areas of knowledge, various types of experience that will inform your teaching, or personal attributes such as patience and empathy.

Discussion

Knowledge: Your disciplinary knowledge is normally the reason why you have been appointed to teach and you will generally have a greater knowledge of the topic than your students. Professional services staff may be surprised by how much they have to offer to academics and GTAs often realise quite early on how far their knowledge has developed since they were at the same stage as their students.

Experience: Your experience is a valuable resource when teaching. You can draw on research experience, work experience you may have had, and wider life experiences such as having lived in another country, hobbies and interests and your own experience of being a student.

Personal attributes: Studies suggest that credibility in the classroom relates to the extent that the teacher is perceived to be competent, trustworthy and caring (McCroskey and Teven (1999). Note that the latter two are about personal characteristics – being trustworthy includes being honest about what you don't know and following through if you say you will do something. Being caring is about having a genuine interest in students and their learning and students are usually quick to recognise this quality. It may be evident in the time you take getting to know your students and the attention you pay to checking their understanding. Other helpful attributes include patience, empathy and responsiveness.

Preparation

Being well prepared obviously helps with confidence. Preparation can involve:

- Ensuring you understand the remit of each session and knowing how your teaching fits into the overall student experience. If in doubt, check with your course leader.
- Preparing a teaching plan or familiarising yourself with one you have been given. This is about *how* you are going to teach.
- Revising the content: i.e. *what* you are going to teach. New teachers often focus primarily on this area although the other areas above are often as important in ensuring an effective session. If students are given lengthy reading lists, check how much you are expected to have read.

For professional services staff, an added challenge can be not being familiar with the subject discipline of the staff or students you are teaching. You may be teaching people who are older or more experienced than you or who are experts in their own field. Remember that they have come to you for your help in a specific area about which they are not confident, and they will not expect you to know their discipline.

One of the commonest fears when starting teaching (and for experienced teachers too!) is being asked questions that you cannot answer. It is important to recognise that you can never know everything and, in fact, people often find it easier to learn from someone who is a little ahead of them than from an expert. You can be open about the limits of your knowledge and say early on, 'I may not be able to answer all your questions but I should be able to point you in the right direction.' (This also makes it easier for students to admit when they don't know something.) On the other hand, you need to be reasonably confident about the core material and be able to explain the most important concepts or demonstrate key skills. So consider this when you are applying for teaching positions or being asked to teach. If you feel unqualified to teach in a specific area, you could ask for support to develop your knowledge or it may be possible to co-teach, at least for the first few sessions while you are learning more. For the most difficult questions, you can refer students to more senior staff, offer to find the answer and get back to them, or guide them as to how they could go about finding answers.

Presenting yourself with confidence

The first session is important in establishing your relationship with students. Remember that how well prepared you are, your body language and your voice all give messages to students about how seriously to take you. If you are well prepared, you should feel more confident and that will project itself to students, even if you are nervous. The 'Beginnings' section in Chapter 5 provides guidance on how to introduce yourself.

Staff new to teaching are often concerned that they lack credibility or authority within the class due to particular characteristics, such as not having English as their first language, being short, or looking young (see Case Study 11.1). Female teachers and those from an ethnic minority may feel they are not taken as seriously as their white male counterparts, and there is evidence to support this (see the start of Chapter 12 for a more detailed discussion).

— Case Study 11.1 —

Reflections on teaching challenges: Kristina Arakelyan, GTA in Music

When I first started working as a GTA, I already had teaching experience but not in a university setting. Two main challenges arose and were at the forefront of my mind as a new GTA. Firstly, I was aware of my age: I was only a little older than my students and was determined to establish myself as a credible educator. To achieve this, I spent some time working on my teaching persona, ensuring that I was dressed appropriately, was friendly but maintained a professional distance. Another aspect was ensuring excellent subject-knowledge to be ready for any questions, some peripheral to the topic, which might arise. Although as a GTA we are not expected to be experts on the modules we teach, I felt that being secure in my abilities and having full confidence when addressing the class could not be achieved without the preparation. My most successful seminars were on subjects which I not only knew very well, but which I was genuinely passionate about – in my experience, the students tend to follow the energy the seminar leader puts in.

The second issue which was very important to get right was creating a safe and inclusive environment, both for myself and the students. Each seminar group was a unique mix of personalities: some groups would be full of active students, and other groups would largely stay quiet, and there were some students who would dominate discussions. I had several teaching tools at hand – using active learning methods, using a 'lead' to prompt discussion, preparing group activities and varied forms of delivery. I found that it was important to gauge the students' response to these tools: as the term progressed, I made note of how each group responded and tailored my seminars accordingly.

Whilst there are some things about yourself that you cannot change, what you can change is how you think about yourself and this in turn can change how students think about you. If you feel you need to overcome anxieties and develop more confidence, you could try the following activities. They come from the field of neuro-linguistic programming, which is based on studies of what successful people do. Not all of them will work for everyone, but hopefully you will find one or more that are helpful to you.

Choosing helpful beliefs

This is the idea that you can choose beliefs that will help (or hinder) you. This may sound strange, but we all have a set of beliefs, often unconscious, that affect how we function.

Reflection

To consider some of your current beliefs, look at the list below and tick those that you think are generally true (and be honest with yourself):

1 Students try to do the least work possible.
2 All students have the potential to learn and develop at university.
3 Students are working hard to juggle their studies, work and social/family life.
4 The university is taking in too many underqualified students.
5 Students try to undermine a teacher that's not up to it.
6 It's impossible to stop students getting distracted by technology.
7 Students will accept me for who I am.
8 Only a few students are willing to put their views forward to the whole group.
9 Students are only interested in what's on the exam paper.
10 I can motivate students' interest in my subject.

Discussion

How do such beliefs affect you? Wiseman (2004) conducted a study that shed light on how self-perceptions can affect people. He compared the experiences of people who believed themselves to be lucky with those who thought they were unlucky and found that the 'unlucky' group had not had any more illnesses, bereavements or difficulties than the 'lucky' group. It was all about perception — a classic case of whether you perceive the glass as 'half full' or 'half empty'. But perhaps a more important finding was how these perceptions influenced individuals' actions. For example, someone who thought they were unlucky in job hunting might see the perfect job but would convince themselves that they wouldn't be successful and therefore that it wasn't worth applying – the one sure way of not getting the job! Relate this to teaching, and, for example, if you believe that students won't take you seriously, you will probably come across as less confident which in turn will give them less confidence in you.

The good news is that you can change your beliefs to ones that will help you to succeed. So, go through the above list again and highlight or underline those sentences that you think it would be helpful to you to believe. Don't worry if you don't believe them (yet).

In this exercise, it doesn't matter whether or not the statements are true because this is about beliefs. We tend to think of beliefs as fixed but you can choose to act according to a new set of beliefs. So looking at the list above, you will probably agree that it would be helpful to believe 2, 3, 7 and 10. If you ticked these statements the first time round, then you already have some helpful beliefs. If you ticked some of the others, you can choose to believe something more helpful; for example, you could change 4 to 'With the right support and dedication, students succeed' or 'Everyone deserves an opportunity to succeed'. Make sure the statements are positive and in the present tense.

You can repeat the helpful beliefs to yourself or write them somewhere and read them before you teach. Over time, you may become more aware of your implicit beliefs as you notice thoughts that slip into your mind and you may wish to reframe them as helpful beliefs.

Visualisations

Visualisations are used in sports psychology and if you listen to interviews with successful sportspeople you often hear them saying things like 'I've been seeing myself with a gold medal around my neck since I was six years old' or 'I've always imagined myself lifting the cup'. You can apply the same technique to teaching as a way to programme your mind for success using Activity 11.2.

Activity 11.2

Visualising a teacher you would like to emulate

Think of a teacher whom you admire and would aspire to emulate – ideally a university teacher that you have encountered. Now follow the steps below:

1 In your mind, imagine that you are watching this teacher. Spend a couple of minutes watching an imaginary video of them teaching.
2 Run the video through again but this time imagine your head on the teacher's body. You can even improve what they did last time and make the teaching better still.
3 Run the video for a third time, but this time imagine you are inside the teacher looking out. Run the imaginary video through from this perspective.

Practise this a few times, including just before you start teaching.

Confidence tap

This is a way of tapping into confidence in other areas of your life and transferring it to teaching. You are aiming to develop an association between a time when you felt confident and a label that you can then apply in a new situation. (If you are familiar with the story of Pavlov's dog, it is the same principle of conditioning.)

Think of a time when you felt confident – it could be a social or work event, a hobby or a family event. It must be a specific time, such as when you gave advice that was acted on, were on a nice holiday or organised a successful event. Choose a label to associate with that event – it could be a word (e.g. party, concert), a colour, or an action (rubbing your fingers together). Now, take yourself back to that event in your mind and re-live it. Imagine you are there: What are you hearing? What are you seeing? How are you feeling? As you re-live it, you should start to feel the same confidence you had then – at this point, label it in your mind with the word, colour or action you have chosen.

Take a short break and distract yourself with something different. Then do the exercise again. If you repeat this several times you will build up an association between the label and the feeling. You now have this feeling 'on tap'. Just as you are about to teach, think of the label and you should feel confident.

Above all, confidence and credibility come with experience and a commitment to reflect and learn from that experience. We discuss this more in Chapter 12, but before that we will look at how you might find support for your teaching and any challenges that arise.

Finding support

Teaching can be stressful and may present professional dilemmas or questions, so it is useful to think early on about potential sources of support for advice, resources or a chance to reflect. You could consider the following options.

Senior colleagues

As a new teacher, there should be mechanisms in place to support you – usually your module convenor, manager or course leader. Don't be afraid to ask for support as senior colleagues are usually accountable for the programme and so have a vested interest in your teaching well. That said, individuals vary in terms of their willingness and availability to help. If they will be absent for a period, ask them to nominate a colleague that you can contact instead.

Peers

Your university may offer peer support schemes where you meet people in a similar role. You will also have this opportunity if you attend workshops on teaching. If nothing is provided, you may like to set up your own support group with colleagues working in a similar context. Having informal opportunities to meet and discuss your teaching in a non-judgemental atmosphere can be helpful. Another option is to set up an online forum for colleagues within your department to share ideas, resources or teaching strategies.

Mentors

Mentors differ from peers in that they are usually more experienced and can offer support and guidance from their own experience and their knowledge of the organisation. They are usually outside your immediate work context so that you can talk openly. You could approach someone whose teaching you admire or ask for recommendations.

Personal contacts

You may find it useful to talk through issues with a partner, friend or relative, particularly if they also have some teaching experience, even if in a different context.

Self-support

Keeping a log or journal in which you reflect on teaching can help you to learn from your experience. There is more on this in Chapter 12.

Literature

There is a wealth of evidence on effective teaching from which you can draw, as well as theories and creative ideas to enhance your teaching. Your university should have an academic or education development centre, which will house relevant resources. It is also worth exploring disciplinary-specific material: check your library to see whether they subscribe to disciplinary education journals. An example of how a GTA has used disciplinary literature in practice is given in Case Study 11.2.

Case Study 11.2

Developing feedback strategies: Eman Ismael, Arabic teacher in a language centre

Corrective feedback has been defined simply as 'responses to learner utterances containing an error' (Ellis et al., 2006: 28). Lightbown and Spada (2013: 216) describe corrective feedback as 'an indication to a learner that his or her use of the target language is incorrect'. Lyster and Ranta (1997) state that there are six different types of feedback: Explicit correction, Recasts, Clarification requests, Metalinguistic feedback, Elicitation and Repetition. When teaching the beginners level, I mostly use two techniques: firstly, 'Recasts', where I reform all or part of a student's utterance and replace the incorrect part with the correct target language form. Secondly, I use 'Explicit correction' to provide the correct form for the learner, clearly indicating that what the student had said was incorrect, for example 'Oh, you mean ...' or 'We usually say ...'.

On the other hand, with the intermediate level I use, firstly, 'Clarification requests' by saying 'Sorry, what did you say?' or 'What do you mean by X?' In this way, the students will rethink about their production and restructure their sentences. Secondly, I use Elicitation techniques, where I ask questions to elicit correct forms: 'How do we say X in Arabic?' – in these questions I usually ask the whole class. My strategy in providing oral feedback didn't change when we started our remote teaching. I still use the oral feedback not only to correct the students' utterances, but to give a positive feedback to their good performance as well.

Pastoral support

Recognise when you need personal support; for example, if you are becoming stressed, anxious or depressed. Teaching can be exciting and rewarding; it can also be difficult and stressful, as can managing dual roles and working to deadlines alongside whatever is happening in your personal life.

It is a strength to recognise when you need help and act early to find support before things get on top of you. Be as kind to yourself as you would to a friend, and remember that the university has lots of support services in addition to those open to the public.

Over to you

All educators encounter challenges and over time you will develop a range of strategies to deal effectively with different situations. Thinking ahead about potential issues and ways of handling them can help, as can discussing your experiences with colleagues. Often, prevention is better than cure, and it is never too soon to start thinking about effective ways of managing your workload and building effective relationships with students and colleagues.

In the next chapter we will explore how to evaluate your teaching in ways that will contribute to your development as an educator. Remember that teaching is a craft you can learn, but it can be a lonely business, so think about where you can find support. When you encounter challenges, be humble, be curious, treat your students and colleagues as allies and do the best you can in the situation. Accept the learning curve, reflect, draw lessons for the future and use your creativity to learn what works for you and your students.

Further resources

Check your university's guidance and whether there are any online forums or peer support groups. You could even consider developing something yourself.

References

Biggs, J. (1999) *Teaching for Quality Education at University*. Buckingham: Open University Press.

Cho, Y., Kim, N., Svinicki, D. and Decker, M. (2011) Exploring teaching concerns and characteristics of graduate teaching assistants. *Teaching in Higher Education*, 16 (3): 267–79.

Ellis, R., Loewen, S. and Erlam, R. (2006) Implicit and explicit corrective feedback and the acquisition of L2 grammar. *Studies in Second Language Acquisition*, 28 (2): 339–68.

Fuller, F. F. (1969) Concerns of teachers: a developmental characterization. *American Educational Research Journal*, 6: 207–26.

Graham, C. and Regan, J.-A. (2016) Exploring the contribution of professional staff to student outcomes: a comparative study of Australian and UK case studies. *Journal of Higher Education Policy and Management*, 38(6): 595–609.

Lightbown, P. M. and Spada, N. (2013) *How Languages Are Learned*, 4th edn. Oxford Handbooks for Language Teachers. Oxford: Oxford University Press.

Lyster, R. and Ranta, L. (1997) Corrective feedback and learner uptake: negotiation of form in communicative classrooms. *Studies in Second Language Acquisition*, 19 (1): 37–66.

McCroskey, J. C. and Teven, J. J. (1999) Goodwill: a re-examination of the construct and its measurement. *Communication Monographs*, 66: 91–103.

Nyquist, J. D. and Wulff, D. H. (1996) *Working Effectively with Graduate Assistants*. Thousand Oaks, CA: Sage

Raaper, R. (2018) 'Peacekeepers' and 'machine factories': tracing Graduate Teaching Assistant subjectivity in a neoliberalised university. *British Journal of Sociology of Education*, 39 (4): 421–35.

Sharpe, R. (2000) A framework for training Graduate Teaching Assistants. *Teacher Development*, 4 (1): 131–43.

Van Lankveld, T., Schoonenboom, J., Volman, M., Croiset, G. and Beishuizen, J. (2017) Developing a teacher identity in the university context: a systematic review of the literature. *Higher Education Research & Development*, 36 (2): 325–42.

Winstone, N. and Moore, D. (2017) Sometimes fish, sometimes fowl? Liminality, identity work and identity malleability in graduate teaching assistants. *Innovations in Education and Teaching International*, 54 (5): 494–502.

Wiseman, R. (2004) *The Luck Factor: The Scientific Study of the Lucky Mind*. London: Arrow Books.

12

DEVELOPING YOUR TEACHING AND CAREER

Learning outcomes

After reading this chapter you should be able to:

- Use a variety of strategies to evaluate and develop your teaching
- Reflect on your developing identity as an educator and how you would like to progress
- Articulate your teaching experience in ways that support your career aspirations.

Introduction

This chapter is about developing your teaching, yourself as an educator and your career, whether or not you see teaching as a major component in future roles. We will start by reviewing the many ways in which you can evaluate the effectiveness of your teaching, and then look at ways of learning more about teaching, potentially engaging in educational research and scholarship, and finally at how your teaching experience can contribute to your career development.

Evaluating your teaching

Evaluation can encompass a broad range of activities involving gathering and interpreting information about the impact of your teaching and how it is perceived by relevant stakeholders, such as students, your department and university. When thinking about evaluation, it is important to consider the purpose for which it is being undertaken, which usually falls somewhere along the following continuum:

Proving   _____   Improving

At the proving end, you may want evidence to convince others such as your module convenor, Advance HE and yourself that you are doing a good job. At the improving end you may want data to inform how to improve your teaching and develop the course or service – and you may want a combination of the above.

Evaluation that focuses on proving is often about accountability. Examples you may be familiar with at national level are the Teaching Excellence and Student Outcomes Framework (TEF) and the National Students' Survey (NSS): see Chapter 1 for more details. You should be able to access NSS results for your area, and the qualitative comments can be useful in informing your teaching. Additionally, universities have internal systems to evaluate the quality of courses as part of their accountability to funding bodies and you should be aware of any feedback that is collected by others about your teaching.

It is important to note, however, that as measures of teaching quality, student evaluations are flawed – studies have shown that high ratings do not relate to improved student learning (Uttl et al., 2017) and student evaluations have known biases (which will be discussed later). For these reasons, you should interpret student evaluations cautiously, and they should not be used by the university to make important decisions about you, such as retention or promotion.

In this chapter, we will focus primarily on the 'improving' end of the continuum: how you can evaluate your teaching as you go along in order to facilitate continuous improvement.

Choosing evaluation strategies

This chapter will outline many ways in which you can evaluate your teaching. Activity 12.1 invites you to think about how you might do this.

Activity 12.1

Evaluation strategies and indicators

Think about a range of different ways in which you can gain information about the quality of your teaching; include both formal and informal methods, for example:

- formal – asking students to summarise key points from a session
- informal – noticing students' body language in class.

Discussion

Formal methods include having your teaching observed by a colleague, reviewing the results of student assessments and gathering student feedback verbally or on forms. Informal methods include noticing levels of attendance, student engagement and the development of student work and confidence over time.

The above strategies require varying amounts of time and effort and this may influence your choice (see Figure 12.1).

Quicker/easier	← →	More time/effort
Noticing attendance	Keeping a record of attendance	Exploring reasons for non-attendance
Noticing the level of student engagement	Monitoring participation in online forums	Reviewing the content of students' posts and evaluating the effectiveness of each forum
Asking students to review the session in the last 10 minutes of class (see strategies below)	Setting up a mid-term evaluation form for students to complete	Checking assessment results and adjusting teaching to address areas of poorer performance
Jotting some notes on your plan about how the session went	Keeping a weekly reflective log	Reviewing your log and discussing themes and challenges with a colleague
Recording your teaching session and reviewing it afterwards	Having a peer or senior colleague observe your teaching and provide feedback	

Figure 12.1 Evaluation strategies

Another factor in deciding which strategies to use is to consider what kind of information you are hoping to gain. Table 12.1 shows a model identifying four levels at which you can evaluate.

Table 12.1 Four levels of training evaluation

Level 1	Reaction	How do the learners feel about their experience?
Level 2	Learning	How well have they acquired the intended knowledge, skills or attributes?
Level 3	Behaviour	How well are students able to apply their learning in real life contexts?
Level 4	Results	What is the impact on the organisation?

Source: Based on Kirkpatrick and Kirkpatrick (2006)

As you move through the model, you can see that it goes from evaluating students' immediate reactions to how well they are learning and the impact of their learning. When starting to teach, you may focus primarily on the first two or three levels. Students' perceptions matter because they influence attendance, participation, learning and ultimately retention on the course. They are also important in the current consumerist climate of higher education where there is a strong focus on student satisfaction and 'the student experience' (see Chapter 1). As an educator, you will of course want to look beyond perceptions to what and how students have learnt and how well they are able to apply that learning beyond the course. The model was designed to evaluate workplace training, so Level 4 was important in terms of how it would benefit the organisation. In the university context you might think about how students' learning could benefit them personally, their community or future organisations in which they may work.

We will now discuss some evaluation strategies in more depth and you can consider which level(s) of the model each one addresses.

Evaluation strategies

Personal reflection

Reflection is an integral part of good teaching practice and important in the HEA application process. During and after teaching you will have an impression of how each session or course is working – particularly when it has gone very well or badly, and most people will naturally reflect on the reasons. You can gain more from reflection by setting time aside after teaching to discuss your experience with an interested colleague or friend, annotate your teaching plan or keep a teaching journal/reflective log.

For discussions with another, or writing a teaching journal, you may like to use a reflective learning framework (see the Further Resources section for references). Reflection can help you to acknowledge your feelings – which may be quite strong, analyse the session in more depth and use the insights gained to inform future planning. An example of extracts from a reflective log is given in Box 12.1.

Box 12.1

Extracts from a weekly log by a GTA in Education teaching a module on critical perspectives on education

Week 2: Key features or arguments of feminist theory

At the beginning, I asked first if any students had questions about the reading since I was aware this week's topic was a very challenging one. This week I was ambitious and tried to include two activities in a 1-hour (online) seminar. For the first activity, students were asked to describe some of the features of feminist theory from the assigned text and post them on the online message board (Padlet). The breakout room discussions about feminism were productive in many of the groups; several students added comments to the Padlet. These comments were anonymous so it is difficult to gauge how many students posted.

Based on the larger group discussion, most students seemed to understand the distinction between liberal feminism and radical feminism and that there is some disagreement amongst feminist scholars. However, when I moved between the groups, some were not speaking at all and did not have their cameras turned on. I don't know if these students had technical issues or were just reluctant to speak. I've realised that it is much easier to 'hide' in online seminars.

Week 3: The concept of powerful knowledge (Michael Young) and criticisms

I decided not to use the breakout rooms today and have a longer group discussion about the concept of 'powerful knowledge'. There were students who had technology issues (wi-fi crashing, background noise), students who were confused and students who did not participate at all. My hope was to avoid the regular issue of some students feeling frustrated and/or disengaged in breakout rooms because their group members had either not read the text, misunderstood the text or chose not to participate (cameras and microphones turned off). I think the larger group format was helpful to mitigate some of these issues. However, I am also mindful that some students were not able to speak who might have wanted to. The ones who did speak (unmute) made some really good points, though most of them were older and more confident UK (home) students so I'm not sure if their comments were as applicable or helpful to the international students.

Conclusion: I think it was good to try this format but I might alternate with breakout rooms each week.

Annotating your teaching plan might involve adding notes about parts of the session that went well or not so well, took more or less time than planned or worked differently than how you envisaged, as well as recording what you would omit, include or change for next time. This forms a record that will be useful to refer back to if repeating the session in future, by which time you would otherwise have forgotten the details.

Reflection can be helpful in prompting more in-depth thought and analysis of teaching. As with all evaluation strategies, it has limitations; for example, you may miss or misinterpret students' reactions, and therefore it is useful to triangulate it with other sources of information.

Monitoring participation and engagement

It is useful to keep track of how students are participating in a course. This includes things like noticing levels of attendance – do student numbers increase, decrease or remain constant across the course? How well do students engage in discussions or other activities during class? Do they come to class prepared? If you are teaching online, how well do students engage with optional activities, such as forums or quizzes? Online platforms collect huge amounts of data about student activity. There are ethical issues around using these analytics to monitor individuals – which you would need to discuss with senior colleagues – but it can be useful to see broader patterns, such as the level of engagement with different elements of a programme, as part of your evaluation.

Teaching observations

Most teachers in higher education will have their teaching observed at some point, often by the module or programme leader, and it can provide a useful alternative perspective. There may be a defined process and paperwork to use or it may be more informal. It is good practice for the observer and observee to communicate about the context, intentions and format of the teaching before the session. After the observation, you would normally have a conversation about the teaching and learning with the aim of helping you to develop and improve your practice and both parties may contribute to a written account of the event.

Peer observations can also be informative, where you and a colleague teaching at the same level observe each other's teaching in order to see what you can learn. This could be a colleague within your discipline or from another discipline: both can provide useful insights.

Finally, you can conduct a self-observation by recording your teaching on video or audio. Be aware that watching yourself or listening to yourself can be uncomfortable at first because we are not used to seeing or hearing ourselves, but it can help you to gain a more accurate impression of how you teach.

You may also have, or be able to set up, 'micro-teaching' opportunities. This is a form of simulation where a group of educators plan and conduct short teaching sessions (say 10–15 minutes) for each other. They may choose to teach part of an existing session, trial a new technique or try teaching a difficult concept. The other teachers act as the students, and experiencing a range of teaching styles from this perspective can be informative. After everyone has taught, there is discussion and feedback about the effectiveness of different approaches and what people have learnt. This can be conducted online or in person.

Assessment results

Part of your evaluation may entail seeing how students perform in their summative assessments. You may be involved in marking their work, in which case you will see directly and can identify what areas they perform well or less well in. If not directly involved, you should still have access to the results and ideally a breakdown of how well students performed in different elements of the assessment, as this can inform future teaching.

Formative assessment (checking learning as you go along) is also an important part of your evaluation and can feed into your reflections and future planning: see Chapter 10 for further information.

Student performance

You may have opportunities to see how students apply their learning, both during the course as they progress from week to week, and in some disciplines, outside the classroom. For example, if you work in one of the health professions, you may observe students working with patients and can evaluate how well they are applying their learning. Or if you work in performance disciplines such as sports, music or drama, you may see be able to assess student learning in a variety of contexts. You may also be able to get feedback from teachers on subsequent modules about the longer-term impact of your teaching.

Student feedback

It is often useful to collect feedback from students yourself, rather than waiting for centrally collected data: you can do this sooner, define the questions yourself and use it to improve the current cohort's experience. Firstly, you need to think about what information you want: do you want to know what and/or how students have learned (the outcomes) or what they think of your teaching (the process), or both?

Consider whether feedback should be anonymous or named: anonymous feedback is often recommended as otherwise students may be reticent to be honest. However this may not be possible if you are teaching individually or with a very small group. Also, having students own their feedback can be helpful for their personal development and can prevent malicious or damaging feedback. Your department may have a policy on this.

In either case, it is useful to explain to students what constitutes effective feedback. You could explain and give examples of constructive versus destructive feedback; for example, not 'The lecturer was boring, terrible slides!' but 'I understand better when you give examples and use visuals in your slides'.

General principles of student feedback

- Only ask for what you will use: students get evaluation fatigue if asked to feed back too frequently.
- Prepare students for feedback: explain why you want the information and what you will do with it.
- Encourage students to develop constructive feedback practices: this is a useful skill that they can apply in other contexts.
- Ask for feedback early enough that you can act on the information: students are more likely to engage if they think they will benefit personally.
- Focus on qualitative information that can help you to improve teaching: quantitative data is also useful if you can identify the reasons for the results.
- Respond to or, ideally, discuss the feedback, either online or when you next meet, for example by summarising the main points and how you will respond (or why you won't/can't).

Strategies for collecting student feedback   Below, we outline some quick and easy ways in which you can collect feedback during a course and how you can use it to inform your teaching.

Online noticeboard or Post-Its   Ask students to post comments to an online noticeboard before they leave class, or to write them on a Post-It note (or 2–3 different-coloured notes) and place on the wall or your desk as they leave the session. Think about what you want them to comment on; for example:

- the most important thing they learnt today
- any outstanding questions or concerns about the material
- what they found most helpful in the session
- one thing they would change if the session were to run again.

You will see that the first two are primarily about the students' engagement with the topic, the latter two more about your teaching methodology. Avoid asking students to provide negative feedback (for example, 'What were the weaknesses of the session?') – instead, ask for constructive comments (like 'How could the session be improved?').

Some online noticeboards offer a 'like' or 'upvote/downvote' function that can be useful to obtain a more representative view of student opinion.

Questionnaires   These can be given in the middle as well as at the end of the course and may include a variety of questions, including ratings and free comments. Examples of different question types you can use are given in Figure 12.2.

Scales:

How confident do you feel about:

	Not at all confident				Very confident
• Analysing primary sources?	1	2	③	4	5
• Conducting surveys?	1	2	3	④	5
• Writing a policy report?	1	2	3	④	5

[Note that while scales allow some statistical analysis of the data, this should be used with caution as the meanings of the numbers are a personal interpretation.]

Categories:

To what extent did you feel the learning outcomes were met?

	Not met	Partially met	Fully met
To analyse the causes of the 1947 partition of India		✓	
To evaluate the consequences of partition.			✓

Continua

I found today's seminar: too hard _____X_____too easy.

The time devoted to small group discussion in today's seminar was:

too much _____X____too little.

Free text:

Please summarise the main points you have taken from today's seminar.

What did you find most difficult to understand?

Figure 12.2   Sample question types for evaluation forms

Questionnaires can be given online and there are a wide variety of survey tools available. These collate the results automatically, but you may need to work hard to ensure that all students complete them. They can also be given out on paper: this allows you to ensure that everyone completes and hands them in but requires you to collate the results manually.

Discussions or focus groups   These can be conducted in various ways, including:

- Open discussion (best for small groups). Listen and note the feedback as you go along, for example on an online document or on a whiteboard which you can photograph afterwards. Be careful just to listen and record: if you start to disagree with the opinions or try to justify yourself, feedback will diminish. You may want to probe at various stages to bring in more people or develop a deeper understanding;

for example, 'Can you give me an example?', 'Hands up who agrees/disagrees?', 'Are there other views on this?' Some people may not feel comfortable to contribute so you could also offer an option to provide written comments afterwards.

- Small group feedback: Ask students to get into pairs or groups of three or four and give them a sheet of paper on which to record any feedback they would like to provide. The aim is to gain a consensus view and to allow students to determine what is important rather than asking specific questions.

- Focus groups: For larger classes, you could ask a representative group of students to take part in a focus group outside class. You may like to ask a colleague to facilitate this if you are not experienced in leading focus groups or if you feel a third party would get more honest feedback. If so, choose someone who will feed back sensitively to you.

Student self-evaluation   When collecting feedback, it can also be useful to draw students' attention to their own role in learning by asking them to evaluate their contribution to the class. For example, you could ask them to rate how hard they have worked or to comment on how they could gain more from the class; a sample form is given in Chapter 4 (Table 4.1).

Interpreting and using student feedback   Feedback can be extraordinarily useful in providing insight into students' learning and perspectives, but it has limitations and issues.

- Firstly, the emotional impact of feedback can be profound. Students can be blunt, even rude, and these comments can hurt, particularly if you have worked hard on your teaching. There are very few teachers, even the most skilled, who have not had negative comments from time to time. Try not to take these kind of comments too personally – they may say more about the student than they do about you. The student may be having a bad day, be angry about something outside class, there may be rifts within the group of which you are unaware or they may have a valid point but lack the skills to communicate it sensitively.

- Evaluations reflect the biases of students: there is a large literature from a range of countries showing bias against female teachers, including a recent, small study of an online course in which female avatars were rated significantly below male ones, regardless of the actual gender of the educator (MacNell et al., 2015). There is less recent data relating to culture or race, but a large Australian study of over half a million student evaluations across five faculties over a seven-year period found that both gender and cultural effects have a negative impact on the scores of women and teachers from non-English speaking backgrounds (Fan et al., 2019). This was true across all faculties, although there were differences in the pattern of impact, with women more negatively rated in science and those from non-English speaking backgrounds (a proxy for culture) in arts and social sciences.

- Depending on your response rate, feedback may be unrepresentative of the whole group – however, understanding individual views can still be enlightening.

- Feedback can be contradictory: after a recent workshop, one of the authors received comments which included:

  o 'The facilitator was excellent and conveyed the topic in an interesting and thought provoking way,' and
  o 'A better facilitator and material that will actually be useful would be great.'

- Students may ask for something you are not able to provide or consider inappropriate. For example, a GTA leading discussion-based seminars was asked to provide a summary of each session. She explained to students that the session was set up so that they could record their own learning, which would be more effective in helping them to make sense of the ideas and concepts themselves.
- Feedback may be difficult to interpret. For example, if a student says something was not relevant when you know it is an important topic, you might wonder why they have that perception. You may not know which student said it or have the opportunity to explore it further.
- Some students may come from cultures where teachers are more revered than in the UK. They may find the idea of offering a critique of the teacher strange and disrespectful, and this would influence how they respond.
- As discussed at the start of the chapter, positive evaluations do not correlate with learning. Sometimes students need time to adapt to new ways of working; for example, a lecturer who required students to write a blog every week and critique each other's initially received negative feedback as students were reluctant to share their writing. However, she persisted and by the end of the term students rated it one of their best courses as they recognised how much their writing had improved.

Given all of the above, how do you interpret and use feedback? This is a personal judgement, but you may want to take into account the strength of views on a particular point – something mentioned by several people may be more important than that only mentioned by one – although not always! You may like to check for clarification with the group on certain points. You can also triangulate with other forms of evaluation, for example what you noticed in the session or feedback from an external person observing your session. It can also be useful to have discussions with colleagues who may experience similar challenges in their teaching.

You may have a wide range of students in your classes and it is difficult to make everything work for everyone at all times. If something doesn't work, treat it as a research finding and try a different approach next time – or you may want to continue and give students time to adapt. Over time, you will learn successful ways to teach your discipline, for example a particular activity, analogy or diagram that seems to help many students understand a key concept. The most important thing is that you are trying to work with your students to improve their learning and they will appreciate your intention.

Review

Activity 12.2 provides an opportunity for you to consider how, in practice, you might evaluate your teaching.

— Activity 12.2 —

Reflection on evaluation strategies

Which of the following evaluation strategies do you currently use and which might you use in future? What has influenced your choice?

Strategy	Use	Plan to use
Personal reflection (log, annotated plans, discussion)		
Evaluating participation and engagement		
Teaching observations (self via recording, senior colleague, peer)		
Incorporating formative assessment		
Reviewing assessment results		
Checking centrally or nationally collected evaluation data		
Collecting student feedback (e.g. via questionnaires or focus groups)		

Discussion

Your choice may be guided by practicalities, time and what you feel comfortable with. Over time, it is useful to employ a range of strategies in order to provide different perspectives and inform how you develop specific sessions and your teaching as a whole. You may like to take into account Kirkpatrick and Kirkpatrick's (2006) model and ensure that you are addressing more than one level.

Further educational development

From looking at evaluating individual teaching sessions, we now look more broadly at other ways in which you might like to further your development as an educator.

Workshops, conferences and self-directed learning

Within your university there will be opportunities to attend workshops and courses where you can learn a range of skills and knowledge relevant to your teaching. These may be stand-alone workshops or there may be a pathway or programme designed for teaching staff at your level. Many professional bodies also offer disciplinary-focused workshops on educational topics. Much of the value of these courses comes from the opportunity to meet and debate different ideas and approaches with your colleagues.

Similarly, you may have university- or disciplinary-based conferences on education where you can hear from practitioners engaged in educational research and development.

There is also a plethora of resources available within and outside universities that can inform your teaching. The university library will house relevant books and journals and there are countless websites offering resources and MOOCs that you may find helpful.

Studying for a qualification

Many universities offer a postgraduate qualification in education or academic practice. These usually provide progression from Certificate to Diploma to MEd, MA or MSc, with each stage taking around a year to complete. The Master's year usually involves a research project, often focusing on developing your own practice.

If you are interested in gaining a qualification, it is worth researching what is available, and considering your preferences; for example:

- Do you prefer to learn with colleagues within your own university or across other higher education providers?
- Do you prefer a course that is interdisciplinary or targeted at your discipline? Some professional bodies and universities offer disciplinary specific courses and qualifications whereas others provide a multidisciplinary experience.
- Would you prefer to learn online, face to face or in a blended learning format? This may depend partly on the practicalities of your circumstances as well as your learning preferences. Blended courses may have residential elements combined with distance learning.
- What is the content and structure of the course? Does it cover topics of particular interest to you? Are there choices within the programme structure?
- Does it contain a practice element, for example teaching your colleagues or having your teaching observed?
- How is the course assessed? What kind of assignments are involved?
- Does successful completion of the course automatically provide HEA recognition, and if so, in which category?
- What is the cost? (Universities and professional bodies may offer courses free to their staff or members.)

Applying for HEA recognition

Advance HE offers staff working in universities the opportunity to gain recognition for the quality of their work via HEA fellowships (see the Introduction to this book for a fuller explanation). As the name suggests, it is a recognition of effective practice, not a qualification or course (although it may be incorporated into one). If not, you make an application according to the process within your university (or centrally through Advance HE), which is reviewed by appropriate colleagues and if successful, you become a fellow or associate fellow of the HEA.

Why might you want to do this? Firstly, the application will help you to reflect on your practice in teaching or supporting learning, for example reflecting on the principles and values underlying your approach and how you know it is effective. You will also gain feedback from colleagues through referees' reports and a teaching observation. Secondly, a fellowship demonstrates to others that you are working effectively to support teaching and learning and thus can be an asset to your career, including in job applications. You are also entitled to put the letters FHEA or AFHEA after your name.

Developing a personal teaching philosophy

When you started teaching, you undoubtedly had ideas and conceptions of what 'good teaching' looked like, rooted in your personal and educational experience, and informing how you wanted to teach. As you become more experienced and reflect on your teaching, you may develop your ideas further. An interesting exercise, which is often required for HEA recognition, is to develop a statement of your personal teaching philosophy. This is essentially a description of your educational values, why they are important to you (usually based on your own educational journey) and how you apply them; examples are given in Case Studies 12.1 and 12.2.

Case Study 12.1

Personal teaching philosophy: Christopher Hazlehurst, PhD candidate and GTA in Strategic Management

My ambition to teach started when I watched the film *Freedom Writers* for the first time in 2007. It showed to me that teaching has a great and profound impact on the lives of people. During my school years, I was subject to persistent bullying. School was a dreadful place for me as I also found that the majority of my teachers handled the situation extremely poorly. When I went into teaching my motivation was to do better. I am convinced that controversial and sometimes divisive discussions need to be held in a classroom because I want to train my students to be able to make informed decisions in life that are right for them, while acknowledging, appreciating and respecting difference. Like Erin Gruwell says at the beginning of the film, 'the battle needs to be won in the classroom'.

In business education, we educate future business leaders. Some of my students may be in a future position where the decisions they make have profound impacts on the livelihood of many individuals and communities. Some might start their own business and will employ people. Previously, there have been many situations where businesses have often acted more in the interest of profit-maximisation than the welfare of stakeholders – the collapse of a clothing factory at Rana Plaza in Bangladesh being one example. It requires moral courage and critical thinking for individuals in those companies to speak up and act courageously. Hence, my mission statement in teaching is to help students develop a critical and forward-thinking and courageous mind to a topic.

Case Study 12.2

Personal teaching philosophy: Abigail Perrin, postdoctoral researcher in Molecular Biology

Some particular methods and principles have been central to my teaching. Firstly, I have found it fundamentally important to engage and involve learners by making my teaching as student-centred as possible. This has meant integrating group work and interactive elements into large group teaching and empowering the students in my workplace to take ownership of their lab projects and personal development. These approaches reliably increase participation and interaction and have often resulted in very interesting scientific discussions.

Secondly, I always aim to emphasise the learning value of an activity over its final outcome of a grade or data and I find that this increases collaboration in my classes and reduces students' anxiety. I also use formative assessment in almost every context where I teach, whether this is by answering students' questions by asking them more questions or by setting specific learning activities that help me gauge students' progress and the efficacy of my teaching throughout an ongoing programme of work. Finally, I use my position as an active research scientist to help my students integrate theory and practice, showing them how the principles and skills they learn are translated into new discoveries. I have seen this 'contextual' approach to promote motivation, interest and enthusiasm amongst the students I interact with.

Research and scholarship

You may wish to explore teaching and learning more deeply by undertaking educational research and scholarship – sometimes called the scholarship of teaching and learning (SoTL). This can take a variety of forms, examples of which will be described shortly, but first take a moment to consider themes or questions that you might be interested in exploring in Activity 12.3.

Activity 12.3

Areas for enquiry

From your experience of teaching to date, what have you been curious about? Are there questions that interest or trouble you? What would you like to understand better? These questions could relate to your own teaching, to how others in your discipline or sector teach, or to students. Examples might be:

- How do other people teach X (maybe a difficult concept or skill)?
- Can I design an activity to make revision sessions more useful?
- How can I help students to understand the academic writing conventions in my discipline?
- Why don't my students prepare well for seminars?
- Do students think my seminars are inclusive?
- How can I engage all students in my large group lecture?

Make some notes on areas of interest and we will return to these in Activity 12.4 to consider how best to explore them.

Methods of enquiry

Within your discipline you will be aware of research traditions and values, for example whether the discipline values broadly quantitative, rationalistic approaches or more qualitative, exploratory methodologies. These preferred approaches relate to broad paradigms about what counts as knowledge and how knowledge can be established (ontology and epistemology). Within education, there are also traditions and specific methodologies that have been developed, some of which are described very briefly below.

Literature reviews: often the first stage, and may be the entire project. There is a large and growing evidence base of research on teaching and learning in higher education, both generic and discipline-specific. Literature can help answer intractable questions, illuminate possibilities and defend practice that is associated with good outcomes even if students aren't enthusiastic about it.

Action research: this approach is about trying to improve your practice by identifying an issue, planning an intervention, evaluating its impact and using this to inform future practice.

Phenomenology: this is the study of how phenomena (such as elements of teaching and learning) are experienced. The subjective views of individuals are sought through methods such as interviews or focus groups.

Lesson study: this is a Japanese model of collaborative research in which groups of teachers plan, conduct, observe and develop lessons to meet agreed goals.

Exploratory practice: this is a form of enquiry developed in language teaching, which focuses on trying to understand what is happening during teaching and learning, rather than to produce immediate changes.

References to further information on these methodologies can be found in the Further Resources section at the end of the chapter. This list is not exhaustive and the choice of methodology will depend on the nature of your question: Activity 12.4 provides an opportunity to think further about this.

Activity 12.4

Designing an enquiry

Take the question(s) or theme(s) you identified for study in Activity 12.3 and consider:

- What is the scope of my enquiry? Does it relate to my own practice or to students or is it a wider question about the discipline or teaching and learning in general?
- Can I distil my general purpose into a specific research question? For example, 'To explore students' views about assessment feedback' would be nebulous, whereas 'To describe the factors motivating students to use assessment feedback in their future work' would be more specific (Cohen et al., 2017: 336).
- What approach(es) or research method(s) could be appropriate to answer this question?
- Will it be practical and desirable to work on this independently or in collaboration with colleagues? If the latter, with whom?
- What outcome(s) do I want? – to improve my own practice, develop greater understanding, publish something, present my work?
- What support do I need? – this may include people, funding and resources.
- What is the time scale?

Discussion

Clarifying your research question, motivation and resource needs will help you to make a realistic plan. As with any such project, it is often best to start small, maybe run a pilot, and then develop further. You may be able to find support from your university's education/staff development unit, and there may even be sources of funding to assist.

Developing your career

You may know instinctively whether or not you want to make teaching a core part of your future career and you may also take into account the results of your evaluation. If you are unsure, you could talk to a careers advisor who can help you to think through your decision. An educational role is an important element of most academic careers and of many other careers, so whatever your path, you will be able to draw on the experience and skills you have gained from teaching.

In this final section, we look at how you can articulate your teaching experience to support job applications.

Representing your teaching in job applications

During your teaching you will have developed knowledge, skills and attributes that will be useful in many careers. Here are some examples:

- Communication
- Creativity
- Collaboration/Team working
- Adaptability
- Technical skills
- Resilience
- Working with challenging people
- Problem solving

- Planning
- Organisation
- Critical thinking
- Stress management
- Time management
- Professionalism
- Facilitation
- Diversity awareness.

These are all highly desirable characteristics that employers look for and are often listed in person specifications for roles. When writing your application, you can give examples from your teaching to demonstrate these areas. When it comes to interviews, remember that your teaching will undoubtedly have developed your knowledge, presentation skills and ability to explain things to others.

To prepare for interviews it is useful to think of specific examples/anecdotes from your teaching experience to illustrate some of the desired skills and attributes. You may be asked questions such as:

- Tell me about a time when you had to solve a problem.
- Give me an example of how you managed in a stressful situation.

Or, if you are going for teaching-related posts, you could be asked more teaching-focused questions, such as:

- Tell us about the kinds of teaching you've been involved in.
- What do you see as the challenges of engaging large groups of students?
- How would you deal with a student that tends to dominate discussion?
- What do you understand by inclusive teaching?
- How do you use technology in your teaching?
- What's your approach to blended learning?

A structure you can use in interviews is the STAR model. STAR stands for: situation (the context), task (what you had to do), action (what you did) and result/reflection (how you know you were effective and what you learnt from the experience). Essentially, you tell a story using this structure. The following example is based on being asked about a challenging experience in your teaching:

Situation: You had a really busy research week when you were off site collecting data every day.

Task: You still had to fit in your regular teaching.

Action: You decided to have students give group presentations that week. You prepared the session two weeks ahead when you were less busy and gave students the details so that they had time to work in groups to prepare.

Results: The students had prepared well and gave good presentations. You had feedback that they enjoyed learning from each other and developing their presentation skills. You were able to manage the session with minimum time away from your research and learnt that with prior planning you can effectively manage a hectic schedule.

A single story like this can often demonstrate a variety of skills and attributes; for example, the above would also be relevant to questions about stress management, prioritisation skills, creativity and problem solving. People often fail to recognise the skills they have learnt, and interviews are not the time to be modest, so think about how far you have come since you started teaching. Focus on the positive experiences you have had and how the skills and attributes you have developed could be useful in the role.

Over to you

We started by looking at the proving–improving continuum. Proving the effectiveness of your teaching can be important both for your department and university and for your career. Improving your teaching is a never-ending process, so the strategies for evaluating and researching your practice will be useful for as long as you teach. Perhaps more important is an attitude of enquiry and a commitment to constantly learn and develop. This is not always a comfortable process but it is important to realise that learning is a collaborative process – students have to engage and take responsibility too and there are wider contextual factors that influence students' perceptions that are beyond your control. Experimenting with different approaches is vital – not all will be successful but you will learn and develop in the process. Think about what kind of teacher you would really like to be and how to work towards this. You are unlikely to find one perfect teaching formula, but through showing interest in your learners' perceptions and development, drawing on educational research and maintaining a spirit of enquiry, you can keep your teaching and your interest in education alive.

Further resources

As the title suggests, the book espouses a reflective approach throughout, with Chapter 14 focusing specifically on monitoring and enhancing the quality of learning.

Ashwin, P. with Boud, D., Coate, K., Hallett, F., Keane, F., Krause, K., Leibowitz, B., MacLaren, I., McArthur, J., McCune, V. and Tooher, M. (2015) *Reflective Teaching in Higher Education*. London: Bloomsbury.

This short article describes four lenses through which you can illuminate your teaching, and includes a critical incident questionnaire to gather student feedback.

Brookfield, S. (1998) Critically reflective practice: *Journal of Continuing Education in the Health Professions*, 18 (4): 197–205.

The following references relate to specific SoTL methodologies that may be of interest to and relevance in your context:

Cambridge Assessment International Education. Getting started with reflective practice. https://www.cambridge-community.org.uk/professional-development/gswrp/index.html (accessed April 2021).
Dar, Yasmin and Gieve, Simon (2013) The use of Exploratory Practice as a form of collaborative practitioner research. *International Student Experience Journal*, 1 (1): 19–24.
Fernandez, C. and Yoshida, M. (2004) An overview of Lesson Study. In *Lesson Study: A Japanese Approach to Improving Mathematics Teaching and Learning*. London: Routledge. pp. 6–15.
Johnson, A. P. (2012) *A Short Guide to Action Research*, 4th edn. New York: Pearson.

References

Cohen, L., Manion, L. and Morrison, K. (2017) *Research Methods in Education*, 8th edn. Abingdon: Routledge.
Fan, Y., Shepherd, L. J., Slavich, E., Waters, D., Stone, M., Abel, R., Johnston, E. L. (2019) Gender and cultural bias in student evaluations: why representation matters. *PLoS ONE*, 14 (2): e0209749. https://doi.org/10.1371/journal.pone.0209749
Kirkpatrick, D. L. and Kirkpatrick, J. D. (2006) *Evaluating Training Programs: the Four Levels*, 3rd edn. San Francisco, CA: Berrett-Koehler Publishers.
MacNell, L., Driscoll, A. and Hunt, A. N. (2015) What's in a name: exposing gender bias in student ratings of teaching. *Innovative Higher Education*, 40: 291–303.
Uttl, B., White, C. A. and Gonzalez, D. W. (2017) Meta-analysis of faculty's teaching effectiveness: student evaluation of teaching ratings and student learning are not related. *Studies in Educational Evaluation*, 54: 22–42.

INDEX